YA KNOW WHAT I'M SAY'N

HEARING THE VOICE OF THE HOMELESS
KRIS BRIDGMAN WITH KEITH BRIDGMAN

YA KNOW WHAT I'M SAY'N
HEARING THE VOICE OF THE HOMELESS

KRIS BRIDGMAN & KEITH BRIDGMAN

ISBN-13: **978-0615944777**
ISBN-10: **0615944779**

 Copyright © 2014 Christian Publishing House

Cambridge, Ohio

YA KNOW WHAT I'M SAY'N: Hearing the Voice of the Homeless

support@christianpublishers.org

Write: support@christianpublishers.org

Kris Bridgman is to be identified as the author of this work.

Editor: Gina Burgess

Christian Publishing House
Professional Christian Publishing of the Good News

For Greg

Dear Reader,

My prayer for this book is that it would reveal the homeless to you through different eyes; to see beyond the ragged, dirty clothes, past the dirty nails and thick beards, beyond the tattoos and addictions and lost-ness, to see a tired soul longing for love, friendship, understanding, and help.

That soul can be camouflaged by the addiction and the hardness that grows from being homeless over time, but it is there. I have found it many times by just sitting, listening, smiling, loving with the love of Christ, and sharing friendship with them.

They don't want to feel like the dirty candy wrapper on the street that gets stepped on, passed by, and ignored. Some may act as if they do not want you to notice them, but I have found they cannot turn down a sincere smile, a listening ear, and a prayer.

Everyone needs to be heard and to be loved.

Everyone needs to hear the Good News of Jesus Christ.

Everyone needs mercy and grace and love.

Come journey with me to the benches of my downtown square and meet the sweet souls God led me to. I pray you will see what I saw. We just might see a little of ourselves along the way and remember the sweet mercy, grace and love we received.

"To love a person means to see him as God intended him to be."

Dostoevsky

"And this I pray, that your love may abound yet more and more in knowledge and in all judgment. . ."

Philippians 1:9

Kris

Acknowledgments

To Ron Hall and Denver Moore, thank you for writing your story, which inspired me to set out to do what the Lord had for me.

To all the blanket donors who gave not only blankets, but oh, so much more to allow me to set out on this God given journey to give to the ones in need, thank you!

To my blog readers who read my stories in the beginning stages and encouraged me and loved me, thank you!

To my mother and sister who read my stories and for being my cheerleaders, thank you!

To our Mayor Bruce Wilkerson, Slim Nash and Alisa Willoughby for reading the entire book before publishing, thank you!

To our dear proofreader, Crystal, for being such a great teacher with love and patience even through the hounding of ellipses from us. We think we got rid of most of them. We hope you are pleased. Thank you!

To all my prayer warriors, for the many prayers you sent on my behalf. You'll never know how much strength they gave me to keep going and to not give up. I love each and every one of you. Thank you!

"To Lori, for making all the phone calls and e-mails that helped make my dream come true, thank you!

To Mr. Andrews, I could not have asked for a better publisher for taking a chance on me, believing in my book, for allowing me to keep my own voice, thank you!

To Greg, for wanting the stories to be told and yelling out to Keith that first day at the park; for your friendship, thank you!

To my homeless and former homeless friends; for sharing your lives with me, being brave to share the stories from your past, for trusting me with such an important part of yourselves, for being so polite and kind and treating me with respect. And to all you men, for treating me like a lady, thank you!

To my husband, Keith, for being such a wonderful encourager, helper, backing me up all the way with my desire to start a Blanket Ministry, to my desire to go visiting underneath bridges and being my bodyguard, to allowing hundreds and hundreds of blankets lining the walls of our home each year, to helping me make this book more beautiful, thank you!

To my Lord and Savior, Jesus Christ, for giving me the vision, the boldness, the guidance, the people, the opportunities, the faith and strength in more ways than one to carry this assignment through. Because of His promise, "I will never leave you; I will never forsake you", I was able to always go forward with His righteous right hand in mine, taking hold of all the opportunities He put in my path. He continued to give me puzzle pieces until the final picture was made. Thank you Father!

To God be the glory!

Foreword by Gina Burgess, author of

Refreshment in Refuge

Within these pages, you will find a startling world of raw compassion. Raw because the compassion is unadorned with worries of what other people may think; the actions illustrated here are ingenuous, very much as Jesus would do. I have heard compassion defined as empathy and love at work, and that describes Kris and Keith Bridgman's hearts as well as their two ministries. However, the book is larger than just two hearts working hard to reflect the brilliant light of *agape* in a dark world.

These are life stories that are certainly heart breaking, there are tormented souls, and there are those who choose a different god than the Lord God Almighty to worship. Some of these people know Jesus, and want to let the mind of Christ take charge, but cannot break free of Satan's sticky web. They wear shackles and chains, imprisoned by their past. What unfolds is the good, the bad, and the ugly sides of the homeless lifestyle.

What Kris has lovingly penned is a result of a real life fast in the vein of Isaiah 58:

6 *"Is not this the fast that I choose: to lose the bonds of wickedness, to undo the straps of the yoke, to let the oppressed go free, and to break every yoke? 7 Is it not to share your bread with the hungry and bring the homeless poor into your house; when you see the naked, to cover him, and not to hide yourself from your own flesh?"* (ESV)

While Kris and Keith do not bring the homeless to live in their home for reasons that will become obvious as you read this book, they have inspired numerous people to bring help and hope to the homeless of Bowling Green. They pray, they bring food, they lift the yoke of bleakness and despair, and they pry open cold hearts by extending the warm fires of God's love to these homeless people. There is a very fast pleasing to God ongoing in this fair city.

A harsh lesson is illustrated in this book as well. Often times we try so hard to live the Christian life in our own strength. We work so hard at eliminating bad habits relying upon our own resources. This is so far from God provided for us, and how He designed for us to live doing the work He planned long before the foundation of the world. Charles Stanley once said, God had to teach him he could not live Christ-like twenty-four seven under his own steam. Only when he could trust God enough to do it for him would he ever come close to pleasing God in the way he lived.

Just like an amputee seems to feel the missing arm, or has an itch on a missing leg, so Satan makes a person feel chains and shackles that have been removed by God Himself. They are phantom shackles, but they feel so heavy and so real. When people live oppressed, weary and heavy-laden, they must be taught how to live free. This book is a strong testimony for the critical need for discipling God's children.

You will find no better illustration of this truth than right here in this study. No doubt, you will tsk at the old Greg, cheer for the new Greg, weep for Dallas, clap for Theresa, root for Tony, gasp, laugh, and pray for them all.

This is a beautiful portrait of compassionate outreach to hurting people. Read and see the physical illustration of the spiritual promises God lays out in Isaiah 58.

Isaiah 58:8 *Then shall your light break forth like the dawn, and your healing shall spring up speedily; your righteousness shall go before you; the glory of the LORD shall* be your rear guard. 9 Then you shall call, and the LORD will answer; you shall cry, and he will say, 'Here I am.' If you take away the yoke from your midst, the pointing of the finger, and speaking wickedness, 10 if you pour yourself out for the hungry and satisfy the desire of the afflicted, then shall your light rise in the darkness and your gloom be as the noonday. 11 And the LORD will guide you continually and satisfy your desire in scorched places and make your bones strong; and you shall be like a watered garden, like a spring of water, whose waters do not fail.

What could be better than living like that?

Endorsements

"Kris Bridgman has literally put her heart and soul into the ministry described in her book. The book is a fascinating journey of a woman who began with a project in mind to help those in need, to a Christian living the Word with the lost souls of our community. It is a must read for anyone with the desire to minister to the homeless to help dispel the misconceptions and expectations of all involved. It is well worth the time for all who wish to help."

Mayor Bruce Wilkerson

City of Bowling Green, Kentucky

....

"I was transfixed by the authenticity of each account of living a life on the fringe."

Brian "Slim" Nash

Director of Community Based Services, Uspiritus (A social service agency that provides a full continuum of care from prevention services to foster care to residential treatment.)

Bowling Green City Commissioner

....

"Like most people, we tend to look at the homeless with judgment, fear or pity. Kris gives a voice to the homeless and allows them to tell their story. 'Ya Know What I'm Say'n' is filled with stories of heartbreak, hardships and a life of bad choices. You will be inspired to get out of your comfort zone, just like Kris, and see the homeless through the eyes of Jesus. You will never look at the homeless the same way again."

Alisa Willoughby

Former Lifeway Christian Bookstore employee

....

"As a Pastor who has had firsthand experience with the homeless in Maryland and in North Carolina, I can say that Kris has captured in her book the heart of Jesus as He looks on a part of our society that is very misunderstood and maligned. My Greg was a man named John in Rockville, MD, and he taught me a lot about the needs of the homeless. If you have a heart (or want to develop a heart) for ministering to the less fortunate in our cities, this book is a must read. We need to look at people with the eyes of Christ (John 9) and see them as people and not problems."

Dr. Thomas Marshall, ThD.; BCPC

Minister; Adjunct Professor, Liberty University;

Editor, Christian Publishing House

....

A wise man named Denver Moore once told me, "Mr. Ron, God don't give you no credit for lovin' the folks that is easy to love." Ya Know What I'm Say'n is about those that are not easy to love. There are hundreds of thousands of sad stories about nameless, faceless souls whom our society has tossed in the dumpsters hoping some government agency will haul them off, and dump them in places that will not mar the beauty of their proud cities. On the pages to follow, walk the streets of Bowling Green, Kentucky with author Kris Bridgman who found a way to show the love of Christ and give hope to many of those so-called unlovable ones.

Kris brings a different perspective to helping the homeless that is most often characterized by showing up at a shelter and dishing out food from behind a counter. She uses the following recipe author Kathy Brunner shared with me that is more satisfying that a pot of spaghetti. Take 2 eyes to see the circumstances, add two ears to hear the needs, 2 hands to deliver hugs, one mouth to voice loving words, and one willing heart to understand. Mix these all together in one serving soul to nourish a sore heart. Food is necessary for survival but only love can offer hope and change lives. Kris' ministry is evidence of that.

Saint Francis of Assisi encouraged his followers to start by doing what is necessary; then do what's possible, and suddenly you are doing the impossible. "Preach the Gospel at all times" he said, "and when necessary use words!" Leading by example, Kris Bridgman is doing what is necessary, what most people consider the impossible as she preaches the Gospel daily using few words while showing the love of Christ to the less fortunate of her city. I've heard it said that most Christians worship one homeless man on Sunday then turn their backs on the first homeless man they see on Monday. Praise God for the Kris Bridgmans of the world who are working to change that image. Denver reminded me daily that you never know whose eyes God is using to watch you, and that sometimes we successful people rise up so high trying to accumulate more stuff that we miss getting to know God. But we can never stoop too low to help a homeless brother or sister and have God miss knowing us. After reading this collection of stories about God's people, see if God is nudging you, like He did Kris, to do the necessary, then the impossible. Recalling the famous words of my friend Denver, "In a way, we is all homeless, just working' our way home!"

Ron Hall

Co-author, *Same Kind Of Different As Me*, and *What Difference Do It Make*, and now in bookstores a new children's picture book telling the life story of Denver Moore, *Everybody Can Help Somebody*.

CHAPTER 1 – Answered Prayer

"Hey, hey you with the camera, come here. I want to talk to you."

My husband Keith was at the downtown square in Bowling Green, Kentucky waiting to guide a photography field trip when he heard someone shouting at him. He turned around and noticed an intimidatingly large man of African American descent sitting on a park bench motioning for him to come over. Had the man been standing, his six foot four or five inch frame and massive bulk would have towered over Keith. At first he felt somewhat uncertain, not sure it was a good idea to walk over there, but something in his heart said, "It's okay, talk to him."

The uneven texture of the brick pathway caused him awkwardly to waver from side to side as he walked over and nervously shook the man's massive hand.

"What can I do for you?"

"You a photographer?"

The man's voice was direct and deep and his jaundice eyes although haggard and tired carried in them a sense of purpose. His clothes were worn and tattered and his shaved head beaded with perspiration reflected the soft evening light. Keith thought the question had a rather self-evident answer, but replied anyway.

"I try to do the best I can."

"You ever take pictures of homeless people?"

In recent weeks, he had taken a few candid photographs of homeless individuals, but nothing of consequence, so the question caught him off guard.

"Well, actually I have taken a few. Why do you ask?"

"I'm homeless, ya know what I'm say'n. There's lots of homeless folks down here, ya know what I'm say'n. Ain't nobody pays us no mind either, they just act like we don't exist and we need help, ya know what I'm say'n. Why don't you take my picture cause somebody needs to tell our story, ya know what I'm say'n."

Keith smiled realizing that this might be the opportunity I was looking for. After he snapped Greg's portrait said, "You need to meet my wife Kris. She wants to talk to someone like you, and your name is?"

"Greg, Greg Thompson, I live in a storage shed just up the road."

....

When Keith told me about the encounter with Greg, there was nothing subtle about it. Sometimes answers to prayers are not so easy to detect unless we're looking for them. God answered my prayers by opening a door into a world few would ever choose to walk through. However, I had no idea how complex and difficult this journey would become.

17

The previous winter I had started Blankets for the Homeless, a ministry that allowed me and other volunteers to connect with the homeless population in our community.

I wasn't sure where or why God was leading me down that path, but I was deeply convicted that He wanted me to do this. I just didn't know how far He wanted me to travel.

God's voice more often than not is subtle and calm, but sometimes He smacks us between the eyes. He smacked me with a book about a homeless man. The title was *Same Kind of Different as Me* by Ron Hall and Denver Moore. It was about how a homeless man was befriended by a wealthy family, and through that relationship, the lives of all of them were changed.

The powerful story so captivated me I read it in a single day. A short time later I discovered that our church had a book club, and the book they were going to review that week was the same one. I signed up immediately. I first learned that my town harbored a significant homeless population during that discussion.

I was shocked actually. I had never noticed anything of that nature before. In reality, I had never looked. From what I could gather at the time, there was a family with children living under the bridge on the north side of town, and there was a cold November wind beginning to blow.

Although it took several weeks that first season, we gathered about three hundred and fifty blankets through donations. Thus the Blanket Ministry was born.

More and more homeless people came into my life by the second winter of the ministry. People who at one time, I would have never noticed much less spoken to. Whether sitting on a park bench, under a bridge, or inside a storage shed they seemed to find me. I began to see them as precious souls placed into my life for a reason.

The more I encountered the lives of the homeless, the more I began to understand their stories. In many cases they simply wanted someone to talk to. Every night as I lay safe and comfortable, they would be on my mind. Questions ran an obstacle course through my thoughts crossing and re-crossing seeking elusive answers. Their stories haunted my heart as they spoke of abuse or bad choices or a myriad of other circumstances that in many cases served all but to destroy what opportunities they might have had to succeed in this world. I could see their brokenness, the despair in their eyes, and in their posture. But, their voices lifted me onto a higher plateau of understanding.

They spoke of their sorrows. They spoke of their family. They spoke of their past and their now. Rarely did they speak of their future. Many were hurting, searching for something, but not knowing for sure what it was or where to find it. I realized God was challenging me to let go of preconceived notions, old fears, discouragements, an old wound not yet healed, to provide a voice for those who had no one to listen to them. Where this would lead, I could only guess. For me a new light began to glow around their lives. For the first time, I began truly to understand what Christ meant when he spoke of compassion.

They needed a voice. The stories they told defined a human tragedy whose cries evaporated into the vacuum of space where no one could hear them. I wanted to write their stories, to give them a voice, but I wanted to do it for the right reasons, not for my own desires.

For six months, I prayed for direction. God's silence dominated my heart. Six months seemed like such a long time to wait for an answer, and like I was inclined to do, one evening I pressed the issue with God, "Please Lord, if this desire is from you, give me some kind of confirmation."

The day Keith heard, "Hey you," was the day Greg became the answer. Over the next few seasons, one point became evident: Lessons are often learned not by arriving someplace, but by taking the journey. It is during that passage of time God will expose us to life realities we would not otherwise experience. He will allow our hearts to experience emotions we would not ordinarily seek to encounter. He will stand with us as we face difficult moments. Too often, we fail to hear what He is trying to tell us, but in time, what seemed like silence will begin to resonate with His voice, "Do you understand now, why I led you this way?"

CHAPTER 2 – Blanket Lady

I stood near the end of the old walking bridge that spanned both flanks of Barren River where it wove through the outer edges on the north side of the city. I heard someone shout, "Look, there's The Blanket Lady."

The Blanket Lady, I never dreamed I would ever be called that when I started Blankets for the Homeless. Having always been a quiet, introverted person, it was not easy to leave my comfort zones. God was teaching me how to step outside myself to view those who were less fortunate as seen through his eyes. What I saw tugged at my heart and challenged my emotions.

Homelessness is not pretty. It carries with it negative labels that society has imprinted on those who are caught within its grasp. In many cases, these are ordinary people caught up in extraordinary circumstances. Most of them simply want others to understand that in spite of their situation, they still have value. Others have simply given up and exist day to day.

Deep emotional wounds and brokenness that are often the result of lost dreams hold many of them captive. None of us are immune from such things. Through this journey, I discovered it is not so much that their lives are lost, it is their sense of belonging, their sense of self-worth that is diminished. For whatever reason, they are forced to look at and live life from a different perspective.

The Blanket Ministry was initiated to fill a basic need. It brought me into contact with many people carrying so many hurts it was almost overwhelming at first. Over time, though, I came to see their deeper needs. They are hungry in more ways than a meal can fill, suffer from cold that no blanket can ever warm, and endure a hollowness than most people can never fully understand. Yet, in spite of, or maybe even *because of*, these needs, an extraordinary God used ordinary blankets, and the most ordinary of people, to transform lives.

A blanket is just a piece of cloth woven together to make a warm covering but God used it to bring a covering of warmth over a city. For some it warmed their bodies, for others, it warmed their hearts, and for still others it melted a vision-blocking veil. It can open the eyes of those who once were unwilling to see, and open hearts with compassion for those who were once unseen.

When the Blanket Ministry began, it ignited a chain of events: A newspaper reporter ran a story then came twenty-four straight days of e-mails, phone calls, and donations that filled the hallways of my home. People I've never met recognized the Blanket Lady from that article placing cash in my hands for blankets. It touched the lives of almost everyone we encountered, not just the homeless, in ways that we never expected. Examples include how it brought a homeless man to reunite with his family, and provided a job for several others. A blanket brought a huge smile to the face of a young girl who was not going to receive any Christmas gifts. It brought a husband along on a journey he never thought he would take, and opened his eyes and heart to make a difference. It brought ordinary people into extraordinary experiences.

Along the way we learned how God could take a blanket, join it with an act of kindness, and turn it into a force that can change hearts. I've heard some speak with callous words about the homeless and needy. It breaks my heart to hear such things. In most cases they simply do not understand, and base their attitudes on their own fears and misconceptions.

Tears of gratitude drip from a soot stained face or the voice of a hardened man breaks from trying to hold back his tears. These kinds of experiences testify to what those misconceptions keep the callous from seeing. When office-softened-hands shake the callused hand of one broken from abuse, and when a man living under a bridge says, "Thank you, for not treating me like trash", I've discovered that when God is part of the plan, miracles can make ordinary become extraordinary.

CHAPTER 3 – Greg – Visit 1

Most journeys begin with an exploratory mission and this was mine. Although I had written down several questions I wanted to ask, I had no real idea how to conduct this interview except maybe just let Greg talk about whatever he wanted to say. I had also considered what to do about protecting myself from whatever else I might find in Greg's territory.

My friend Carolyn could hardly be considered a bodyguard. She was maybe an inch taller than me but about the same size. Both of us looked like twigs when compared to Greg, who could easily have snapped us into smaller pieces if he so desired. My first sight of Greg as I walked towards him made me think to myself, "Whoa, he's big!" Nevertheless, he carried a warm genuine smile. But Carolyn and I noticed right away his red, sleepy looking eyes and the smell of alcohol drifting our way. He had been drinking.

A few minutes into our meeting though, I realized no bodyguard was needed because the sweet soul of this gentle giant began to emerge. As he began to tell me his story a deeper more interesting character revealed himself. Over the next hour or so he sped through forty six years of a hard life and it became apparent I would need much more than one interview to dig deeply enough into his life to understand who he really was.

There was more to his story than words could define. His words simply revealed the details of his life, things like cancer taking its toll, his lack of education, his time in prison, but it was the language of his body, which revealed the most about him. His eyes cast a sense of searching, a sense of desperation, and lost hope. He had fallen so deeply into a hole because of life choices, climbing out seemed all but impossible. His outward countenance expressed defiance, yet his posture indicated someone beaten down by circumstances.

He spoke about his desire to become a person who can take care of himself, but his life circumstances reduced the possibility realizing that desire. He clung to what dignity he could retain, but in his mind, wearing a colostomy bag reduced the strength of that dignity. He was searching for a greater purpose, but a GED earned in prison for an education limited his ability to find a way toward greater endeavors. Although he was not highly educated, his powers of observation were strong as he could read the body language of the people around him.

"See that guy over there. He's homeless."

"How do you know?"

"He got that beat down look, know what I'm say'n. He got that far off look in his eyes as if he is look'n for something. You can just tell, know what I'm say'n."

Few people ever spoke to him, and even fewer showed any degree of kindness or compassion toward him. This lack of connection most likely stemmed from fear that came from little or no understanding.

My heart broke as he spoke of the one great loss in his life. His daughter at age nineteen died from the effects of abusing chemical inhalants. He did not reveal many details about that time, but in his eyes one could see the pain he carried about what happened. He lowered his head fighting back the tears, and became very quiet as though he did not want to talk about that part of his story. I fought along with him to hold back emotions that were difficult not to release, and did not press him for more details.

Although Greg had sought help for his situation, what he found time and again was superficial and temporary. What he needed was something to allow him to regain a sense of self-sufficiency and a way to rise above the stigma of being homeless. He had become a survivor in a system that only sustained the status quo. He needed more. He needed to regain his pride. There was an inner strength in him that remained untapped because life had suppressed the best of what he could give and at that time, only the worst of what he had become showed.

Except, he spent time feeding the squirrels as that was the only way he knew how to offer something in return. Simple things like this gentle act showed a soft heart, a caring soul, and a spirit worth knowing. I asked him, "Do you want to tell me anything else?"

"People just walk past me, won't even look at me, know what I'm say'n. I could be a bug and they act like they don't even care."

I told him that I cared and I was listening and wanted to know more.

One of the few hopes he carried was that he hoped he would go to Heaven and see his daughter again. I told him I didn't want him just to hope, I wanted him to know that he would be there one day. I wore a yellow plastic bracelet with the scripture from John 14:6 (KJV) imprinted on it.

"Jesus saith unto him, 'I am the way, the truth, and the life: no man cometh unto the Father, but by me."

I asked Greg if I could give it to him and he lifted his large forearm and let me slip it over his hand onto his wrist. He smiled as he turned his wrist so he could read it again. We ended our time together with my prayer that he would accept this promise completely in his heart one day, he would *know* that one day he would have a permanent home, his old life would be washed away, and he would never have to be called homeless ever again.

After I said "Amen", I noticed that he still kept his head bowed and whispered his own prayer. When he raised his head his expression was different from when I first met him, he seemed to be more at peace as though he was beginning to understand that there was something greater than his circumstances.

Greg carried within him a melody that had been suppressed by bad choices and consequences. I did not yet fully understand the depth of the melody he carried or the intensity of the consequences of those choices. All I knew was that God had opened a door into the life of a man looking for redemption. Like a giant puzzle yet to be assembled, this first visit offered a glimpse of what the final image would become.

This first exploratory visit ended leaving a vast array of questions unanswered and many more yet to be realized. I could not offer him much tangible help, but did leave him with a bag of food and an offer of friendship. I wanted him to know that he did have a higher purpose, and that was giving his story a voice in hopes that it could be shared some way, somehow to help others. He showed a genuine concern for younger kids and how their choices if not made wisely, could lead to a desperate life. He told me he wanted his story told to help others because that was the best way he could give back.

I once asked God what it was he wanted me to do. On that opening day with Greg, he showed me the first corner piece of the puzzle.

CHAPTER 4 – Greg – Visit 2

Living without hope can make one tired, but never under estimate a smile, a handshake, and a friendly hello. As simple as those things are, they can bring a sense of belonging to someone, who for whatever reasons have lost that part of their lives. Greg began to teach us about the value of those simple gestures early in our relationship.

Many homeless are without one important thing in their lives, touch. Even a handshake will transmit more than the physical act might otherwise suggest. That need for closeness we all have, but the homeless lose closeness when they are in most need of it. Over time, that lack of touch begins to settle deep into their hearts, hearts that grow cold and indifferent to the world around them. Even on a hot summer day, the frigid atmosphere of their lives can harden a heart into deep despair. The longer it settles, the colder they become as a person until they no longer care, no longer seek out a close relationship. Thawing that coldness from their lives requires more than a physical touch, it requires an emotional bond.

We were only beginning our relationship with Greg. At first, we did not understand just how cold he was inside, nor did we understand why. Even so, early on mostly through his eyes we recognized a spark of warmth there that had not yet been extinguished, struggling to glow warmer against a damp and empty life. A cold life can wear down the strongest of hearts.

Greg looked tired sitting on the park bench. Just getting by day to day will do that to a person. He sat with a noticeable lean forward with elbows resting on his thighs and head positioned with a downward pose. His faded green shirt appeared clean but tattered with holes dotting across the back and along the bottom edge.

He straightened to an upright position when we came into view, and seemed genuinely pleased to see us. I was pleased to see that he was sober. At the end of our first visit, I had asked Greg to please not to have been drinking before our visits, as I wanted him to have a clear mind. This was the first of many times he showed respect to my wishes and to me. I sat on one side of Greg, and after greeting him Keith stood nearby leaving the two of us to talk in private.

On this warm day, the downtown square buzzed with activity. A bridal party posed for pictures around the fountain, sweethearts walked hand in hand along the shaded sidewalk, someone was walking his dog. In front of us, behind us, around us, they passed going about their day.

Greg and I must have looked odd to them. Here was a petite, middle-class, white woman sitting next to a large, dark, homeless man. I can imagine what some might have been thinking. A few stares did settle on us. I paid them no mind. Greg didn't say much at first and there seemed to be longer than comfortable pauses in our initial conversation.

During one of those pauses, I looked toward the ground, and noticed our shoes positioned on the paved path. A few leaves scattered across the gray surface broke the dull flat color. I could not help but wonder that we were so different yet similar in so many ways.

The path that we were seated near seemed like a metaphor of our lives. Along its length there were forks leading one direction or another and scattered here and there were bumps and small pits and broken pavement undercut by large roots of the giant shade trees surrounding the park. How many roots in Greg's life undercut his path I did not know, but I knew enough to understand that the route he chose was filled with potholes and numerous detours.

In his youth Greg chose one path, I chose another. He grew up in a broken home with his mother, as I did. He went to church at an early age, same as me. At age twelve I made a life changing decision to follow Jesus, a decision that has held true ever since.

30

At age fifteen, Greg thought he was a man and no longer needed rules in his life. People who encouraged him to live a life dictated by personal desire, alcohol, and drugs influenced him. He robbed a person, was caught, and served time in prison. After being released, he fell back into the grasp of those same people. It wasn't long before he was in trouble again with more time spent in prison. The same cycle repeated itself a third time, just more severe in nature. In all he accumulated around fifteen years in the custody of the state of Ohio.

His deep baritone voice made it difficult for him to speak softly, but in as soft a voice as he could he said, "Once you're in prison, you ain't never the same again. I thought those people I hung out with cared 'bout me, ya know what I'm say'n. They didn't. They just wanted to use me, they didn't care what happened to me . . . never did . . . ya know what I'm say'n?"

I'm not sure why at the time, but after hearing him speak about his time in prison and the characters that helped to put him there, I couldn't help but think of a verse from Ezekiel, *"And I will give you a new heart, and a new spirit I will put within you. And I will remove the heart of stone from your flesh and give you a heart of flesh."* Ezekiel 36:26 (ESV)

According to Greg, he never grew up understanding real love. There was a gap in his life, where his father held little if any influence over him, and what influence there was, was mostly negative. He always told me he loved his mother, but would always shake his head saying he could never live with her; there was just too much friction. He had sibling love for his sisters, but they were all off in their own worlds, and Greg wanted to be in his. He shared with me the only real love he had ever experienced was for his daughter, but even that was denuded by distance and time away. It took a tragedy to make him realize just how much he loved her, by then it was too late. I know he loved his mother and sisters because I would be sitting next to him at different times when he would use my phone to call one of them. He showed concern and care when one sister had surgery and every time he hung up, he would say "I love you."

I believe it's just natural to have a love for our families, even if we feel distanced for whatever reasons. Down deep I think he knew there was love, but he didn't always know how to process it, and maybe others were too involved in their own emotional needs to show it the way he needed it and could understand it.

His perception of love came from the cast of characters who steered him toward the kinds of behavior that got him into trouble. Then they abandoned ship no longer having any use for him. He didn't understand that real love will lay down its life for another; it will sacrifice for another. Real love is what builds a heart, never tearing one apart. I suspect his friends never sacrificed much for him.

Because of his choices at an early age, his chances of becoming a person who could contribute something productive to society were greatly diminished. He found himself trapped. He desired to become a man who could take care of himself. He wanted to distance himself from his past, but instead ran into walls of discontent that prevented him from doing much more than simply surviving day to day. His past no longer resided in the past. It followed him every day of his life. It haunted his every doing, his every desire to forget about those days. It thwarted his ability to move forward. Instead of it being something to build upon, it became an anchor embedded in quicksand, which threatened to suck him into its depths. His old nemesis alcohol became his life preserver.

"Most people like me down here on the streets do drugs and alcohol, ya know what I'm say'n. They don't want to face their realities . . . it ain't pretty, it's not nice living out here like this, know what I'm say'n. Better to medicate and not feel so much, not see so much."

Not feel so much, not see so much. How profoundly those words resonated. The fact that life could become so impaled by circumstances dictated by poor choices that it could cause a person to no longer want to face it caused me to realize that except by the grace of God, I too could have taken a similar path.

"Someone got beat down the other morning over an orange! One had it, and another wanted it, know what I'm say'n. An orange and somebody beat up someone, know what I'm say'n. Most of us homeless have a rule, ya know, of common courtesy. We try to share what we have, know what I'm say'n. But, that don't always happen. Some just want to take." Greg looked away for a moment and appeared to contemplate his situation, looking for the words to express the difficulty of living on the streets.

"I'm luckier than most, I live in a storage shed, know what I'm say'n. I can get out of the weather. Others have to live under the bridge, one guy I know lives under a trailer, some in parks and in the woods, ya know what I'm say'n. I've seen people have to get inside porta-potties to get out of the weather cause they ain't got no place else to go."

I couldn't help but think, "How many of us would feel lucky to live in a storage shed?"

There was another long pause and I watched Greg twist his massive hands, opening and closing them appearing to do so in time with his thoughts.

"A few months ago I met this lady, Ms Brown, from Life Fellowship Church. She invited me to come. I thought about it for a long time. I liked the idea it was a small place I could walk to real easy, not too big, know what I'm say'n. I thought about how I had started out life without Jesus and noth'n ever turned out right, know what I'm say'n, so I decided to go. Been going now for two months ever Sunday morning and Wednesday night, know what I'm say'n. That's when you and your husband came around. For the first time I 'm start'n to feel hope."

His posture changed to a more upright position and he held his head just a little higher like he realized that maybe for once he had made a good decision. It was like he was asking for my approval without asking for it. He could probably see the smile on my face, and that was approval enough for him.

I asked him what his thoughts on God were.

"I believe in God. I believe in Jesus too, I believe he's God's son, know what I'm say'n. I believe in good works too, that's why I feed the squirrels 'cause that's all I know how to do, only way I can give back, know what I'm say'n. I try not to be selfish, I share when I can, but I don't have much."

I could see in his eyes a brightness that wasn't there before. It was as though some kind of light was beginning to shine within him, yet it struggled to glow at full intensity. He wanted it to shine. He just did not seem to have enough understanding of how to fan that tiny ember into a larger flame.

I asked him, "Have you ever prayed the sinner's prayer of repentance, and asked Jesus to come into your heart?"

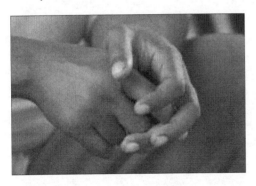

"I've done that, several times," he said with an air of confidence yet he looked away as though he was uncertain of what he had just admitted to.

I did not know at the time where he stood in that regard, although I do believe he had prayed that prayer. My impression was that he really did not understand what forgiveness was, and that he still carried with him a sense of guilt from past transgressions.

There were just too many things in his life, which he either would not or could not discard. These things had crushed his sense of self-worth, and it was so distorted that his connection to what Jesus had actually done on the cross for him was not yet strong enough to overcome all the weight of a guilty conscience pressing down on him.

By this time in our conversation, I was beginning to see more deeply into his life. He was a man held captive by remorse, but whose entirety of existence was formed by a constant barrage of one bad choice after another. These choices generated a conflict inside of him. Somewhere down deep there was a man with a good heart who was trapped. His good heart, his sweet soul could at times claw its way to the surface under the right circumstances. But, it was an untrained goodness almost child-like in nature possibly held down by fear. This innocent goodness rarely had an avenue of expression in his life, and maybe that is where the conflict came from. Somewhere along the way the goodness was redirected away from where he was in the moment.

As our time on the bench ended, I handed him a sack of food that contained a loaf of bread, a jar of peanut butter, an apple, and an orange. He laughed when he saw the orange.

"Weren't we just talking about an orange?"

I laughed and said, "Don't you get into a fight over it."

"You know, I just want to live like a normal person. I don't need a lot of money, know what I'm say'n. Don't need no fancy house and fancy things, I just want a place of my own, a place I can call home. I just want to have some dignity, know what I'm say'n. I wouldn't mind mak'n it month to month, that's not so bad. It's the day to day liv'n that's hard."

When I thought about it, I couldn't imagine living day-to-day. My heart broke for this giant of a man. I had no answers for him, but I could offer him friendship and a return visit for another conversation.

Before we parted I asked him one last question, "Can you sum up your life in one word?"

He thought for a minute before answering tilting his head and pursing his lips trying to find the right word, "Screwed!" He hesitated like he had said something he shouldn't have then looked at me eye to eye. "Hopeful ... I'm seeing hope."

My husband offers the following perspective that he saw as he was taking pictures.

'Do ya know what I'm say'n?''...a question and phrase that was repeated often as Greg spoke of his life and situation as a homeless man. It was almost as though he wanted, no, he needed to make sure his words were heard, and as he spoke of a life filled with bad choices, tragic outcomes, and discouraging experiences, I began to understand more clearly what the phase *do ya know what I'm say'n*, actually meant.

He spoke with a deliberate cadence often struggling to find the right words to define who he was as a 46 year old, homeless man. Words describing how his difficult life might have taken a different path had he chosen more carefully when he was younger.

There were a few times during his talk that I could see in his eyes and expressions how hurt he was because of what happened to him. I sighed a few times as I began to understand just how repentant he was at having done the things that he did that sent him spiraling into a lifestyle that essentially destroyed any potential he might have had to make it in this world. When asked how he would have done things differently, he reflected on his early years when he was fifteen maybe sixteen years old, and said he wished he could start over, change what he had done. When asked to sum up his life in one word or phrase...he thought hard for a minute before answering. What he said surprised me, *"Screwed... hopeful.... but I'm seeing hope."*

When I first met him, I was a bit intimidated by his presence and gruff voice. But as I got to know him, I could sense a need for dignity and understanding. It came from inside of his eyes, and from a heart that was hurting, a heart that needed to heal and find rest.

When we finally parted, my instinctive feeling about our conversation could be summed up in one familiar word— hopeful. Hopeful that we could continue to speak with Greg, touch his life in such a way as to help him regain any lost sense of dignity, and find a way to help him heal his hurting heart. He is a big man physically, but inside he is a child of sorts, one who long ago lost his innocence, yet one who still needed to find his path in life.

Mike Yankoski in his book Under the Overpass ends his story with this: *"Sometimes it's easy to walk by because we know we can't change someone's whole life in a single afternoon. But what we fail to realize is that simple kindness can go a long way toward encouraging someone who is stuck in a desolate place."*

CHAPTER 5 – Greg – Visit 3

It was a typical, hot, mid-August day when Keith and I made our way to the downtown square. We found Greg sitting on a bench in the cool shade of one of the large trees in the area. A live band was playing and multitudes of people strolled here and there in time with the rhythm of the music. Several tents and booths were scattered across the park for some kind of a craft fair. Greg usually shied away from crowds, but on this day he did not allow all the activities to deter him from our scheduled meeting. We brought chicken dinners for the three of us, but only Keith and I ate. Greg placed his to one side, very appreciative, but seemed anxious to start visiting with us.

 He started off by telling us about how he had met our neighbor Maryellen the previous week. Maryellen is not a person inclined to allow a chance to greet someone to pass her by. She had learned about Greg from our conversations and when she saw him sitting on one of the park benches, well, her personality took charge and a conversation between the two of them took place. Greg seemed genuinely pleased to have met her. In fact, a number of people who had read my blog stories about meeting with Greg, pictures included, began to recognize him, and stopped to say hello. That ordinary people would come up to him, an obviously homeless man in tattered clothes, and strike up a conversation seemed to resonated positively with him.

As we were talking, I noticed the beauty of the downtown square. This sanctuary is where curving brick sidewalks reflect the late afternoon light, and flowers glow with a resonance that almost seem to shine from within. Birds sing, squirrels play, and music from the masterpiece of nature harmonize with the symphony of park concerts. Summer will find busy people stopping simply to enjoy for a moment the calmness that prevails here.

Greg appeared almost at peace during those long hours he would sit in the park. To me, it did seem as though he wanted to find a measure of peace in his life, but his life history had been anything but that. And as it was so often in his life, he allowed the drama of alcoholism to overwhelm the small measure of calmness he did find.

From our previous talks I began to see a pattern in his life choices, a pattern that followed an all too common uncertain path. Growing up was a chaotic adventure for him, a journey that blasted him with confused and distorted worldviews of what it meant to be a man. It was filled with conflicts and admitted selfish pursuits often at the expense of those he encountered along the way. Those pursuits often butted heads with designed protocols the rest of the world adhered to, and when they butted too hard, something would break. This breakage led to incarceration and lost freedoms, and that time eventually led to the situation he found himself in when we met him.

Even so, I saw in Greg an almost boy-like demeanor struggling to resurface. He would often talk about fishing, playing games, and sports especially basketball in which, with his six foot four or five inch frame, he excelled when he was younger. He also enjoyed cooking, but was not currently in a situation where he could do much of that.

The kind of cooking he was doing now was a physical chore for Greg. "I have a microwave, but no electricity. I have to carry it outside and down to the other end of the storage area and plug it into the socket on the light pole, know what I'm say'n. That's where I heat my soup, then, I have to carry it all back."

Somehow those good things in his life never took hold in such a way as to steer him clear of the troubling events that eventually overwhelmed his life. Now, as he faced life living in a storage shed after having treatments for colon cancer, he realized for the first time the errors he made at a young age. As a result, he seemed to navigate to places that offered a shelter of comfort, a respite from his life, from his existence as a convicted felon, alcoholic, and homeless man. He sought beauty and clarity, but often looked for it in the wrong places. The park offered an element of both, which he used to define what beauty and clarity meant.

"I invited someone to go to church with me." He said with an air of goodness about him.

"Church? Which church is that?"

"You know, that small church just across the road from where the shed is, know what I'm say'n, the one with all the flags out front."

"Oh yes, I remember."

Although I did not know much about that particular church, it did seem to have a positive impact on him. I was impressed with him for doing such a thing. He had never had a very close relationship with God, so for him to make that kind of a commitment was a dramatic change in his way of thinking. Then for him to ask someone to go with him was a reflection of the change that was taking place in his heart.

Many years ago I heard how a small seed can crumble the hardest of sidewalks once it takes root. In my heart I felt that somehow a small seed had been planted in Greg's hardened heart, and now it was taking hold and starting to crumble the stony coldness that had resided there for so long. As I looked around the park, I noticed the beauty growing all around, I could only wonder if Greg would ever find the beauty, he so desperately sought but seemed never to find.

An ordinary pond, located a short distance from my home, served as a place of healing for me. There I found solitude and calmness as I talked with God and sought healing for my broken heart. Just as the pond held special meaning for me, this downtown square offered a similar kind of respite for Greg.

Each time I saw the light reflect off the shiny surface of the benches, my smile grew a bit larger because they reminded me of the beauty of the conversations I had with Greg, and the friendship that started to grow because of simply spending time with him. Only God could bring something like this together. Only from Him can boldness come from someone normally timid and shy. Only from Him could the rough texture of this man soften respectfully to talk about his life. Joy is what resulted. Things such as these are the beauty that comes from God. I wanted so much for Greg to find not just that beauty, but to replace the hardness and ugliness that had been his life with the change that can come only from knowing this kind of splendor. It doesn't matter if we're homeless or live in a mansion. We're all searching for the same thing.

We're all homeless in a way as aptly stated by Denver from the story *Same Kind of Different as Me*, "The truth about it is, whether we is rich or poor or something in between, this earth ain't no final restin' place. So in a way, we are all homeless – just working our way toward home."

There was a noticeable pep in Greg's spirit, not the defiant, depressed demeanor, he portrayed when we first met him. In our first meetings he had been slumped over. Now he was sitting up straight with a big, genuine smile. He seemed relaxed, happy, and hopeful. It is amazing how we all crave those simple things in our lives: a handshake, a pat on the back, a simple hello. Greg responded positively to those things. It had been so long since anyone had genuinely done any of those things for him.

As we finished our time together and walked away, I turned back toward Greg and said, "I'll see you again next time? I don't want to lose you."

A huge grin spread across his face, a happy smile, one that says, 'I belong'.

"You won't lose me, I ain't goin' nowhere."

His words reminded me of another verse I've read many times.

"*...lo, I am with you always, even unto the end of the world.*" Jesus – Mathew 28:20 (KJV)

He ain't goin' nowhere either.

CHAPTER 6 – Prison Doors

Too many times I allowed my fears of rejection to dictate my actions, or rather lack of action, when it came to following what God was calling me to do. Through those fears I became blind to his will desiring instead to remain safe in my secure home with my family. Fear can become prison doors as strong as steel if we allow events of our past and uncertainties of our future to temper them, but fear can provide us with a greater strength if we allow God to temper them.

What I've learned is that God is patient even in our insecurities. In our immaturity, He allows us enough seasons to mature into a stronger understanding of why he wants us to face certain challenges.

Prison bars and comfort zones do not blend well, and yet I believe we get comfortable in what we know is not good for us. Comfort zones can also become prison bars if that is all we know. Greg spent many years behind real prison bars because of his actions. Even when he was eventually released each time, he returned to the same environment that put him there in the first place. As bad as that environment was, it was actually a comfort zone for him because that was all he knew.

Greg and I were so different in many ways, yet the same in others. His comfort zones eventually led him back to prison multiple times in multiple ways. There was the hard, cold, steel bar kind then there were the addictions, the kind of prison with invisible bars that were just as incarcerating. My comfort zones led me to a different kind of prison, not one made of steel bars, but one just as confining, just as limiting. My bars were called extreme shyness, timidity, and insecurity. Although these bars were much softer than his, I was still locked in silence, hidden, unable to step out; it was where I wanted to reside, but not where God wanted me. God started to bring me out of those limiting zones more than fifteen years ago, and as a result, limits became amazing adventures. However, certain comfort zones continue to linger in my life, but stepping away from them has become easier.

Yet, here we were, two different people with two different backgrounds and life stories, sitting on a park bench talking about the difficulties of his life as a homeless man. Somehow, in God's infinite wisdom, he understood that the two of us needed to connect. I suppose the experiences I had suffering behind the prison bars of my own, helped me to empathize with Greg's situation. He no longer wanted to blend into the background. He had called out, "Hey! You with the camera!"

God asked me to come forward and speak to him. He was ashamed of what he had become. God asked me to let go of my fear, and help him find peace. He was a man who had tried to harden his heart, but God saw in him a spark of warmth that needed someone to help him rekindle it into life.

"... let your light shine before others, so that they may see your good works and give glory to your Father who is in Heaven"

Matthew 5:16 (ESV)

I used to have trouble understanding this verse. At first glance one might think it was about boasting to the world about what you do for the Lord. That was the last thing I wanted to do. But, God showed me that this verse is not about me, but about Him. What it means is to show His strength and His works and His power through our lives. He

45

unlocked my prison doors once I began to understand that message, and I was able to step outside of that limiting cell of fear.

Prison doors carry different meaning for different people. Even a well dressed, successful, church-going person can be locked behind invisible bars the outside world never sees, or they can be as strong as the ones Greg had to deal with. Too often our prison bars are made of an unwillingness to forgive, anger, resentment, addictions, or any number of similar emotions and conditions.

As a believer, I must always remember that Jesus has already unlocked those prison doors and all I have to do is open them. When we focus on ourselves, we will fail to see that the door is jarred open. Fear is the mechanism that Satan uses to blind us from understanding the truth of God's word and to place our trust in that word. What we will find is that He is standing on the other side of those prison bars reaching out His hand to take hold of ours.

"Do not fear, for I am with you; do not be dismayed, for I am your God. I will strengthen you and help you;

I will uphold you with my righteous Right Hand."

Jesus brought Greg and me together for a purpose neither of us knew at the time. Within my own power, I never would have thought to find myself on a park bench with someone like Greg, a big, bad, ex-con dude, and sharing Jesus with him. He would never have thought of finding himself on a bench next to a white Christian woman talking about Jesus, oranges, and prison. Nevertheless, Jesus is who brought us together and made us friends. Isn't that just like God? Although he was no longer behind steel bars, other prison bars held him captive and I prayed that he would someday find a way to break free of that bondage and take the Almighty's hand.

CHAPTER 7 – Greg – Visit 4

"No, I want to hear the whole story," Greg insisted. My son Christopher came with me for this visit. It was one of those beautiful late summer days in Kentucky, with a bright blue sky and warm sunshine, as well as a cool breeze floating across the Fountain Square Park. Very different from the weather conditions that contributed to the story that Greg wanted to hear.

On our previous meeting, I mentioned to Greg that I wanted to share a true story with him that showed the power of prayer and the power of God demonstrated through a cottonwood tree. It was an awesome story that had I not lived it myself, it would seem almost too incredible to be true, but it was.

"It's a long story Greg, I'll try to give you the shortened version", as I didn't want to lose his attention with such a long story.

"I want you to tell me the *whole* story, know what I'm say'n, it don't matter how long it is, I got plenty of time, know what I'm say'n."

By his subtle words, he reminded me just how long his days were, and personal stories like this were something he craved. Secretly, I was glad he wanted to hear the story about how a tree fell down—twice—and the impact it had on my family. I prayed silently God would use it as He had so many times in the past.

....

"Well, I need to give you some background so you'll understand why the tree was so awesome in more ways than one. Some years ago when I was very young, my mom and dad split up, and this split caused much grief for my mom and

48

my sister and me. He eventually remarried and continued with his life while my mom struggled with emotional issues, barely able to hold a job, barely able to provide for us. I was too young to understand all the issues involved, all I knew was that our home was no longer the happy home I remembered it being at one time.

The strain on my mom eventually proved too much. She lost her temper with me much of the time, and that was hard. She eventually went into mental institutions to get help. Because of her emotional state, I was removed from my home to live with my paternal grandmother. For nine years, I never once saw my mother. Inside the confused and uncertain emotional state I was in, my thoughts were always that I wanted her to be happy. She just didn't need to be in my life.

As I grew older, I silently wondered why my dad was not in my life. I saw other dads with their kids. It hurt. About the only times he stepped into my life was on a birthday and at Christmas, but then only for a few hours at a time. Other than that, he seemed to never have the time or desire to stay connected. Instead he spent all of his vacations and time off with his new family and his wife's children. My stepbrother and sister knew him better as dad than I did. I was hurt by my dad's lack of attention. Mom and I just did not understand. People should have explained more to me, but they didn't. During those nine years apart from my mom, my sister diligently prayed for our reconciliation.

I lived with my grandmother until Keith and I were married in 1981. I was an inexperienced nineteen-year-old at that time, and Keith was ten years older. We started our life together simply trying to make ends meet.

Over the next several years, my mechanical involvements with my dad remained sporadic and still no relationship with my mother. Then a strange event happened to me, one that I can only now reflect on as an answer to my sister's prayers, and how God's timing with our life events is always perfect.

My mom had recovered from her emotional issues and had completely turned her life over to God several years prior to this day. One afternoon while dusting my dresser in the bedroom, out of the blue I heard the Lord's voice in my spirit saying, 'It's time to call your mother.' I immediately went over to the phone and called her. I don't know how I remembered the phone number after nine years, but I did. Keith and I lived in a small apartment in Tulsa at the time, just a few miles from where my mom lived. One phone call, and we were laughing, crying, and sharing our lives again. We've been best friends ever since. That was 27 years ago. Yet, my dad remained distant and superficial in my life.

As Keith and I grew in our marriage, as young couples often do, we moved, first to Arkansas for almost five years, where our first son Tim was born, then to Edmond, Oklahoma where our son Christopher was born. Within a year, we were able to purchase our first home. It was small with a small yard that dropped off into a drainage ditch on the backside. Out of that drainage ditch, grew several large cottonwood trees that stretched close to sixty feet high. Late in the afternoon on a hot summer day, those cottonwood trees provided a nice shade across our backyard.

During the next six or seven years, my relationship with my dad and stepmother remained about the same, although time dulled the pain somewhat, deep inside I still harbored a sense of loss and longing to have had my dad in my life. I wanted to love my dad. I wanted to love my stepmother, but what I knew as love for them, was in reality only mechanical respect for the man I knew as my dad, not a man who was ever my daddy, and a stepmother who seemed distant and disconnected in our relationship. I began to realize that in many respects, I was blaming my stepmother for my dad's reluctance to share his life with us.

Unknown to me at the time, my dad began to express signs of regret for having been distant to his children. During one of our annual Christmas gatherings, he revealed to Keith that he knew he had not been a good father for remaining out of my life for so long. He was a prideful man, but he made a remarkable statement for someone so stubborn. He was glad I had married someone who loved me so much and wished his life with his family could have shown more of those same kinds of traits. Keith took this to heart, and more than once when I would get down about the situation, he would remind me of what my dad said. Even my stepmother began to loosen her tight cordiality and demeanor. What few token visits we made she seemed more genuine and accepting, which made all of us more comfortable. But it was too little and not nearly often enough.

During this time the Lord began to work on me directing my life and those around me toward an event no one foresaw. I began to grow more spiritually, learning more about and from God's word. I sought personal time with Him often praying from inside my closet to remove myself from distractions. Small events of faith began to show in my life, like the time my lawnmower would not start and I asked Christopher, who was only three or four at the time, to help me by placing his hand on the mower with mine and we asked God please start this stubborn machine. It roared to life on the next pull. Then there was the time Keith had given Christopher a pocketknife that he cherished, but somehow he had lost it in the backyard, I felt so sorry for him because he was almost in tears over it. We looked and looked but couldn't find it, so we prayed together right there on the ground saying we knew the Lord could see it and please

51

show it to us. When we looked up, the sun glistened off the blade and he found it on the ground under the swing. Simple lessons of faith that would one day be well served in Christopher's life.[1]

As simple as those things were, I was emboldened by them and began to feel closeness to the Lord that I had never felt before. At one time, I was an extremely shy person who lacked confidence, but the Lord revealed to me that even as timid as I was, with Him, I could do all things.

God led me out of a comfort zone to join an evangelism program at my church where I learned to share the gospel in an easy manner. After going through the program, I began to grow concerned about my dad and stepmother's salvation. So one day I put my fear aside, and presented the gospel to them. The Lord prepared the moment in such a way that it defused many of the tensions and anxieties I felt.

Their response was remarkable. They recognized they had not always lived in God's will, and had let things keep them from church. They seemed sorry about that then, but verified they had both made a personal commitment to Christ many years ago. They never realized just how important that was to me and this conversation lifted many of the concerns I had about them, and broke down many barriers. I told them about the lawnmower and the lost knife and they seemed fascinated. A few weeks later, my

---

[1] It is very important that all Christians have a balanced understanding as to when and how much God miraculously involves himself in our lives, so as to not have false expectations. Please see:
http://bible-translation.net/page/does-god-step-in-and-solve-our-every-problem-because-we-are-faithful
http://bible-translation.net/page/why-has-god-permitted-wickedness-and-suffering

stepmother called and wanted me to pray for her lawnmower because it wouldn't start. I did, and it started.

During this time, my dad began to show flu like symptoms that just would not go away. The doctors thought it was pneumonia and started antibiotics. The symptoms grew worse. Further tests revealed the truth. It was lung cancer. My dad had quit smoking many years before, but too many years in the habit had finally caught up with him.

One thing I must admit about my dad, the courage he showed during this time demonstrated the kind of man he was, exhibiting his true nature. He uttered few complaints as he underwent radiation and chemotherapy. The side effects were awful and broke him down physically and emotionally, yet he remained confident and resolute. A few years earlier, my sister survived ovarian cancer. Her survival deeply moved my dad, and contributed to the softening of our relationship. I think it helped him during this time.

My stepmother became a rallying point for strength standing with him through the darkest and longest of days. As a result, my respect for her grew, and I began to understand this person that I once resented was truly a loving and caring individual. My love and respect for her also grew as a result.

The cancer spread to my dad's bones, and the doctors said the odds were not good that he would beat it, and it was time to get all of his affairs in order. I experienced a range of emotions I had never felt before. Inside of me still harbored those disappointing lack of memories, yet I experienced an unexpected rekindled love toward my dad.

I shared time with my sister, my stepmother, and step sister spending long hours at his bedside helping take care of his needs as his life slowly ebbed toward its end. Eventually, he was placed in a hospice care room because of complications and because my stepmother was physically worn out.

One night, I told her to go home and get some rest, I'll stay with him. As the evening churned into the late hours I had dimmed the lights and gazed over at my father as he slept. Maybe because I was tired, maybe because Satan was attacking me, but for some reason all those old hurtful and painful memories from the past resurfaced. I cried out silently, "You were never there for me. Why should I be here for you now? Why should I care?'

The anger and fear that boiled inside of me broke my heart and I felt alone, vulnerable, and defeated. So I reached out to the only comfort I could find. I prayed.

"Lord, why am I having these feelings again, I don't want them. I want to love my father, but he was never a father to me, he was never there when I needed him. Please Lord, please remove these feelings from my heart, I no longer want them in my life."

I raised my head as tears slid down my cheeks, and I gazed upon the emaciated face of my dying father. Within my breaking heart a rush of compassion overflowed, and what started as tiny tears, became a flood of released fears and lost dreams. Within my heart I know I heard the Lord speak these words.

He may not have been the kind of father he should have been, but now in his time of need, I expect you to be the kind of daughter I created you to be.

With those words filling my soul, all the bitterness, all the anger I ever carried for him dissolved into forgiveness and compassion. The past no longer mattered, it simply mattered that he was my father and I was his daughter and he was in need of forgiveness from me. By granting him that forgiveness, I was released from the chains of bondage that had held me captive for so many years. I felt a freedom I'm not sure I even really knew I needed.

During this time Keith had remained in Edmond while I was in Tulsa attending my father. It was spring, and the storms that so often blow across the Oklahoma landscape began to stir into life once again. An unusually violent storm with high winds and torrential rains rolled across the plains of central Oklahoma from the northwest. The next morning Keith called and said something had happened. One of the tall cottonwood trees had blown over. A giant ball of roots and soil had broken loose from the slope that angled down into the drainage ditch. The width of that root ball was much wider than my outreached arm span. After checking the property line, it became clear that the tree belonged to us and it must be taken down. We could not afford that kind of expense. We just did not have the money to deal with this disaster.

My emotions began to tumble. I was tired from being up all night, and it seemed that Satan was throwing everything he could at us. When I finally made it back to my mother's home, I stepped into my 'reserve' prayer closet and simply asked the Lord to take care of it. The next evening, I told both my stepmother and dad about the tree, and I wasn't sure how we were going to deal with it. I just prayed and asked God for help. In their troubled state, they could offer little but concern. On the evening of the third day, another storm blew across central Oklahoma, this time coming from the southwest. It was as violent and as strong as the previous one.

Then next morning Keith went off to work like he always did, and came home at noon to fix a sandwich. As he was eating, he opened the backdoor to look at the tree. He stopped for a moment not sure what he was seeing. From where he was, it looked like the fallen tree was now standing upright again. That was impossible. It had been ripped from the ground, and now it was standing as straight as a new tree. He walked over to the fence and peered over the top. No limbs were broken, no more hole in the ground, no root ball protruding. The second storm had blown the tree upright again, and it was in perfect condition. The ground did not even appear broken. The Lord had stood up our tree!

When Keith called, he buzzed excitedly about what had happened. Several other people witnessed this tree resurrection as well. I told my dad and stepmother and about praying in the closet asking the Lord to intervene in the issue. Their eyes opened as wide as a child's eyes in disbelief, but it was true. A miracle had happened in my backyard. And then another miracle immediately happened. My stepmother and dad asked if I would come over to the hospital bed and hold their hands and pray for them. They had never showed an interest in prayer or anything regarding church, the Bible, or even God before. It was something I had always wanted to do with them. It was all I could do not to cry as I took their hands; we bowed our heads and prayed.

Greg was looking at me the whole time I was sharing, listening so intently. People were walking by us but I don't think Greg ever noticed. I continued.

Every day my dad grew weaker and every day, he would ask about that tree, "Is it still standing?" he would ask when I would walk into the room. When I verified that indeed it was, a sense of comfort and peace fell upon both of them. In a way, it seemed that old cottonwood tree became a symbol of hope for them, for now they knew for sure that God was watching over them. It provided a calming sense of assurance.

Within a couple of weeks, the doctor's prediction came true. I stood with my sister and brother, stepmother and step-siblings gathered around his bed. With one last breath, he left this world to be with God. I wept in sadness, and yet in comfort knowing that he had claimed Christ as his savior. We as a family had claimed reconciliation. The love that I had so wanted from him had been rediscovered and we shared those last few days within the shade cast by the story of a cottonwood tree.

Over the next year, I continued to grow in a relationship with my stepmother. In an odd turn of events, she was also diagnosed with lung cancer. For the next several months as she slowly deteriorated, and the prognosis grew dim, she in a feeble voice would ask,

"Is your tree still standing?"

Great comfort would fill her sunken eyes each time I would assure her that the tree was still standing, healthy and strong, good as new. She would smile and close those tired eyes and drift off to sleep. Within a couple of weeks, she too went on to be with the Lord having died with the knowledge of God's grace, and in comfort knowing that something wonderful and awesome was awaiting her arrival.

A week after her funeral another one of those storms blew across central Oklahoma. The winds kicked up blowing in gusts upwards to 70 miles per hours. My son and I stood at the back door and watched as our tree bent with the wind, hoping it would continue to stand. Then we heard a crack and watched as the resurrected tree crashed to the ground.

We carried a sense of sadness over its falling, and at first we did not understand why God would allow this tree that had all but been ripped from the ground to stand tall and strong once again only to allow it to fall during this storm.

Then it became obvious to both of us that this tree no longer had purpose. Its purpose was to provide my dad and stepmother with a visual miracle in which to understand the glory and grace that God offers to all who call upon His name. It became a confirmation to me that even though my earthly father was now gone, my Heavenly Father is always there for me. I have this feeling that in some way, the felling of this tree was my father and stepmother's way of letting us know they were okay in Heaven, they were with the Father, they didn't need the tree anymore, and neither did we.

When the sun broke free from the storm clouds later that next morning, the tree that fell twice reminded me the door on one era of life had closed, and another door of reconciliation and warm memories opened.

....

Greg remained quiet as I finished the story. It was obvious the Holy Spirit was working on him from the look on his face and the tears streaming down his cheeks. I knew it was a time to simply let Him work.

Greg held his head low between his legs almost perpendicular to the ground. His massive hands cupped around his eyes and stretched across his forehead. His tattered shirt fluttered in the breeze. I looked over to Christopher and he cast a shallow smile my way fully understanding the significance of the moment. The park, which had been filled with its everyday noises and commotions suddenly seemed quiet and subdued for several minutes. Greg finally raised his large shoulders and turned toward me tears casting sparkles across his face, which he wiped with his hands.

"I want that. I want to know I have it, that it's for real. I want to be saved, know what I'm say'n, but I don't know how. Can you help me?"

"Would you like to pray with me?"

"I don't know how."

"I can help you with that, if that is what you truly want."

"It's what I want, more than anything."

I wanted to be sure that he understood what he was saying. I told him he was admitting he was a sinner and acknowledging he could not save himself. He was asking Jesus Christ to come into his heart and save him. He was acknowledging in faith that Jesus Christ rose from the grave three days later. He nodded yes, and bowed his head low with his hand once again covering his eyes.

"Lord I know I'm a sinner. I want you to forgive me. I know you died on the cross for me and that you rose again three days later, and I want to live for you, the rest of my life, amen."

A huge lump filled my throat and tears welled up. I was so happy. When I gazed into his eyes, what were at one time sullen and lost, were filled with peace and joy just as though he had never experienced such a powerful moment before. Christopher couldn't stop smiling, and he jumped up to snap a picture of the moment.

We sat for a while longer and talked about his new life, but time came when we had to part ways again. I gave him a big hug and he stood tall and straight with a giant grin across his face as we walked away. He waved to us as we drove around the corner. The next day I returned with a friend as I wanted to ask Greg about following up with being baptized.

"I knew you were going to ask about that" he said, "but that's okay, 'cause I'd like to do that right away. Will they baptize me in your church?"

"I'm sure they will, I just need to ask Pastor Jason."

"That's good then, but, uh, how, uh, how am I suppose to get there, it's too far to walk, know what I'm say'n, and you and Keith ain't suppose to be given rides to homeless people, I understands that though."

"Well, I think we can make an exception in this case," I reassured him.

I spoke with our pastor that afternoon to get the testimony sheet that the church wanted filled out. Keith and I brought it back to Greg that evening and made plans to pick him up the following Sunday morning.

As we prepared to leave, Keith said to Greg, "You know Satan is going to come after you now, don't you?"

Greg replied with confidence, "Let him try, I got my armor on now."

Now I was smiling big! Keith shook his hand and hugged him. Greg pointed at Keith and said, "You are now my brother in Christ." He pointed at me and said, "You're my sister in Christ, but, you better go now, 'cause I think I might cry."

Keith and I walked to the car with a spring in our step and big smiles on our faces. We thanked God for Greg and what God was doing in his life and for the privilege of letting us be a part of it.

One verse comes to mind when I remember the events of that day.

"*The LORD sets the prisoners free...*" Psalm 146:7 (ESV)

Greg was now free from his past and had hope in his life, but Keith's words of warning to Greg were to prove prophetic.

CHAPTER 8 – Stirred Waters

This will be a day I'll never forget, know what I'm say'n?"

I'll never forget that day either, the day Greg was baptized. When we picked up Greg that Sunday morning, August 28, 2011, he was waiting for us carrying a huge grin and radiance across his face that had been missing a few days before. He didn't say much as we drove toward the church other than the normal greetings and some small chitchat, but as we pulled into the church parking lot, I've never seen such a large man appear so nervous.

"How many folks did you say would be watching?"

"Oh, somewhere between six and seven hundred, in the 11:00 service anyway," I answered.

Greg sighed rather deeply. Then he cast a subtle grin through pursed lips toward me. He looked out the window at the hundreds of vehicles parked in the parking area and seemed at once pensive yet determined. Large crowds always bothered him, and we were a bit nervous for him too knowing that this experience was going to challenge him in ways he had never been challenged before.

"Whatever possessed you to think that I'd ever want to stand up in front of seven hundred people and do this?" Greg asked. He was wearing the cleanest shirt he had, a rather torn and faded green t-shirt that hung loosely over the top of his baggy jeans. His tennis shoes were worn and tattered as well, the souls flattened by his great bulk.

We laughed. I reassured him that he would do just fine, "It will be over before you know it."

As we walked up the steps toward the side entrance, he fell in behind us. When we entered the hallway that circled around the sanctuary, we met several people that knew about Greg's conversion and most of his story. Yet, in spite of that, they graciously greeted him and gave him hugs and words of encouragement. I was never more proud of my church, for Greg was an intimidating man with a broken past, yet they accepted him with open arms. He responded warmly to their overtures, and seemed to calm down some.

We had about a thirty-minute wait for the 9:30 am service to end, so we sat in the prayer room because he wanted to remain out of sight. I think he felt somewhat embarrassed by his clothes knowing that many people in our church would be dressed in their Sunday best. Keith and I purposely dressed down for the day anticipating that he might feel more comfortable if we did so.

Eventually the 9:30 am service ended. About six hundred people filed out of the sanctuary, many stopping to speak with Greg and us. A few, once they learned that Greg was going to be baptized in the next service, decided to stay long enough to watch. He seemed appreciative. One of the people we saw was Miss Francis, one of the founding members of our church. A year or so prior to that day she and Greg had actually become friends while he volunteered at a local charity organization called Hotel, Inc.

Miss Francis was genuinely fond of Greg. The feeling was mutual for he felt a close connection with this kind and gentle older lady. The two of them met in the hallway and we could tell right away that Greg carried a degree of respect and admiration for her. She was so thrilled that he was there, and the fact that she was there helped Greg calm down even more. Knowing someone in a strange place certainly provided an element of comfort for him. They talked alone for several moments until it was time for us to meet in the baptism prep room.

Several friends of ours were there, helping Greg with the gown, and showing him what and where and how things were going to work. As simple as those instructions were, knowing what to do seemed to make him feel even more at ease. Pastor Jason arrived, and with his jovial and personal style of greeting people connected with Greg right away. We left them to find our seats situated where we had a good view, and where Keith could take some pictures without interfering with other peoples view.

As I sat in the pew waiting for the service to begin, I reflected on some of the blessing moments I often listed in my journal.

Park benches in the shade

Being thanked just for listening

On bended knee with husband in prayer

Chord of three strands not easily broken

The privilege of praying the sinner's prayer with my friend Greg

Younger son beside me witnessing a soul being saved

Friends willing to go with me to interview the homeless

Testimony sheets filled out

Friends in church pew with me holding hands and hugging

Witnessing peace all over the face of one who had only known chaos

Where we were sitting, we could see almost the entire congregation, balcony included, and in this 11:00 am service, the sanctuary was filled to capacity. I began to feel nervous for Greg knowing that this kind of environment was exactly the kind of situation in which he would feel lost and uncomfortable. I prayed that peace would fill his soul and that the moment would be special beyond anything he could imagine.

The time came for him to step into the baptismal and he followed Pastor Jason into the shallow pool of water. I was never more proud of my pastor during this moment as he spoke in a gracious and loving way about Greg's life in a way where Greg's dignity remained intact. I had been somewhat concerned about how he would handle that story. He spoke of how Greg had lived a difficult life, a life not honoring God, and how his life had been a world filled with chaos. He spoke about that day on the park bench. He spoke of how Greg came to understand the saving grace that was offered to him through faith in Christ, and now that his heart was changed, he was ready to turn away from that old self. Through those few moments that Jason was speaking, I could not remove my eyes from Greg's face. He stood with a peace and joy that only a man who had been forgiven of so much could ever have. He closed his eyes and held his head high. His massive body towered over Pastor Jason, who was a former college football quarterback and was no small individual himself.

Jason turned to Greg and asked if he believed that Christ had died for his sins, that He was raised on the third day and that by his faith in that belief, he understood he was now a new man with a new heart.

Greg said with confidence, "Yes I do."

With those words, Jason held his arms and as Greg knelt into the water, he submerged him. Suddenly, Greg's feet lost contact with the bottom and he lost his balance. Jason struggled to hold on as Greg stumbled and splashed trying to find his footing. My heart skipped a couple of beats and I said to myself, "oh no..." Jason almost went under himself, but he held on, and soon Greg found his footing. At that moment we witnessed something that I have never seen before in our church or in any church that I've ever attended. The entire congregation stood and began to cheer for Greg. The noise that roared from those cheers was the loudest spontaneous noises I've ever heard in a church. People were cheering and clapping and hollering.

Jason turned to Greg and said, "Take it all in. All of that is for you."

Greg stood there for a few long seconds absorbing the moment. I could see he was deeply moved by what was happening. The peace on his face began to glow with an aura that surrounded his massive shoulders. For in that moment, Greg experienced the compassion, love, connections, and happiness that he so desperately needed in his life.

My heart leapt with joy, and my eyes filled with tears as my friends who surrounded me hugged my shoulders. I couldn't stop smiling or crying.

We met Greg, escorted him to the service, and when it was over, Greg said once again as we walked across the parking lot on that hot August day, "I'll never forget this day. This is my new birthday. This is the way to live cause people need to live for Jesus."

"Is there anything that we could do for you?" Keith and I asked.

"No, I just want you to keep doing what you've been doing, just keep being my friend, ya know what I'm say'n."

"You've got it Greg, we'll be friends forever."

Greg's life, as he often put it, had been lived in chaos, but on this day, for the first time in all of that uncertainty, he was able to see clearly the life God intended for all of us to have. He may have been homeless on this earth during that time, but he knew now that a mansion awaited him in a home he would possess for eternity.

As powerful as that day was, as wonderful and joyous of a moment we had witnessed, as confident in our hearts that

Greg's decision had been real and purposeful, what lay ahead for him and for us we could never have foreseen. I am convinced that Satan will attack hardest those who threaten him the most. If that be the case, then Greg must have been one of Satan's most powerful threats.

CHAPTER 9 – Jane

Her aqua blue eyes were the likes of which I've never seen before. They were astonishing eyes, brilliant, bright, and glowed with a blazing hue that immediately caught the attention of anyone graced by the opportunity to look into them. Through those eyes, I caught a glimpse of a strong woman simply trying to get by as someone living on the streets, and through those eyes I discovered just how weary and worn down a person can become by a life lived in such conditions. As bright as they were, they were tired eyes. I'll call her Jane.

The weeks following Greg's baptism, he became one of my strongest supporters, who seemed determined to help with, and was fascinated by, the process of compiling information for this book. It became our project. As a result, he often arranged for me to meet with other homeless people he knew. On this day, my friend Shannon and I were searching across the main part of downtown looking for a lady Greg had mentioned.

We searched in several locations to no avail, and I was beginning to get discouraged that at least on this day I would not connect with anyone. I tried one last place, a hidden spot tucked into the corner square of a downtown church, and discovered Greg sitting in the shade under a protective overhanging awning. With him was a middle-aged woman who I discovered was Jane.

She tied her once blond, but now grayish hair into a ponytail to keep it out of the way. It appeared to be quite thick and a bit unkempt. She wore a dark loosely fitting top decorated with small dots. Her posture indicated tiredness, a kind of low-leaning, slumped forward position trying to find a comfortable place. She was attractive, but seemed to have lost the ability, or desire, to keep herself up physically.

Greg was genuinely pleased to see us, and always the gentleman he moved over to another bench to allow Jane and me some privacy. Shannon sat on one end of the bench and allowed me to do most of the talking.

Compiling reference information for a book such as this requires not only persistence but also a measure of tact tempered with compassion. My memory being somewhat limited, it was important to take notes and, when possible, to electronically record the conversations for future reference. Understandably, that became an issue at times. I never assumed it would be okay; I always asked permission first. Usually I let Keith do all the photography but he was not always available so I had to use my limited knowledge to do the best I could to take pictures. Making a visual record proved one of the more difficult and contested parts of the process. So many homeless do not want their photograph taken. We understood this and always approached the process with discreetness and respect for their desires.

We learned a great deal through trial and error during the interview process. What became evident is these precious souls do not want to be treated like a project. That was never my intent. Walking a fine line between obtaining the material and treating them with respect was a challenging part of what I was doing. Treating them with value was foremost important. Gaining their trust took time most often accomplished by demonstrating a genuine and consistent nature of concern. Once they became comfortable with your intent, in most cases they would open up to the photographs and the recording of the interview.

Jane was no exception. She was friendly but reserved, cautious yet willing to speak about her situation. She was reluctant at first about having her photograph taken, even of just her feet from the knees down.

"I'm not presentable enough. No, I don't want my picture taken."

Greg couldn't help but pipe in. Even though he sat some distance from us, he could still hear what we were saying. "Jane, we got to move forward, know what I'm say'n. Can't stay in the same way."

Jane cast a sharp look toward Greg, and he took her cue as if he understood he needed to leave us alone. He stood and walked away out of sight.

I backed off the photograph, and asked her to tell us about herself.

"I'm from Franklin (KY) and came to Bowling Green looking for a job. I've done lots of jobs, dishwasher in the schools and restaurants, housekeeping jobs in motels, cleaning lady, you know, things like that."

I acknowledged her with a nod and waited for her to continue.

"I've lived in lots of places, Tennessee, Oklahoma, Kansas City, and Nashville. That's where I ended up homeless, Nashville, for about a year, been in Bowling Green for two months now."

She paused for a moment to collect her thoughts then continued. She appeared not to want to discuss the particulars about how she became homeless. I didn't pursue it; I just let her talk.

"I grew up in the country. My daddy worked on a farm six days a week. We never had much money, but we got by. My momma got sick with cancer and couldn't take care of my two-year-old brother, so I had to drop out of school in

71

the eleventh grade so I could help raise him. I never went back to school, but when I was forty-nine I got my GED."

She seemed proud of the fact that she finally did finish her high school education. Lack of education is one of the most dominant traits that contribute to homelessness. A wide variety of situations cause people to drop out prematurely a good percentage of them not unlike what Jane described.

"When we were kids my brothers and sisters and I went to church, but momma and daddy stayed home. Sunday was his only day off so he just wanted to rest. My grandfather and great grandfather were both preachers."

I asked her about Jesus in her life.

"I got Jesus okay. I know I'll be in Heaven one day. I can't remember the exact day it happened, but I was twelve when I was saved, all us kids were."

She held her head up high with those words, her radiant blue eyes shining in the reflected sunlight. Then she lowered her chin and looked toward the ground with a more somber look on her face.

"Then the preacher ran off with one of the deacon's wives, and I had to wait to get baptized. My brother is a Baptist preacher in his town, and sometimes he picks me up so I can go to church, but it's been a while since he last did that." Again, she paused as if to reflect more deeply on her life searching to recall events that might be of interest or shed a degree of importance upon who she was as a person.

During the interviews I've done, it has become a great revelation just how important it is for people caught in the homeless trap to regain a sense of value about who they are. Even small victories in their lives carry with them a significant impact that becomes more valuable the deeper and longer they remain in their homeless state. It is almost as if they search for those meaningful, but often obscure events, sometimes lost in the chaos of their lives, but rarely forgotten. They just need something to jar loose the lid from their locked storage chest of memories. Simply listening and possessing a caring heart will go a long way in helping them regain a sense of historical perspective and meaningfulness from their lives so they can move forward.

"I got married when I was eighteen, but it didn't last. Two more times I was married, and two more times they failed. I had a miscarriage once. My husband elbowed me in the stomach, and I lost the baby."

Her brilliant blue eyes filled with tears, and I experienced a damp blurriness in my own eyes. I can't imagine how devastating that must have been for her.

She changed directions with her next statement. "Never had a driver license. Never had a car so I never learned. No money or time to do things like that. Always a bill to pay and work to do. I usually just took the bus. This church right here where we're sitting gives us free bus tickets every month, but I still have to walk a lot."

I glanced down at her feet, which were swollen, and her worn out shoes were untied to reduce the pressure on them.

"Is being homeless scary?" I asked her.

"Not really. Being scared is a weakness, and I don't want to be that way. I want to be strong."

In many ways I could see her strength, yet in many ways she was broken and lost. If being brave is defined as moving forward in spite of fear rather than an absence of fear, then she certainly demonstrated that concept. I'm always amazed at how adaptable the human spirit is.

"I don't drink or do drugs or nothing. Others say I'm boring because of it. Had to fight my way out of a bar once; I didn't like that. So I stay away from those places now. I got too much trouble as it is, don't need no more. I've been in jail a couple of times, once for sleeping in a doorway and once for trespassing."

She seemed rather matter of fact about the jail time as though it were no major concern, and something that happened because of her situation. She didn't appear to be angry about it nor was she remorseful about it. She directed her reaction as not wanting to go there again.

"Don't always believe everything you hear about all those help organizations. People there think they are doing good things, but they're not. Yeah, you got a roof over your head, running water and all. But some of those people are not all that good. They holler at you for no reason, and if you don't do what they say they want to send you off to a sanitarium."

"What about Hope House or Hotel, Inc.?" I asked. "They have some really nice people there."

"I know about those places. They're better than most, but I don't want to go there unless it's a last resort kind of thing. I get food stamps so I can buy food, and don't need other handouts. Jesus said, 'What comes out of your mouth condemns you', so we shouldn't be judging others."

There was another short pause as she gathered her thoughts and I gathered mine. Most of the time I have a list of questions I work from, but sometimes I just let the conversation flow. A few questions just naturally entered the conversation.

"So what gives you hope?"

"Jesus. Knowing He will let me do what I need to do."

74

"What do you want people to know?"

"Jesus can get you through everything, no matter how hard life is, He will give you strength."

"Do you have any dreams for yourself?"

She paused for a moment. Her blue eyes became teary again. She directed her gaze away from our location as though she saw something far away.

Finally, she said, "A home where I can have all my grandchildren together around me."

She has four grandchildren and two great-grandchildren. Although she never revealed their names or spoke about her own children, I could tell that family was an important element in her life, one disrupted by circumstance. One of the common issues I encounter with the homeless is family. Sometimes the issue is bad, and other times it is just lost in a haze. Other times family is what holds them together, yet family issues often prove to be one of the driving forces that can cause people to crumble emotionally.

Not being a psychologist, I find it difficult to look at the problem from an analytical point of view. Being a mother and a wife, I can empathize why family carries such a powerful influence over a person's emotional wellbeing. Too often broken emotions are caused by selfish desires, and those desires require little to fester into a full blown case of distrust and anger. Although Jane did not reveal much about her family, only the good parts from what I could gather, I felt as though there were deeper issues here that she held in reserve just for herself to ponder.

As our time together ended, my friend Shannon and I took Jane's hands. We prayed that the Lord would continue to watch over her, keep her safe, and provide her with an answer to her dreams. When we finished, Jane's blue eyes were puffy and inflamed. As I gazed into those windows of her life, they filled with a watery sparkle. She blinked hard once. Then tears dripped down her cheeks in a long, sustained flow that wove across the lines of her face. We hugged.

I'm always torn inside after an interview like this. They reveal so much about themselves to the point that it not only affects their emotions, but mine as well. Most people never know who these people are. Few rarely care, and even fewer attempt to find out. With limited resources, I can do little. What I've grown to understand is that it is not always the volume of what you do that is important, it is the quality of what you do that matters most. For someone who, for whatever reason, has lost a part of who they are, simply sitting and speaking with someone else can often lift their spirits. That gives them a sense of value even if only for a day, gives them something they would not ordinarily experience.

Jane appeared reserved at first, offering short, cliché comments about her life, a tightly closed bud. After a while the budding flower, opened into a full bloom. Trust became the nurturing soil that provided life to a relationship. Sometimes that soil becomes depleted of nutrients and requires external substances to revitalize it. Even so it takes time for a nutrient starved life to rebound into a healthy vibrant person again. Until that occurs, relationships are difficult to build with people who have constructed so many protective barriers. Dealing with such difficult issues was not something I was prepared for initially, but I learned that compassion travels a long way to break down those barriers. The distance traveled often becomes the most important part of the journey.

Before we left, Jane untied her ponytail and brushed out her hair. She wiped the tears from her face and her angelic eyes began to sparkle once again.

"You can take my picture if you want to," she said.

"You have such beautiful eyes. Thank you for allowing me to capture their radiance." I will never forget the haunting sadness locked inside the beauty of those piercing blue windows of her life.

My conversation with Jane opened my eyes to an important aspect of gaining the trust of the homeless. Discovering the windows from which to peer into their lives became a constant challenge as many times those windows were locked shut, or clouded over. Removing the locks, cleaning the grime from their surfaces required more than simple conversations. What it required more than anything was consistent, quality time.

CHAPTER 10 – Richard – Visit 1

"Every time we take two steps forward, we get knocked back ten. It just isn't right. It's hurtful to be looked down on and called a bum." It was a powerful statement coming from such a young man, but as I explored deeper into the world of the homeless, I began to see the different faces that defined this devaluing state of life.

Richard, one of the youngest I met along the way, was twenty years old from Boston, Massachusetts. He looked more like a college student who should have been enjoying football games and life as a university student. Instead, he survived on the streets.

The day after my talk with Jane, I found Richard sitting on a bench on the downtown square. He seemed somewhat shy, maybe a little embarrassed about his situation. It wasn't easy for a young man to admit he was homeless. Young men are supposed to be strong and fearless, providers and doers of great things at least that is what society teaches. For Richard, the challenges of life revolved around when his next meal would be available.

"I was seventeen when I first became homeless. My mom's boyfriend and I didn't see eye to eye, and my mom chose him over me. It was the middle of winter with snow on the ground when I left. All I was wearing were flip-flops, shorts, and a hoody."

My desire as I heard these stories was to do so with a pure heart and without judgment. I had to hold back my desire to express how appalled I was at the thought of a young boy having to leave home under those kinds of conditions.

"My dad wasn't there when I was growing up. He spent a long time in prison after an armed robbery. I grew up in a good home though. I love my mom, and I just want her to be happy. I think mom was just lonely, and needed someone, and that is why she connected with the guy. My mom and dad were never married, never intended to."

The fact that Richard spoke fondly about his mom was encouraging to me. It spoke strongly about his personal strength, and ability to see the good even through the haze of lost dreams and heartbreak.

"I tried to get into a homeless shelter at first, but they wouldn't let me stay there, said I was too young at seventeen. Eventually, I got into trouble and ended up in jail. While I was in jail, I tried to contact my mom but I never could get hold of her. After my time was up I got out and found a job as a roofer. Made pretty good money for a couple of years, even had my own place. But, the economy turned bad and I lost that job."

"How did you end up in Bowling Green?"

"I had some friends down here, and a chance came up to get a new start. So a buddy and I caught the bus, and moved in with them. It lasted a couple of weeks, and we got into an argument over twenty dollars, and had to move out. We walked around for two days until a police officer stopped us, and we told him our story. He sent us over to the Salvation Army, and that ended up being a good thing because we didn't know anything about what was here in this town. He actually did us a favor, and was a friendly man, and helped us get situated, for ten days anyway. Then we will have to move out again."

"When the ten days are up, what then?"

"I'm not sure. When you're out on the streets you can get burned by a lot of people. Sometimes they come off really nice, but it's really only you and no one else. You don't have people to confide in or do things for. It feels good if you can do something good for someone, and make them happy. But it's a real de-motivator to not have anyone to do something for."

"Why not do something good for yourself?"

"Because it feels better to do something good for someone else. I never thought I would be homeless in a million years. I miss my mom and sister. It's like I don't have a family any more. I've been alone for three years now."

Even though his demeanor was typical of most twenty-year-old males, I could tell his heart was broken. He needed to feel important, to belong to something larger than what he currently faced. I try to remove myself from emotional connections when I talk with these individuals, but it is impossible to do so completely. As a mother of a son about the same age as Richard who walked away from home a few years ago, I fear that my son may also find himself caught in this same kind of trap. Why Richard is disconnected from his family I will never fully know, but I do understand the pain he must feel because the pain of a lost son hovers like a heavy fog over my heart every day. Richard's heart must also be clouded by the heavy mist of uncertainty and loss.

"I wanted to be a nurse and actually enrolled at the University of Massachusetts, but I had to drop out because I ran out of money, and couldn't get any more. I came to

Bowling Green with three bags, but had to ditch two of them because I was tired of carrying them around. I have to walk everywhere. Makes it hard to get a job and stay clean. No one will hire you if you walk in after being outside all day."

"Are you able to get enough to eat?"

"Salvation Army provides three meals a day as long as I'm staying there; cereal in the morning, something like soup and a sandwich at noon, and another sandwich for supper. It keeps you going, better than nothing, but I still feel hungry a lot. I am thankful for what they provide."

I couldn't help but notice one of his eyes appeared somewhat different than normal. I was hesitant to ask him about it when he volunteered an explanation.

"I had cancer in my eye when I was little and lost it. My mom was so loving then, and treated me so well. Sometimes she was stern but we had a good family then and I remember the good times and dinners together. She invested time in me. All that changed when the new guy came into her life. I have no hard feelings, I just want her to be happy. I love her so much, I could never hold a grudge."

He looked away and then toward the ground as if thinking back to younger, happier days. He paused as he gathered his thoughts. I waited for him to continue holding back my own tears. He is a strong young man in so many ways, yet caught in the middle of clouded circumstances that altered his life's path.

"My sister is a real sweetheart, beautiful, I love her to death." He extracted two small, somewhat crumpled and faded pictures of her and himself from his wallet.

I see two small happy children who in their youth were innocent and vulnerable. I could tell he cherished those pictures, and proudly displayed them as if to say, "See, I had a good life at one time." Clinging to the goods things from a happier past is a common trait I've seen in many homeless people I've talked to.

As I held the pictures closer so I could see them more clearly, he said, "I don't know where either she or my mom are now. I guess they must have started over fresh somewhere."

I passed a comforting pursed smile primarily to keep myself from crying, but also to show a sense of understanding to him. As I looked at the photos more closely, I asked him if they had been taken in a church.

"Yes, we went all the time when we were little, I was even in Royal Rangers, but now," he paused and reflected on his next words, "but, now I don't know, I think I'm losing my faith. I don't think it's completely gone, but not much there anymore. I've read the Bible, I don't understand everything in it, and I don't understand why a loving God would allow people to be homeless, to have all the heartache that they do. I know a lot of homeless people who have just given up on God, but some haven't."

Losing one's faith is an element that infiltrates into the hearts and minds of many homeless. I've seen both sides of it; some who cling to their faith and use it to find strength in hard times, and others who discount it to rely on themselves to get by. Often those who blame God for their situation do so because they fail to understand the relationship aspect of their connection to Him. They do not realize that God is not the reason for their situation. He is the answer for them.

Answering the question why do bad things happen to good people has always been a difficult question to answer. Ultimately, what it boils down to is that man is a sinful creature, and that sin is what has separated us from God.

Satan is the cause for the pain, the anguish, the heartache in this world, yet he has so deceived the world that we too often want to point the blame at the very thing that can save us.

"There is not much available here for homeless people," Richard told me. "Salvation Army makes you leave after ten days, or you have to pay five dollars a day after that. That don't sound like much, but to a homeless person with no income it might as well be a million dollars. In a few days, some buddies back in Boston are going to wire me enough for a bus ticket, so I'll be heading back up there. I hope to get back into nursing school, but I don't know, the nursing profession frowns on people who have tattoos."

His arms were covered in tattoos and I could see one along the side of his neck. There may have been others hidden under his clothes. They were works of art.

"I wish I had thought first before covering myself in them, but when you are down and out, depressed and heartbroken, it's hard to think that far ahead and make wiser decisions. Homeless people are just regular people who are going through some rough times. We try to get back on our feet, but it's a struggle, sometimes struggles make you stronger though."

"You know Richard, I spent nine years separated from my mother and because of prayer and faith we were able to reconcile what happened and reconnect. My oldest son who is not much older than you are walked away from his family, and only because of faith and prayers we've been able to move forward. It's what gives me hope every day. I'll be praying for your faith to return and to be stronger than ever, and I'll pray for healing and restoration for you and your mom and sister."

His reaction was one of genuine appreciation as he thanked me multiple times, and hoped that our interview would help provide a voice for the homeless. Richard was a sweet kid who made some bad choices and found himself caught between circumstances that offered him little control and even fewer options. His basic instincts about God are still there, yet clouded over by the depressed state of his situation. I was fascinated by his tattoos, as they were amazing works of art, but works that demonstrated a darker side of his emotional wellbeing. The next time I spoke with him, those tattoos became an avenue that opened more doors into his life.

CHAPTER 11 – Richard – Visit 2

Maybe because I brought the cold, soft drink to him, or maybe Richard was genuinely glad to see me again. Whatever the reason, I met Richard again the next afternoon on that same bench, and anticipated peering more closely into this young man's life. He was such an intriguing young man.

"When I lost my eye to cancer, I was five years old. The bills were enormous because of the cancer treatments. My real dad was already working three jobs trying to take care of all of us, but there was never enough money. That's what caused him to commit armed robbery. He didn't hurt anyone; he just wanted to provide for us. He got caught and went to prison for a long time, so I never really got to know him."

My parents split up when I was little, so I too grew up without my dad for the most part. It was for different reasons, but I felt as though I understood the sense of loss time and regret he carried around with him.

"After many years he was finally let out, and moved to Virginia. We talked on the phone every day for a while. I was seventeen by then, and had moved out. He said when I turned eighteen I should come down and live with him. He would find me a job. We could go hunting and fishing, and do guy things like that together. I missed out on all of that stuff while he was away. But, after a while, he quit answering the phone. For a long time I kept trying, but I could never get hold of him; he just disappeared. I found out later that he married someone and now had another family. At least he's a dad in somebody's life, just not mine."

"Did your dad ever go to church with you when you were little?"

"No, he wasn't a believer in God, and never went. My mom was a diehard Christian always going to church, Bible studies and women's groups."

"So, what happened to her?"

"I think she just needed to be in love, and ended up with the wrong guy. She doesn't go to church anymore. At one point I believed, but after everything that has happened I lost my faith. When I was in college, I studied the Bible in a class and it seemed like there were a lot of inconsistencies, contradictions, and fairy tale stories. I even asked pastors questions, but could never get answers that satisfied me. I prayed a lot, but I've never heard no voice. When I became homeless at seventeen I prayed all the time asking for help, but it never came. I saw a lot of other people getting help; most of them didn't deserve it. I was trying to do the right thing, but I never got no help."

The homeless get down and need help. It is common for them to turn to God thinking that he is supposed to be a circumstantial gift giver of sorts, to pull them out of their plight. I shared with Richard about how God doesn't always answer prayers the way we think He should. Many people never live for Him to begin with, never acknowledge Him in their lives, and have never repented and stepped out in faith. They may know about him intellectually, may have heard Bible stories, may even have been told to live their lives a certain way. But none of that is what saves us from our deserved punishment.

The Bible story is about creation, a fall from grace, a rescue, and then restoration. Once we understand who we truly are as sinners, then we can understand more clearly why

86

Christ came into this world to pay the price for our sins. By believing on him, and believing that he conquered death, the he will enter into our hearts and we can begin to step out in faith to live a life of freedom.

"I believed at one time, and had faith, but I never prayed for forgiveness or repented of anything," Richard said.

"You know Richard, Satan and his demon angels know very well who God is, they believe who He is, but have still rejected His authority. Christianity is based on faith, and the more time you pursue him, build your personal relationship with Him, the stronger that faith will grow, and the more real he becomes. He wants you in his circle, but you have to let go of the things that hold you back and believed with all of your heart that Christ was who he said he was, then that free gift of grace will be yours."

Richard wanted God to show himself to him. He wanted to see it firsthand. He kept returning to how he asked over and over for God to let him know he was going to make it, and everything would be okay. He wanted to hear an audible voice. That voice never came. He keeps asking God to come to him when in reality God is already there. Richard just needed to see Him inside his heart, and not just his mind.

"I guess I'm just sitting on the fence, I believe, but I'm having a hard time buying into it through these tough times. My first tattoo was a big cross with the face of Jesus in it. That was a happy time for me, then things went bad. My tattoos changed to things like upside down crosses. I was angry. I hope I can get my faith back, and by doing so my life will get back on track. Maybe this is all a test. If I pass, the doors will open up for me."

I've never been a big fan of tattoos, but I wanted to show an interest in what seemed important to him. I asked him to tell me about them.

"The Gemini one represents my Zodiac sign, and here's the one with the cross and Jesus inside. I got this one when I was eighteen, and started dating this girl who helped me regain my faith. I really liked this girl. We went to church together and she helped me keep a straight path."

This was a clear indication that he was relying on another person for his faith, and not relying on the power of genuine faith in Christ to sustain him. His eyes were focused on her, not on Christ.

"And then she cheated on me, three times, and ran off with all of my money. I got mad, and started hanging out with the tattoo crowd. I love art, but it's more like a shield I use so people have a hard time reading who I am."

The demon skull was put on after he started getting angry at God. The artwork was remarkable, the message frightening. A stark contradiction appeared between the messages he was attempting to portray in the art of the tattoos and the soft demeanor he presented during our conversations. The two did not blend well. Somewhere inside of Richard's heart, a war between faith and conflict raged. His outward expressions indicated a gentle soul. His words presented a story told from a perspective of sadness. The artwork presented the battle that raged with in his life. I asked him to explain what each tattoo meant.

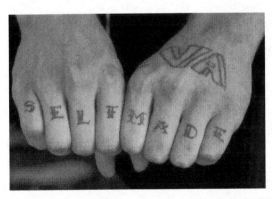

The letters on his fingers, "self made", represented how he survived while being homeless. The jaguar because it's his favorite animal and his mom liked all the jungle stuff. The dagger through the head represented all the mental pain he had gone through. The five-eyed wolf was a sign of strength and perseverance, the goat skull with the upside down cross in it because he was angry. The woman with a blindfold over her face represented him walking through life blindly having no sense of what to do.

The skull, candle and a rose; the rose represented the love he had for the two friends who died in the military, they were like brothers to him, the skull represented their death and the candle, he said represented the fact that their memory is always burning in his head.

The teardrop under the eye is because of the sadness of losing his friends and family.

Out of Step With The World represented lyrics from a favorite band and I believe the interpretation is in the words.

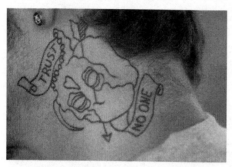

Trust no one represented all the times he was burned by friends and family. His motto right now is be nice to people, but don't trust them.

I asked him if he trusted me. He said, "I trust you, you are nice. You get vibes off people and I can tell you are nice and a good person. You're doing the right thing."

I've never understood someone wanting to cover himself in tattoos, but after talking with Richard, I believe I have a better idea of why. In his case, these images are images from his life, a visual crying out to take the place of hidden tears and anger resulting from life experiences. They are an attempt to say to those who meet him, "I have value. Don't throw me away like my family did. I am someone with feelings and dreams. I am searching for answers to questions I haven't asked yet. I am seeking to find my way and these images engraved on my body tell my story."

Jesus doesn't look upon the outward appearance of a person. He looks at what resides in their heart. I can only imagine what He might find inside of Richard's heart. What I discovered was a searching young man who needed an anchor in time from which to balance his life choices. If the anchor is locked into the truth of Christ's love, then life will balance and be in equilibrium. When it is locked in uncertainty and false promises, life balance become skewed and distorted.

Before we parted I said to him, "Don't give up on the Lord and don't give up on people. I want you to find hope and love and happiness again in your life."

We sat silent for a minute, his gaze not focused on anything in particular. Then he turned toward me. "I think I will pray that prayer someday. I'm just not ready yet."

I prayed for him, and when we were done, I gave him a motherly hug, and wished him well. I trust that Richard will rediscover truth in his life based on the certainty of God's love through faith in Christ. The talks that we shared offered an opportunity to sow new seeds of truth across the depleted fields of his life. A few days later Richard returned to Boston.

Lord, I pray that Richard will trust in You with all his heart and lean not on his own understanding; in all his ways that he will acknowledge You and that You will make his paths straight (from Proverbs 3:5-6).

Maybe then, Richard can add a tattoo claiming he found the One he can trust for life!

CHAPTER 12 – Matthew

It is inevitable when talking with homeless individuals to run across situations and people who remind me of my own family. After spending several hours talking with Richard, his friend Matthew walked into my life, and through him I witnessed again the devastating effects rebellion casts upon a family. His was a story that reminded me of my own son.

Matthew was twenty years old as was Richard, he was from Boston. I first met him on a hot summer day after he had already walked over eight miles. With a stout physique, he was tired, sweaty, and beat down, yet he was willing to sit with me, and talk about his life.

"I grew up in a Christian home. My father is a pastor and our home was very strict. I didn't like all the rules."

He was home schooled for most of his younger years, and as many home-schooled students often do, he excelled academically and was able to graduate from high school a year early.

"I played little league baseball for six or seven years for city teams, but I didn't have a lot of friends. When I was twelve I began sneaking out of the house to get away from all the rules I had to live by. Not far from where we lived there were a lot of homeless people. Usually by the time I got away from home, most of them were drunk and usually passed out. I would steal the liquor they had stashed in the bushes, that's how I started drinking. That kind of behavior caused me to become belligerent at home. It caused a lot of problems because of the way our home was, my dad being a pastor and all. By the time I turned sixteen and had a car, it opened up a whole other level of rebellion because of the freedom it gave me. It got so chaotic at home my parents gave me an ultimatum; change my ways or leave. I chose to leave."

Matthew's life choices caused so much chaos at home. I could not help but reflect upon how our own home suffered through a rebellious, chaotic turn of events. Our oldest son was rather like Matthew. He was raised in a Christian home and taught values that should have served him well through his life. He was a happy boy growing up, smart, a quick learner, caring, and kind. He didn't have many friends growing up, not that he was left out of opportunities to develop them. He was involved in many activities and sports. It was more a situation where most of the kids his age seemed less mature, so he tended to shy away from them. He was a very conscientious boy rarely giving us reason for grief. We were a happy and close family.

I'll never forget the day when my son was about twelve years old, throwing his hands up in the air and proclaiming, 'I love my life.' The world was his for the taking. But by the time he turned seventeen, he began to hang around friends, who challenged his perspectives about what he was taught. He eventually, was faced with making choices about his life, and in our perspective, he chose poorly. He walked away from a four-year scholarship, walked away from our home, and out of our lives. It became a very confusing, heart-wrenching situation. I thank God for not leaving us. I thank God for not leaving my son. His eye is on the sparrow and I know He watches him.

I came back to the present when Matthew shifted his weight on the bench. I asked, "What did you do after you left home?"

"Sometimes friends would let me stay with them. I mostly just slept on a couch, and had to scrounge for something to eat. I did a lot of walking around looking in trashcans. Sometimes I'd find something. Sometimes I wouldn't. I actually went an entire week without eating hardly anything at all. Not exactly what I intended, but you get used to it."

Since my son left home I've discovered there were times he went hungry as well. It broke my heart to hear of such things. To have such a loving son fall into such a chaotic and disruptive lifestyle was almost more than my family could bear. What sustained us through this trial by fire was the strength we gained through our faith in Christ. Where unthinkable events brought pain and heartbreak, what lifted our spirits in the midst of this despair, was the control God demonstrated to us during those most uncomfortable days. Matthew told of the difficult days he suffered through. As I listened, I could only imagine how much pain his family must have felt during that same time.

"When I was eighteen I was able to move in with some other friends for a few months. I managed to get into trouble, you know, drugs and drinking and getting into a gang. I was arrested a couple of times, even went to jail for a couple of weeks. I knew a lot of the police officers in town,

94

and well, they came to bat for me and all of my charges were dismissed. I was let go. After that I wanted to straighten out my life, so I got a job for while, but got laid off and ended up homeless again. That's when Richard and I found out we had some friends here in Bowling Green and we could come down here to get back on our feet. That lasted about two weeks until we got into an argument and they kicked us out."

He and Richard were waiting for friends back home to wire them bus money to get back. I wondered if those friends would come through.

"How much money do you need for the bus tickets?"

"About a hundred eighty dollars each. I've got thirty dollars in my pocket and forty dollars on a card."

Keith and I have two basic rules we adhere to when working with the homeless; we don't hand out money, nor do we give rides. Even so, the mother instinct in me wanted so much to give them the money they needed to get back home. It is difficult sometimes not to do something like that, but as is often the case, doing so can be counterproductive especially if done as a spur of the moment reaction.

Maybe God had other ideas in their situation. It was obvious that God was at least an element in their lives at one time anyway. I did not want to interfere with His plans, so I held back making the offer, and decided to pray about it. More importantly, to pray for God to provide what these two boys needed most.

Matthew continued, "When I was back in Boston I would panhandle, and might end up getting five dollars at any one time. That was enough to at least get a fast food meal and something to drink."

Matthew's mood gradually changed from being matter of fact to being more contemplative. I could see by his body language as he told his story, that he realized just how poorly his life choices had turned out for him. He would turn away and stare off into the distance, and other times he would look down not wanting to look at me directly. There seemed to be a pride issue with Matthew.

Not wanting to appear weak, he rarely accepted handouts. Although his life was pretty much in disarray, his pride prevented him from returning home to reconcile with his parents. The story of the prodigal harbors valid truths, even for events played out in today's world. For him to return home without first obtaining a repentant nature probably would have only caused more grief for the whole family. My job was not to judge, nor was it to offer advice, I simply listened, and I became an advocate for the plight of homeless individuals. My mothering instincts wanted to reach out to these two young men, and hold them close to give them the love they needed so they in turn could learn how to love back. My intuition, probably coming as a hint from God, said to refrain from doing so for His plans for these two boys were well in hand.

"Can I give you a sack of food?" I asked him.

"No, I'm all right. We'll be heading back to Boston in a few days, and things will get better for us then. I am going to get a job, and eventually I'll get a place of my own."

"What about your dreams? Do you have any life dreams that you hope to fulfill someday?"

"Yes I do. I'd like to get into law enforcement, maybe security. I'd like to get into the military where I can get some training that might help focus me toward those things. There are always circumstances worse than my own. That's what helps me get through the day knowing that I'm better off than some. I heard about an older man in the shelter who was in the army, and now he is back home and homeless. That just don't seem right."

I could tell that Matthew was troubled by the veteran's story. In some ways, showing that kind of concern indicated a strong level of inner strength. Many homeless that I work with have lost that aspect in their lives. They have been so beat down, so absorbed by their own circumstance, that showing compassion for others no longer resonates within their lives. In spite of his circumstances, Matthew tried to stay positive, and carried a good attitude. As a child, he became a Christian. His rebellious teen years distorted the goodness that was in him, and he allowed bad influences to affect his life choices and to take over his world.

"You just gotta learn from your mistakes," he said.

"Do you still have faith in God?"

"I don't think about that much, just trying to get by day to day. I don't pray much anymore either. I used to, but with my circumstances, I just couldn't see how it was helping so I stopped."

"You know, I'm reminded of what the Bible tells us, that we are not promised an easy life, but that Jesus will walk through it with us, that He will never leave us, and I hope that you will not forget that."

"I'm just making it day by day. I don't understand why most people think that homeless are just lazy, and don't want to work. I used to think that way myself, but now that I've been there, my perspective has changed. It's not as easy as some think. People get depressed, and that can make everything worse. I know I'm where I'm at because of my own choices. If I could, I'd go back ten years, and change everything. I would not become the rebellious teen I was, I would not smoke or drink. I know now that all the rules my parents laid out for me were for my own protection. I wish I could go back and change all that," Matthew reflected.

I understand about the rules. My own son rebelled against rules in his late teen years. Yes, our home had rules when our boys were young for teaching values, character, discipline, and respect for us and for others. But we tempered those rules with grace.

As an older teen, he thought he knew better what was right for him, and he managed to throw away a free college education. He also brought sickness and pain to his family and to himself.

Too many teens do not understand how foolish it truly is when it comes to making disruptive life choices. Even worse, they do not comprehend the heartbreak it bestows upon their family. Moreover, so many out there do not understand that rules are not a bad word. It allows us a life of freedom. It's when rules go out the window, that chaos ensues and what they perceive as freedom actually binds them in bondage.

Matthew can never change his past as he desires. He can determine his future. Because of his circumstances, his character has been hardened. His nature changed. He is now one who carries daily regrets and heartache. I believe he knows what to do to resolve those issues, though. Pride will have to be laid down and repentance move into the heart. I have a feeling his parents, just like Keith and myself, are standing at the door with open arms. I pray Matthew and our son will step over those thresholds, right into forgiveness and grace.

He listened intently as I shared those thoughts with him. "I'll consider it," he said with a smile when our day ended. Then I asked Matthew if I could give him a hug.

"Oh no, I'm not one of those touchy feely sort of guys, I don't want you to do that."

And so we parted for the day. The next afternoon I was once again sitting on a bench at the downtown square when Matthew and Richard walked up to us. I spoke with Matthew for a short time asking if he had anything else he would like to share.

"Yes I do, I'd like to share something with you." He turned his head away, and gazed toward the far end of the park watching the movements of another young man, and a young lady who was with him. He swallowed heavily as if to remove a lump from his throat.

"When I was sixteen I worked as a counselor at a summer Christian youth camp. We'd work all week and then have the weekends off. One weekend one of the counselors threw a party. There was drinking and people were getting drunk." He seemed somewhat embarrassed by that statement. I could guess the reason why.

His expression grew more pensive as he spoke, "At the party I met this girl, and we spent time together, if you know what I mean. When the summer camp was over, I found out she was pregnant with my child. She lived with a really bad father who was drunk all the time. After the baby was born, it was boy, she was walking down the stairs carrying her son when her father, in a drunken state, shoved her and she fell. When she hit the bottom, my son was thrown through a pane glass door. He died as a result. She suffered a broken hip and a broken back. I just wanted you to know about that part of my life." He seemed deeply affected by the events surrounding his child, and the child's mother.

My heart felt ripped apart by Matthew's story. My eyes grew blurry with the tears that I tried to hold back. It is difficult to separate doing a job and connecting with someone emotionally. We never know what pain lies deep inside of someone. Homeless individuals are a stoic breed, but they are not invulnerable from broken hearts and events that would affect anyone. It gives them a deeply human element. An element that few ever realize exists.

After Matthew finished his story, we walked over to where Richard was sitting. I thanked them both for sharing their stories with me and I asked my friend Carolyn, who was with me on this day, if she would pray for them. She asked the Lord to provide them safe passage and to guide them in the way they should go. Richard gave me another hug. I looked at Matthew understanding that he was not inclined to reach out for such a thing, but he surprised me.

"Oh, come here. I'll give you a hug." His trust was beginning to return. A little genuine warmth, compassion, and a listening ear will go a long way.

The next day, Richard and Matthew returned to Boston. I pray for these young men and for my son to once again wait upon on the Lord.

> "...but they who wait for the LORD shall renew their strength;
> they shall mount up with wings like eagles;
> they shall run and not be weary;
> they shall walk and not faint."
>
> Isaiah 40:31 (ESV)

CHAPTER 13 – Thomas

"I guess you just get immune to it, the homelessness. It just becomes your life after a while, like doing twenty years in jail, it becomes your life. It becomes all you know. You remember that movie *Shawshank Redemption* with Morgan Freeman? A man got out of prison at eighty years old, and hung himself because he didn't know anything but prison life. Homelessness becomes the same scenario. I know that makes no sense to people but that's just the way it is."

Thomas came into my life because Greg convinced him that he should speak to me. At thirty-eight years old he was originally from Maine but has lived, and been homeless, in ten different states. He was a thin man, but well groomed with dark eyes and closely cropped hair. There was gentleness in his face. For most of our conversation, Thomas never removed his sunglasses. I see this often when speaking with homeless individuals. They need something to hide behind, and dark glasses provide a barrier that prevents others from penetrating into the recesses of their soul through the eyes. I felt the gentleness I saw in his expression obscured the turmoil that seemed to boil inside of him. As always, I asked if I could take his picture.

He said, "No."

Over the last five years he had drifted around Bowling Green in search of something that would elevate his life from one of despair to one with meaning and purpose. Six months before I met him, he was divorced from his wife who now cares for their three children ages five, nine, and ten.

You can tell a great deal about a person through their body language and how they present themselves. All through our conversation Thomas kept drinking from a water bottle, a water bottle not filled with a nourishing liquid, but one filled with a clear alcoholic substance. As discouraging as it is, alcohol seems to provide a measure of false strength for many homeless. It provides them a temporary and artificial means to prop themselves higher so that the trials of their daily existence do not seem so bad. Unfortunately, in most cases the alcohol actually creates the opposite effect and holds them trapped inside a world characterized by a dazed stupor where any hope of escape is lost in the fogged over effects it produces. I could see this in Thomas right away.

"Both of my parents were alcoholics, but they seemed to function okay most of the time. When I was thirteen, they didn't care if I drank, so I did. They removed the shelves from the refrigerator and replaced them with kegs of beer so anytime I wanted I could just tap into it," Thomas told me.

Often I am surprised at the background homeless people reveal. Thomas needed to understand that life choices will have far reaching effects. I said, "You know Thomas, life is made up of choices even at thirteen. Did you think about the consequences of drinking at that young age?"

"My parents didn't care, so why should I have?"

"So the answer is yes, you did have a choice, you chose to drink, like your parents did," I persisted

"I guess you could say that." He said with a smirk across his face.

He grew quiet for a few moments and turned away. He lifted the water bottle and swallowed another gulp. The pungent aroma of alcohol floated around us but he seemed oblivious to it.

"I was in Special Ed from kindergarten on until I was sixteen. I wasn't a troublemaker or nothing. I just had trouble understanding things. When I turned sixteen, I was kicked out of school. They said I just didn't have it in me. I was more of a doer than a book learner. That's why I worked in construction for a while. I could do that. Then things began to change and instead of operating machines with levers and mechanics, they wanted you to do things with computers and joysticks. I don't know anything about that stuff and they didn't take the time to train me, so I was let go."

I didn't say anything. I just let him talk and eventually he came back to the topic of alcohol.

"I was in AA once, but didn't like it. The guy teaching it had only been sober for three months. I had been sober for five months at the time and it just didn't seem right that he was leading this class having been sober less time than me.

"They put me in rehab, twice, and it was pretty rough. You had to work all day with strict time rules. You ate when they said to eat. You slept when they said to sleep. I didn't like that. I wanted to get my GED, but I couldn't because they never gave me any time to do so. I wanted to learn how to stay sober, but they wouldn't teach that, they just made you work. For nine months I was supposed to go through that, but I quit after five. I just couldn't take the crap any more. Seems like all they were interested in was money. I wanted to learn something, but they weren't teaching anything." Thomas seemed to grow somewhat irritated as he spoke about his rehab experience.

I've spoken to a number of homeless people who have similar stories. Alcohol controlled their lives and even when they attempted to break free of its grip, the cure would become too much for them to deal with. Instead, they would return to their comfort area, to what they knew best. In spite of the detrimental effects the alcohol had on their lives, it was just easier to hold on to that element than to give it up.

"Tell me about your parents," I requested.

"I did okay until my mom died in my late teen years. She seemed to hold everything together, hold the family together. Have you ever noticed that?"

"I understand. I'm a mom too."

"They never showed me any kind of affection. No hugs or kisses or saying I love you or anything. It just wasn't their way. They pretty well let me do what I wanted. A few years later my dad died and everything went downhill after that. I was on my own." His mood changed somewhat after he spoke about losing his parents. Their loss thrust him into the world with no other emotional or physical support. It was a world he was not prepared to deal with and so he clung to the one thing that gave him a degree of comfort, alcohol.

"How do you survive day to day?"

"I can eat at the Salvation Army. At least here in Bowling Green you don't go hungry like in other places. Too many churches and other places that will give you food, mostly canned stuff and that gets a little old sometimes, but you gotta be thankful for what you can get. I can't stay at the Salvation Army anymore because my time is up, but I can eat there at noon."

"Where will you stay tonight?"

"I guess I'll find me a place behind one of these buildings or in an alley someplace. Don't have too many options." Once again he turned away and took another drink from his bottle. His gaze floated around the downtown square as if he was sizing up his place-to- stay options for the night.

"What are you teaching your kids?"

104

"I don't get to see them much, but I want to teach them not to start drinking." He shifted his gaze toward the ground and a half-grin half-grimace tightened his face.

"But, I drink around them though. I do want to teach them to do the right things. My ex takes them to First Baptist Church. That's where I see them mostly." He raised his eyebrows as if he suddenly understood a good thing his kids were doing.

"When you are in church do you listen to the sermon?"

"Oh yeah, I read all those words on the big screen and listen to the preacher, but it mostly just all goes over my head. I don't understand much of it. It just don't sink in. I try to make it stick, but it just doesn't."

"Do you want to go to Heaven?"

"I gotta do that. I don't want to go to Hell. I know all about the sinner prayer, I've prayed it many times, but I guess the alcohol is stronger." Again he dropped his gaze toward the ground and lifted his shoulders with a gusty sigh. In a moment he popped his head upright with a big smile on his face and asked me, "Do you have Jesus in your heart, it's great isn't it?"

"Yes I do and it is a great feeling."

"That's how I feel when I'm drinking. I feel greatness when the alcohol gets into my system."

"But Thomas, the greatness I feel in Jesus doesn't make me sick. It doesn't contribute to me being homeless. It gives me peace and hope. Does the greatness you feel from alcohol give that to you?"

"It's greater than anything I can control. I've prayed that prayer you're talking about, many times, but I guess Jesus just doesn't want to come in."

"You're wrong about that Thomas. He's there waiting for you and wants to come in, but you have to surrender and let him in. You have to truly want it from the heart, not just your mind. Just saying the words is not enough. Everything about your life you must let go of, and allow him to take control. Then He can change your life."

I paused a moment to let those words float around inside of his thoughts. He looked away, dropped his head again. Even though we can never know for sure what is going on inside another person's heart, whenever I have an opportunity to share about God's love to someone, especially a homeless person who appears trapped inside the confining grip of alcoholism, I ask God simply to use me as a messenger to do his will in this person's life. I alone am unable to change anyone's life. It is God through Christ who does the changing.

"Do you want to quit drinking?" I asked.

"Sometimes I want to and sometimes I don't, I just feel like I need it to get through the day."

I paused a moment before answering him. I wanted to be careful to choose the right words. "Alcohol is the main reason you are homeless. Wouldn't that be reason enough to make you want to quit?"

"Sometimes I care, and sometimes I don't. You know, when I was working hard all day I just wanted to come home and relax, and have a cold beer. But, then it would always go downhill. I couldn't stop. You lose everything, and you think why did I do that, then you do it all over again. Alcoholism is crazy like that. I just don't understand it. My body craves it. I need it to get through the day." A few moments passed in silence. Then he said, "I guess you just get immune to it, the homelessness. It just becomes your life after a while."

I could tell he was slipping toward a more depressed state, so I redirected the conversation into a more positive topic by asking him if he ever had dreams about what his life might become.

"No I never think about that. I would like to be a better person, but the alcohol just stinks. Half of me wants to quit and the other half doesn't want to. I wish someone could teach me how to let go of it. People tell me to pray about it, but it's gonna take a lot more than that. I've tried to do my part. I try to do the right thing and always get kicked down. Sometimes I wonder if that's God's will or if he's just trying to teach me a lesson."

By this time, Thomas was tired emotionally. The emotional juggernaut that rolled across the hills and valleys of his life left deep ruts of confusion and contempt in its wake. When he peered deep into his heart, he realized what he needed to do, yet alcoholism had long, demonic claws dug in against his attempts at making sense of his life.

Doing the right thing rarely becomes the easy choice. The most destructive things, unfortunately, become much easier to follow. Alcohol distorts even the most noble of attempts to correct the deviations of life. Thomas was right in one thing; it will take more than just praying about it to correct this tragic deviation that controls his life.

I hoped I could trigger a desire within him to look at his life from the perspective of what his future could become as opposed to what his life is now. So, I asked, "Thomas, just what do you want in life."

After thinking for a few minutes, staring down at the pavement, he finally answered. "I want to get a good job again, and get back into some housing. Then get the classes I need. Not just classes for the sake of taking classes, but an education that addresses my personal needs and issues: Anger management and getting off alcohol. I need to learn how to live without it."

"Can I pray for you before I leave?"

"Please do."

For the first time Thomas removed his dark glasses and bowed his head. I prayed for healing from the alcohol; that he would find his place in this world free from its bondage. When I finished, we both raised our eyes, and his glistened with moisture.

"Thank you," he said.

Although most of the interviews I made with homeless people lasted maybe, an hour or so; much is revealed during those few moments. It is relatively easy to see through someone who is not being honest about his or her situation. At the same time, after the trust factor is established between the two of us, honest reflections often pour out of their hearts. Moments such as those make it difficult not to connect with that person emotionally. From their stories the depravity of their lives reveals the heartache and sorrow that becomes bottled up inside. Too often what keeps it bottled up is alcohol, and the control it exerts. It tends to numb or thwart desires, hopes, and dreams to overcome their situation. Listening to and encouraging them with a simple act of kindness can penetrate deeply into their hearts, and even if for only a moment, help them to release their lives from those inner fears and demons.

Thomas gave me a genuine hug.

I never saw him again after that day.

CHAPTER 14 – Bruce

I was immediately drawn to the eyes of the people I met, for those windows revealed the hardness of their lives. When Greg first came into my life his eyes dimly reflected something distant and hollow. His life all but destroyed by alcohol and drugs had hardened his behavior, but I could see a sense of longing and searching for something better in his eyes. After he prayed that prayer while sitting on the park bench, a different glow resonated from within him. There was a genuine change that became readily visible through his eyes. No longer were they hollow, no longer did they stare vacantly without hope, his was a changed life that seemed calmer and less aggressive than before.

Greg became my scout. He knew and had many contacts with homeless people across town. He directed one after

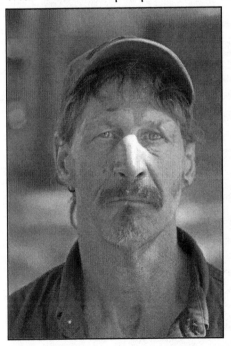

another in my direction, sometimes at inconvenient times. I'd receive a call in the middle of the afternoon and Greg would be sitting with someone who wanted to talk to me. I wasn't always able to just stop what I was doing, but I made exceptions and would find time to meet with them.

Bruce was one of those. When I first met him, what stood out more than anything was the sadness that tinged his steel blue-eyed gaze that pierced my heart. He was in his mid-forties and was originally from Indianapolis, Indiana. He stood about six feet tall, and wore a beat-up, red, baseball cap, and dressed in a dark blue shirt that was probably way to heavy for the summer heat. He was thin, with a carriage that was rough and physically strong. I noticed all this as he walked toward me sitting on the park bench.

At first he told Greg he did not want to meet with me. After Greg and I chatted for a few minutes, he changed his mind, "It's nice to meet you," he said somewhat reluctantly.

"Thank you for talking with me," I replied. "How long have you been in Bowling Green?"

"About fourteen days. My sister bought a Greyhound bus ticket for me so I could make the trip. I've been staying at the Salvation Army, but my time ran out, and now I'm living under the bridge." He pointed to the north where the Old Louisville Road bridge was located about two miles away.

"Why did you come down here?" I asked him.

He cocked his head to one side leaned forward placing his elbows on his knees; a position that looked rather uncomfortable. Then he leaned back against the park bench.

"I couldn't get my social security disability back home, so I came down here to see if I could get it. Both of my parents are dead and the rest of the family moved on, I was left with nothing so I ended up homeless."

"How long ago was that?" I asked.

"Oh, maybe ten months ago. I can't live with any of my family. We don't seem to get along. I hope to go back to Indianapolis soon. I've been here long enough, maybe six weeks. People are weird here. You ask them something and most will tell you to go to Hell, some will help, but most won't." He turned his head away, and paused for a moment before continuing. "I haven't worked in over a year. Last job I had was a janitor, but I started having seizures and they let me go."

"What about school? Did you finish high school?"

"I dropped out my senior year. Just needed two credits to graduate."

"Just two? Why did you drop out when you were so close?" I was surprised why he would do something like that. Not unlike so many other homeless people I met, his behavior patterns followed a similar path of poorly thought out choices that generated far reaching negative effects.

"I wasn't any good at math or English and I knew I just wasn't going to make it. I said the heck with it. I'll go to work someplace and ended up at a car wash. Stayed there for a year and half. After that I became a janitor and worked there for six years, and then my seizures started. I started taking meds for them and they do the trick, they keep me from having them."

"What about getting your GED? Did you give that a try?"

"Nope, too much of a hassle."

"What about your future, what do you want to do?"

"Right now I just want to go back to Indianapolis, get on food stamps, and hopefully live until I'm seventy two." For the first time he laughed.

I thought it sad that he had no more ambition than to live on food stamps for the rest of his life. That is one persistent if not glaring element I've seen in many homeless people. They have no future nor do they seek to find one other than to survive day to day.

My intent has never been to judge, yet there are times I wonder what the mechanism is that leads to this situation. Do they give up on having a future because they are beat down living a homeless life, or are they homeless because somewhere in their early upbringing the idea of making a life for themselves was suppressed?

"What about your family? Will you meet up with your sisters when you get back?"

"Maybe my oldest one, the one who bought me the bus ticket, but the rest of them", he pauses and his expression tightens, "they're just a bunch of snobs and knuckleheads, been like that my whole life."

"When you were younger did you ever go to church?"

"We went as a family every Sunday. The kids had to go. Dad fired up the car, and had all four doors open. We kids better be in there. I went to church all the way through being a junior in high school, then I quit going."

"What did you think, about church I mean?"

"It was all right," his demeanor changed as a big smile spread across his thin face. I took this as a cue that something good must have happened during that time.

"We always had something to do. The pastor's right hand man always had something for us to do. I remember one Sunday all us kids were told to bring our dirty clothes, you know, the old ratty stuff, something extra we could get dirty. They took us to a friend's house and we painted the garage and all the trim, and replaced a couple of rotten boards. It was nice to help someone."

I took a quick glance into Bruce's steel blue eyes. Their appearance changed from the tired, searching look they had when I first met him to a gaze filled with a sense of pride. I could tell that the simple act of kindness he and the other kids performed made a lasting, positive, impression upon him. He continued with his story.

"I learned that you gotta ask Jesus into your heart. I've asked nine thousand times."

"It only takes once." I instinctively blurted.

"I know, but I like to keep Him awake up there."

I've heard similar statements from homeless individuals. They know what to do, but do not understand that to make that kind of commitment comes from the heart and not from the mind. Mechanically saying the words carry little if any value. They search for the meaning of the words, but have yet to grasp their significance. I've prayed that God would open doors, and they give me the words to say. Many times the doors remain closed, but sometimes, they open wide, and I step through.

"I don't believe He ever sleeps," I answered and he chuckled, "Did you ever pray that prayer, asking Jesus into your heart?"

"Yep! I ask him for help all the time. I always say, 'Jesus are you going to help me?' and sometimes he does, sometimes he don't."

A solemn expression settled on his face.

"It's hard making it day to day. It gets old. I'm about ready to jump off that bridge into the river."

"Oh my, please don't do that." I said.

"Oh, I probably won't."

Bruce changed the subject when he continued, "I don't do drugs, but I've been an alcoholic for thirty two years. I've tried to quit, went to rehab for sixty days, got off the bus, crossed the street, and bought some beer. I had the shakes so bad I felt terrible, and I just wanted a beer so bad. My dad drank all his life. I guess I will too. I steal the liquor most of the time 'cause I don't have enough money most of the time to buy it."

I must have looked shocked because he chuckled again after he looked at me.

"They got all those people walking around inside, they can't keep their eyes on just one person."

"Have you ever been caught, or in jail?"

"Yep, twice for intoxication, just got out the other morning. I stayed in for five hours, then they brought me breakfast, and then said I could go."

The longer Bruce spoke about his life and addiction to alcohol, the deeper my heart went out to him. Even though he had asked Jesus into his heart, his actions and addictions clouded over and obscured any good that may have come from it. The fruit of his life was soured by the need for alcohol and the effects it imparted on him.

I was compelled to ask one question, "Do you know that Jesus loves you?"

"Yep."

"How do you feel about that?"

"He's a good man. At least he's on top of things most of the time."

"If you could go back and change anything in your life, what would it be?"

"I wouldn't change anything."

"Not even the drinking?"

"Yep."

"You think the drinking has made your life tougher?"

"Tough! Whatever the good Lord throws at me is tough, even if I'm not drinking. It's the drinking that helps me relax."

"What if you could talk to kids around fifteen to sixteen years old? What advice would you give them?"

"I'd tell them, 'drink outside not inside."

"You wouldn't tell them not to drink?" I was surprised by his answer.

"They're gonna do whatever they want to do, and I'm gonna drink no matter what because I like it too much. Nothing is gonna affect them, so I'm not gonna say nothing. They can do whatever they want. Who knows if they graduate or not if it will help or hurt them?"

"Let me ask you this, do you have any dreams, something you want to accomplish in your life?"

He looked at me like I was crazy, "I just want to get back home and have a place of my own."

"Is there anything you want people to know about homelessness?"

"Whatever you do, do it with somebody."

"Is it lonely for you?"

"Yes it is!' he yelled.

"Do you have any friends here?"

"I did back home, but I keep to myself here."

Time was beginning to get away from us and before I knew it, the church bell on the next block began to chime indicating that another hour had passed.

"I listen to the bell that rings in town. Every ring means another hour. That's how I keep track of time," he said after the chiming had stopped.

I began to hear inconsistencies in his ramblings, so I began to wind our conversation toward conclusion. I felt like I was losing his interest. I thanked him for talking to me, and as I do when speaking with my new homeless friends, I asked if I could pray for him.

He immediately removed his baseball cap and bowed his head. I reached out and touched him, placing my arms around his shoulders. When I finished, I backed away noticing something I had not expected. His head was still bowed and he was praying. I waited for him to raise his head, but he continued to remain in his pensive posture. I touched his arm and asked if he was okay.

He pursed his weatherworn lips, and slowly raised his head. Those steel blue windows were filled with tears that streamed down his wind burned face. He smiled, replaced his ball cap, and walked away.

A lump rose inside my throat as I watched him fade into the distance. During our conversation, he seemed so absorbed by his alcoholic nature that I subconsciously believed that he was a burned-out soul. However, the Lord does work in our lives in so many unexpected ways. As I watched him wipe the tears from his eyes, put his hands in his pockets and silently step out of my life, I wondered how long it had been since someone had touched him in a loving way. I wondered how long it had been since someone prayed over him.

I felt my heart sink with a heavy sadness, and I had to sit down on the bench by myself to gain some composure. It would be so easy to write off someone like Bruce, a man lost in his world of alcohol, with no future, no hope of ever elevating himself to a position where he could understand why his life was the way it was. His life was so sad; it broke my heart. The demon of alcohol so consumed and dulled his soul he simply had no more will to fight against it. He looked like he was on the brink of giving up for good, barely holding on to what dignity he could still muster, barely clinging to memories of happier times.

He said he grew up in a small town even attended a little country church where there weren't many classes for young men. However, I pondered, it doesn't take a class to disciple someone. It takes people. Too many young men fall through the cracks, even in well-meaning churches.

I returned home that day and hit the floor on my knees praying for all the others out there in the world that Satan is hunting and hurting. I pray for their protection and for their eyes and hearts to open up all the way to the One who is standing near waiting for them to call out. I prayed for a totally surrendered heart to Him who can give life and give it more abundantly. I wanted that to be their desire, not "What are you going to do for me?" attitude.

I never saw Bruce again, but did discover that a friend of mine and her husband were at the downtown square the next day, and spent some time talking with Greg. They offered him a sandwich, but Greg gave it instead to Bruce who had been sitting nearby.

Bruce stepped over to my friends, held out his blackened, greasy hands and asked them to pray for him. They gladly did so. Was Bruce touched by our prayer? Was he seeking answers and was God working on his heart? I may never know, but my prayer for him was for God to touch his life and break through his hardened shell to soften his heart so that he can find peace and freedom from the addictions that rob him of all the hopes he has forgotten.

CHAPTER 15 – Dawn

I felt haughty stares that day in September. The coldness in the stares did little to dispel the heat of the day, but they certainly pierced like arrows. Ordinary people seemed to find it difficult to reconcile within themselves why an ordinary person like me, would actually sit with a trio of homeless people as we were sharing lunch together. As uncomfortable as it made me feel, I could only imagine the indignity the daily recipients of this kind of behavior feel.

It was on this hot Indian summer day I met Dawn, a fifty four year old grandmother from Idaho. She became stranded in Bowling Green a few days before we met. What started out as a perceived vacation became a nightmarish ordeal that left her on her own and homeless. Once again, my friend Greg showed he seemed genuinely concerned about Dawn's situation, and because of his efforts, Dawn came into my life. We sat on a park bench in the downtown square. Greg moved away to another bench to give us some privacy, and her friend Anita, who was also homeless, sat beside her.

"So, how did you end up in Bowling Green?" I asked after a few moments of casual chatting.

"A friend of my son-in-law is a truck driver. I've known him for about two years. He offered to take me on a road trip while he traveled to another state to drop off a load and pick up a load. My gut told me not to go, but everyone around me pushed me into going saying it would be fun, like a vacation. I thought to myself, 'Well, he's a friend, so why not?' It was a big mistake, him being married an all."

"So what happened?"

"A few day's into the trip he decided he wanted to be more than just friends. I didn't. When we stopped in Franklin, twenty miles or so south of Bowling Green, he paid for me to take a shower at a truck stop, and he'd wait for me. My stomach was in knots, but I needed a shower. When I came out my bags were sitting on the ground and he was nowhere around. He left me there stranded. I had no money and didn't know what to do. I didn't even know where I was or where to go. The people running the truck stop were nice people, they gave me ten dollars, and another truck driver gave me another ten dollars. I was able to call the police and tell them what had happened, but all they could do was drive me to the county line where the police on the other side took me to the Salvation Army here in Bowling Green. That was four days ago. I've got two weeks of clothes, a cell phone that has no service, and a laptop that is almost out of juice."

"What about a bus ticket back home?" I asked.

"A ticket is two hundred dollars. I don't have that much, and all my family back there don't have that much either so they can't help me."

"Could they not pool together and come up with enough for a ticket?"

"My little sister is about to have a birthday and they all wanted to celebrate by going to the casino..." She never finished her statement as tears began to slide across her face and her voice stumbled.

Usually it is easy to see through someone who is not being completely honest as sometimes their behavior becomes rather stoic with little emotion attached to it. Dawn on the other hand demonstrated a genuine heart-felt disappointment when it became apparent that her family was not going to help her. Anita reached across and patted her on the shoulder, and I held her hand. After a few moments, she gathered her composure.

"My husband died two years ago. We were married for twenty-eight years. Things sort of went downhill from there. My family blamed me for what happened to him, I don't know why. I took care of him for eight years while he was sick, did everything I could, so I don't understand, I just don't understand why they blame me."

"How many children do you have?"

"Four, now. One is thirty-seven, one twenty-nine, one twenty-seven, and one is twenty-six. Another son who was thirty-eight passed away."

She took a deep breath, and held it for a couple of seconds before releasing it. Moisture again welled up inside of her eyes, and rolled across her cheeks, finally dropping to the ground. I took in a single, deep breath trying to fight off the emotions that were generated inside of me.

"Why would my family want to go to a casino and leave me stranded?" Her tears flowed more freely now accompanied by a noticeable sobbing. I counted in my head and realized that she must have been sixteen when her first child was born, an obviously young age to be a mother.

"I'm not sure I really want to go home." She said half muffled between the sobs. "Maybe I should just stay here."

"I've been to some of the churches but they said they preferred to keep the money inside the community. What money they had must be used to help local people. I don't understand that. Back home churches will help anyone who needs it, local or not. The Catholic churches help the best. I was raised a Mormon and my grandmother was high up in the church. Mormons are good to help people."

She paused for a moment turning toward Anita. They exchanged a smile, and Anita again provided a comforting pat across her shoulder.

Dawn continued, "One of the churches here downtown gives away sack lunches every day to those who need one. They fill them with Vienna sausages, applesauce, crackers, and a drink. I really needed that one day as the Salvation Army fed people tuna fish and I'm allergic to tuna."

The local Salvation Army provides many good services for the community and especially to homeless people. Even so, many of them complain about the policies they have. Instead of simply living off a handout, homeless individuals are encouraged to look for a way to better themselves. Those policies are enforced for reasons of safety as well. But even I sometimes question why they do certain things.

"The Salvation Army is okay, but I don't like the way they make you leave during the day. I have a hard time walking because of arthritis in my hips. Carrying a lot of weight makes it hard to get around. When it's hot like it is now, it just wears me out. There are times I need to take a nap but have no place to do so."

"What kind of work did you do?"

"I'm a licensed LPN in Idaho and I was going to school to finish my degree in Social Work. Because I'm stuck here, I'll miss the next semester. Maybe it don't matter, I'm not sure I'm strong enough to finish."

"Finishing your degree would be a great accomplishment and will probably open doors for you. That alone could make you stronger." I said.

"Maybe I'm being tested right now."

"Do you have a strong faith in God?" I asked.

"I used to, but I'm not so sure now. I just want to help people, but not as a nurse or working in hospitals. My husband died in one and I don't like being inside them anymore. I want to help children with anger and fear issues. I think that is why God is testing me like this, so I can help them more."

"I think I understand what you mean. A lot of times it is going through the valleys that make us stronger." I said.

She chuckled, "I'm ready to climb out of this valley. If I stay here I would like to go back to school but I would need financial aid and not being a resident makes it harder. I want to teach autistic children to read. It feels good to help and I like that kind of challenge."

"If the bus ticket money became available, what would you do?"

"I'd probably go home. I have a house there, just renting, but I'll probably lose it now, but I could get another one. If I go back I will be different. I won't be so giving to my family," she said with a tightened jaw.

"Has your relationship been good with them until now?"

"Off and on good. They don't like me being so giving to others, but I like to give, but now," she begins to sob again, "but now I have to receive."

She sobbed shortly before regaining her composure and wiped her eyes before continuing.

"There needs to be more resources here. After ten days at the Salvation Army you have to leave or pay five dollars a day. That's a lot of money for a homeless person."

I was reminded of Richard who said the same thing.

"They need people to channel the homeless to the right places. With Daily Labor, you might get a job for maybe a day, and you might not. I want to work, but they send you here and there to 'ask' for help. What we need are places we can go to 'get' help. I don't know my way around, I don't know the streets, so that makes it hard to get around."

"Have people been helpful to show you around?"

"Ummm, some do, but most just ignore you. I've asked younger people how to get someplace, and they just walk away. Older people tend to help more."

"What do you miss the most about Idaho?" I asked trying to redirect the conversation to something more positive.

"My seventeen grandchildren," She sighs and slightly shakes her head left and right, "All my kids fight a lot and say mean things to each other. It will never change."

"I wouldn't say never," I told her, "Things can always change."

"I don't think they will, they are set in their ways." Again she begins to cry. "One of my sons is bad on drugs, in and out of prison because of it. He lives in Oklahoma now part of a gang and on meth. I don't want to be around him because

I'm afraid I might get into trouble because of his behavior. He can't even read or write."

I was surprised when she said that, "How come?"

"I worked twelve hours a day. None of our cars ran so I had to catch the bus early and it would be late for I got home. I thought he was in school, but he wasn't. My husband just let him do whatever he wanted. He had an evil side to him. He'd let the children call me b— all the time. He was not the good husband we all want, but I loved him anyway. I made most of the money, and paid the bills. He spent most of his money on drugs, rarely helping to pay the bills."

"You said we needed more services here. What kinds of services would you like to see in our community?"

"People need a place to go during the day. We need something to keep us busy. I like to sew. I'm a good seamstress, and can design clothes. That would allow me to give back to the community. People could donate material, and I could make stuff to sell or to give away. There is a lot of talent in the homeless world that's just going to waste."

"What kind of things would you make?"

"I would make turbans for the hair, sundresses, winter pajamas, clothes. I can also knit things like slippers, hats, gloves, I can even make coats. I used to sew all my kids clothes, we couldn't afford store bought clothes."

In the middle of her conversation, her leg began to shake which caused her to redirect what she was saying. "See that? People think I shake because of nerves but it's not nerves. I have sewn on those old grandmother type sewing machines in the cabinet where you use the foot trundle back and forth. I did that so much that my leg just keeps doing the same motion."

For the first time in our conversation, she laughed out loud. It was good to see her laugh for a change. Her emotions being tugged the way they were, needed something to bring them back into balance.

"I know this is your first time being homeless, but is there something you would want people to know from what you have experienced?"

Without hesitating she said, "I would tell them you just never know when it is going to happen. People need more compassion and understanding. Someday they could be in the same boat. I never thought in a million years I would be in this situation, but here I am. What hurts most is that people think you're bad, and they will not associate with you."

Her tears began to flow again followed by muffled sobbing.

"I know you're not a bad person." I said as I reached across the bench and gave her a hug. She clung to me tightly and sobbed for another few moments.

"It just makes you feel degraded. People look at me differently now, like there is something wrong with me. There are a lot of homeless here. I'm not really homeless I'm displaced, very displaced! I have a home. I just can't get to it. I don't understand why the churches here cannot help people like me get back home. I've been through a lot, but this is almost too much. I used to see homeless people back home holding signs, 'will work for food'. A lot of them had children. I never gave money, but I would buy them food, sometimes a small cooler and fill it with stuff. That's just the way I am; I like to help others. I once stood in line for four hours to get some free coats, and I gave them away to the children in the neighborhood. It made my heart feel better."

She paused for moment to gather her thoughts before continuing.

"I've had a rough life and its getting rougher, but it's gotta get better, I just need direction."

"Do you believe in the power of prayer?" I asked.

"I don't know. I used to."

She dropped her head and looked toward the ground as if to reflect on an aspect of her life that once held an important place, but over the years had been shoved aside because of circumstance and uncertainty.

"Can I pray for you?"

Without hesitating, she said, "Yes."

I held her hands, and prayed for the direction she needed to come. When I finished I thanked her for sharing her story with me. Then I turned to her friend Anita, and asked if she would share her story. Anita soon opened up and revealed a remarkable story that I will share in the next chapter.

Summers are characterized by humidity tempered with heat in Kentucky. This day was no exception and after Dawn and I finished our conversation I realized just how hot it was. Neither Dawn nor Anita possessed the physical stamina in this heat to walk back to the Salvation Army for their noon meal, so I invited them to join me at the sandwich shop across the street. We asked Greg to join us, which he readily did.

In a short time, we had our sandwiches, and were sitting inside the air-conditioned lobby. That is when the unwarranted stares began. I couldn't help but feel a little angry, and at the same time feel somewhat saddened by their unwitting expressions of contempt. Had they listened to Dawn's story, if they had known of the transformation in Greg's life, if they took the time to understand the nature of who these people were, would the stares they cast our direction possess the same level of condescension?

As I pondered on Dawn's story, the fact about how life choices often bring pain and disruption to our lives became apparent once again. I wish that her choices could have been different beginning when she was a sixteen-year-old mother. But that was her choice and the path she chose to travel. Ultimately, those decisions led us to the pier where we have landed.

A week later, I discovered that some people from BRASS, a non-profit organization that helps women, met Dawn during the lunch hour at Salvation Army. They bought her a bus ticket, and she returned home.

CHAPTER 16 – Anita

"I played Russian Roulette when I was twelve. We put one bullet in a revolver, spun the chamber and I took first turn. I was lucky. The other boy was not. The gun went off and the bullet passed through his brain. The rest of us ran off."

I sat in bewildered silence as Anita spoke of this horrific experience. So stunned by the words and her matter of fact recounting, I was unable to respond. I can only imagine what kind of impact that must have imparted on her life.

When Anita sat with a comforting demeanor for Dawn as Dawn spoke about her life, I sensed this fifty three year old was a pleasant and gentle lady. I asked her if she had anything to share. The stories she retold were not the kind of stories I expected. I should have known better for I am always amazed when a homeless person finds the courage to face the demons from their past.

"I'm originally from Tennessee," Anita began, "and was living with my daughter, but the landlady did not want two families living in the one place. So I had to leave. That's how I ended up on the streets. That was about four months ago.

My fiancé at the time was about to go to jail because of drugs and alcohol related things, and he didn't want me staying in a shelter down there, so he thought I'd be safer at the Salvation Army here in Bowling Green."

Anita spread a pleasant, grandmotherly smile across her face, the kind of smile that makes strangers feel at ease and welcome. I could tell she was uncomfortable physically as she kept fidgeting from one side to another. I asked her about her health.

"I've got diabetes among other things. My shoulder was busted and my ankle was crushed back in the year 2000 because of a car wreck. The diabetes has caused me to have neuropathy in both of my legs. They are numb from the knees down and it makes walking difficult. I can't reach very high or lift very much either. A few years ago I had a heart attack, and the doctors put in two stints."

"How do you get along from day to day?" I asked.

"I get a social security check and some disability plus Medicare. It's not much, but I get by mostly."

"Tell me about growing up as a child."

"I went to church some, started when I was eight years old. My mom didn't care if I went or not and my dad was an alcoholic," she snickered under her breath before continuing. "He was always either in jail or just gone all the time. We never knew when he would be home. I'm half Indian. When I was little the racial violence was bad at times. Life was hard for a little girl who didn't understand such things. Not long after the Russian roulette incident, a friend of mine invited me to church. The preacher's message really spoke to me that day, and I experienced a sinking feeling inside that was never there before. It was like something was missing and I needed to fill the void so I invited Jesus into my heart that day, and he's been there ever since."

For quite some time she spoke about how hard things were even with Jesus in her life. In time she grew up and was married. I hear this kind of thing often about how someone at an early age makes a decision for Christ, and they are left to struggle on their own often because their living environment doesn't change. Too often the church does not follow up with discipleship to encourage and teach. Anita never did address this issue directly, but from the way she talked about her struggles it became apparent that she was never adequately discipled to help her understand more clearly what her relationship with Christ could be.

"My husband became a paranoid schizophrenic, and had lots of problems with drugs and alcohol because of it. I worked long hard days all week as a floor manager in a plant and I was away from my children a lot. For some reason, the state declared me an unfit mother, took them away, and placed them in foster care, and the trailer I lived in was condemned. That's when I fell into a deep depression and that is also when Satan tempted me to start drinking. But I didn't because I had seen what it had done to my father, and I was determined not to follow in his footsteps. You know, the drinking don't make the problems go away, they're still there when you sober up, and the drinking just adds to them."

I was proud of Anita for not falling into the same trap that so many homeless people fall into. In most cases, the alcohol drove them into homelessness, but she managed to avoid it. What she shared next was another shocking story I didn't expect to hear from this pleasant and friendly lady.

"When I was thirty five, the depression was taking a toll on me so I decided to end it. I found some railroad tracks and laid down on them waiting for a train. Eventually one did come, and I closed my eyes waiting for the end. But just above where I was laying the train veered over onto another set of tracks."

I said nothing, and just allowed her to find her own words. I could see from her expression that as she reflected on the near miss encounter with the train, she realized just how close she had come to succeeding in ending her life.

"Another time I walked out into the Mississippi River and wanted to dive in and let the river carry me away. On that first try there were a lot of people around and I just couldn't do it thinking that someone would interfere. I tried a second time with the same result. Then as I thought about trying for a third time, I discovered I was pregnant. I couldn't do that to a baby," she paused and stared away for a moment, "I guess Jesus just didn't want me to go yet. There is some reason I am still here, I just wish I knew what it was."

I struggled to find the right words. Many times the words do not come to me, and I've learned to simply let it go and allow my guest to reveal as much or little as they desire. Anita appeared relieved that she had failed in her attempts to take her own life. Secretly, I understood her statement about Jesus not wanting her to leave. For me to say so would have added nothing to the emotion of the moment. She changed the subject to a more happy time.

"For many years I had been a 'Gospel Balloon Artist and Clown.'

"Please, tell me about that."

"I would go into a church, in Kansas City, and do routines for the Sunday school children's service. I'd dress like a clown and give gospel messages. I went to several different churches doing this, some would not let clowns inside, but most would."

She continued talking about that happy time in her life not unlike what so many of the homeless I've spoken to will do. They cling to the one thing from their past that provided them with a sense of purpose and meaning. It becomes a lever they apply to lift themselves to a higher place of self-esteem. It becomes a commodity they share with others that serves to identify something positive in their life. In many cases the memory has faded into obscurity because of circumstance, and only resurfaces when people take the time to acknowledge that their life has value. Those old happy-time memories are the most valuable thing they retain. Those memories are unique to them alone that no one can take from them. Too often just as quickly as the memory surfaces, it fades again and the reality of the present fills their life with fogged ambiguity.

"Can I ask you something?" I said, "Because you knew the gospel and because you had an alcoholic father, why is it that you were attracted to a man like your fiancé who has so many issues with drugs and alcohol?"

"I felt God was telling me 'this is your man'. I couldn't get away from him. Every time I turned around there he was. I even moved away to another county and there he would show up. I felt like God wanted me to help him. He told me once that if it had not been for me, he would have been dead by now. I know he cares for me because it was important to him that I was safe while he was away. He said he wants to do his time and then help others as a counselor and teach children about the dangers of drugs when he gets out."

"Are you ever angry about your situation now?"

"Not angry so much, just frustrated. I want to do so much but it seems that Satan keeps throwing stumbling blocks in my way. I want to help people too, volunteer at the Salvation Army, I love to cook. The Salvation Army will often serve cereal for breakfast, but there are people like me who can't eat that. I'd love to make them biscuits and gravy. I taught all six of my kids how to cook."

She kept sweetly smiling at me during our conversation. There was genuine warmth that prevailed from within her. She demonstrated kindness and compassion, yet at the same time an element of chaos in her life constantly stirred her existence into a thick broth of uncertainty. Somehow she persevered through it.

"You seem to have a peace about you even after everything you have gone through, and being homeless too. Do you think that is from God?"

Without hesitation she blurted out, "Yes it is! I know God is going to take care of me no matter what. We've been through a lot together already and there is more to come, but he'll provide. That's his promise to me."

Our conversation ended shortly after that.

I am always amazed at the stoic nature homeless people possess. I can't help but wonder if it comes from some inner strength or, simply because of their situation, they do what they have to do to survive. Anita, in spite of her physical infirmaries and lack of resources, showed a gritty determination to press on.

Anita became a friend that I occasionally ran into. She was always friendly and warm and eager to talk and show me the crafts she was making. On one of those days I ran into her, she said she had made me something and handed me a gift I treasure to this day, a beautiful beaded necklace with a silver cross hanging from it. I asked her to please put it on for me. I was honored to wear her gift. She beamed, looking proud.

With help from some of our friends and other organizations in town, she eventually moved into a small apartment. Those apartments became a focal point of future events neither of us could have imagined.

CHAPTER 17 – Susan, Jim, and Baby

"I'm not looking for a handout. I just need some help to get back on my feet. I need a job where I can support my family."

Homelessness took on a different face the day I met Jim and his wife Susan with their two-year-old son. What started as a routine interview evolved into an emotional struggle as their story unfolded like a bad novel.

Children hold a special place in my heart, especially children of a homeless family. What is already a complex struggle is made even more complex when dealing with the needs of a child from the perspective of an empty plate.

From the beginning, Jim's eyes cast a pleading look of despair that was tempered with a sober inner strength to persevere. The boy clung to his mother seeking comfort as if even in his youthful ignorance of their situation, he understood that life was not right. His emotional and cognitive development having already been impaired because of a lack of involvement with other children his own age, it was apparent that he needed more stability in their family. It wasn't that Jim and Susan were unaware of this; they fully understood the situation. Time after time of being turned down for a job withers even the strongest of men, and Jim was one of the strongest. He was a former Navy Seal.

"I was in the Navy for twelve years, and was originally a FAA certified Air Traffic Controller. I eventually qualified for and became a Navy Seal about the time of the Granada affair in 1983. In 1991, I was involved with Desert Storm monitoring the burning oil wells behind the lines. There was a firefight and I was seriously wounded. Because the wound messed up some internal organs, it caused me to become a diabetic. As result I was eventually discharged from the Navy. After that I worked as a police officer for a long time until I just got burned out. I didn't want to carry a gun anymore. So I left. I've been a certified plumber ever since, but plumbers jobs are hard to get now, that's why I'm out of work."

Jim was forty-nine almost fifty when I met him. He was still very fit with muscular arms and shoulders and stood about five feet eight inches tall. In many ways he was a delight to interview as he was articulate, educated and presented himself well. Susan was too. Neither of them fit the preconceived profile of a homeless person, but as I have learned, homelessness does not discriminate. Circumstances can overwhelm anyone.

Jim continued with his story, "I was told there was lots of work in Montana, so we packed what little we had and drove two thousand miles. I had to take a certification test and after that was told I was to make twelve dollars an hour.

137

One day later, I was let go because the company who hired me did not want to pay certified plumbers wages."

Jim leaned forward placing his elbows on his knees and ran his hands across his eyes. Susan looked on with a sense of overwhelming what-else-is-going-to-happen look in her eyes.

"We didn't have much money left, but decided to head back to Tennessee. We stayed for free at RV parks at night sleeping in our truck, and ate what we could. Along the way we ran into good people who helped us. We got food from a food bank, and lived off the land camping at campgrounds as we could. One lady at an RV park said she had to go somewhere on an airplane and couldn't take all her stuff so she gave us a lot of it. Inside the cooler she gave us, was some food and personal things like soap and wipes and one hundred dollars cash."

I noticed Susan's eyes filled with tears as he spoke of the generosity they encountered along their journey.

He continued, "By the time we got to Bowling Green our money pretty well ran out, and so we were stranded. We've been staying at the Salvation Army, but our time is about to run out. We've been out every day looking for work, any work, but it's hard to do that with a child."

Susan spoke up, "We're doing the best we can. I spent over two hours in one store just filling out the application. I had to take personality tests, which I understand having to do, but most places won't allow you to bring a child in with you so Jim and our son had to wait outside in the heat inside the truck until I finished."

Jim broke in, "I applied at a plant the other day. Took three hours to go through the process, and I'm just waiting to hear from them. I might actually get that job, but it will be a shift job working late and with no place to stay, that makes it hard. Right now we've got a quarter-tank of gas and twenty dollars to our name."

They did not phrase the words in such a way as to imply they were asking for a handout to help them. I understood right away that was not what they were doing. They were simply telling me about their situation.

I asked, "Have you tried any of the churches to ask for help?"

"Not yet", Jim said, "we want to make it on our own."

As we talked about the possibility of approaching local churches for assistance, I asked them what kind of religious beliefs they had.

Susan spoke first, "I grew up in a troubled life. I was a member at one time in a Protestant church but felt they were never there for me. I felt they looked down on me because I was from a single parent home. When the youth went off to do things, I could never go because we could not afford for me to. I went to the church for emotional help, and they were not there for me. I never felt at home in the church."

Jim added, "I graduated from a full Protestant Gospel Church School, a private school. My adopted father was an ordained minister who beat me black and blue every day. I can remember hearing my mother scream, 'You're going to kill him!' She was super religious, a real fruitcake. She was super annoying with it, always in your face, to the point where it was downright aggravating. The minister of the church school was a fraud, a homosexual."

"So was school a bad experience for you?" I asked.

"No, I didn't even know about the minister until later. I received a very good education. I went on to college but did not graduate there because I decided to go into the Navy instead."

"What about now? Do you believe in God?"

Jim was quick to answer, "No. We are spiritualistic, not religious. My grandfather was a full-blooded Canadian Cree. We choose to believe in their way. In the Cree belief, the father does not teach until his father has passed away. It is always the elder, who does the teaching. I learned through the peace that grandfather displayed and taught, through love of the land and living things, in the air, the wind, the water," he motioned with an arch of his hand in front of him, "that is life.

"When we were in Wyoming and Montana we lived off the land; caught fish from the river. You would say," he gently pointed his hand at me, "that God provided the fish, but we believe we were lucky enough that there was a man who caught the fish for us. His good spirit was what had voluntarily gone out and got us the fish. I'm not a Christian. I'm not religious in that way. The man liked to fish and we like to eat fish. We believe there is good in people no matter what religion, if any at all. It is about the spirit, the person. Many people who call themselves Christian are not good people and a lot of people who are not Christian are good people."

Jim paused for a moment and shifted his gaze toward Susan. She smiled back with a reassuring nod, silently confirming that she understood and agreed with what he was saying.

He continued, "We are very positive people, we have to be. Our lives have been very difficult since our childhood so we believe in the day to day. As long as we keep a positive attitude and outlook, tomorrow will be fine. We don't plan because we're tired of being disappointed. I can't put faith in something I don't agree with and that I see so many conflicts in. We are Pantheists."

Later I did some research on what Pantheists believed. This is what I found. *It is the view that the Universe (Nature) and God divinely are identical. Pantheists thus do not believe in a personal or creator God. The central idea is the Cosmos as an all-encompassing unity and the sacredness of Nature. Canadian Cree's believe animals and humans possess a Spirit. Because the Spirit is eternal they believe when they die, it is only physical death and the journey continues on. When the body is no longer viable, the Spirit ascends into another realm. Traditional Cree spirituality strongly reinforces the principle of a circle of life, the essence of which is found in Spirit.* http://www.sicc.sk.ca/saskindian/a89mar11.htm

Susan said to me, "We don't believe we'll come back as a hamster or anything like that" she says chuckling, "But neither do we believe in a Heaven or Hell."

I've run across a variety of religious and non-religious beliefs from homeless people. This particular one certainly was unique. They seemed well versed in its history and personal revelation. My intent on this day was to interview, but, I silently hoped that God would open a door in time to allow for another opportunity to share the truth about God's love with them. Well-meaning Christians too often do more harm than good as was the case with Jim's upbringing. I certainly did not want to contribute to their misunderstanding of what living as a Christian means.

I asked Jim to describe what it was like to be homeless.

He responded, "It is easier to fight as a homeless person when you are single, but with a family and you are suppose to be the bread winner and head of the home, its rough. To see your wife and child experience such tragedy, it is heartbreaking. But witnessing others going through this is heartbreaking also."

"Are you surprised by the number of homeless people?"

"No, we are not surprised, with the way the economy is, it's just hard. Seattle is at the top of my list for caring for the homeless."

I said, "Seattle is a much bigger place, so it's probably easier for them to take care of the homeless there."

"I disagree. In a smaller community where there are less people, less crowds, it should be easier to help. I have never seen so many churches in such a small square mileage area as it is here in Bowling Green. I am surprised there is not a better system here."

Jim continued to share his observations. "Homelessness comes in all shapes, sizes, colors, from the professional to the mediocre. It doesn't take but one unfortunate experience to put someone on the streets. They can be those with mental problems and substance abuse. They really need the care and understanding. We are not looking for handouts. We just want help so we can help ourselves. We just need somewhere to turn to show us how to help ourselves in this situation. Salvation Army has been great in putting a roof over our heads and meals, but it has been very difficult. There needs to be a better support system. We get more understanding from each other (other homeless people) than we do from others. The other homeless help us more in telling us where to go to apply for jobs, how to get around in the city, etc. than do the professionals who are supposed to be there to help us."

I asked, "What could be more helpful in this town for the homeless?"

"Transportation is a big problem. Most are on foot. Those of us who have a car cannot afford the gas. We still have payments left on our vehicle and it's about to be taken away. People who are older get so tired of walking all over town looking for jobs and having to go here and there, that they are worn out, and just don't have the energy the next day to get out there and do it all over again.

"Phones are another problem. If they have a phone, they can't afford to keep minutes on it. If they don't have a phone, just having enough money to use in a pay phone can be too much for them. When you're looking for a job, people may have to make as many as 8-10 calls a day. That's a lot of phone change to a homeless person. The professionals who are trying to help could give better directions. We are not from this town and do not know the streets. The people have given us awful directions and we have wasted what precious gas we have left in our truck trying to search for the places that we need to find. Childcare would be wonderful. It is so hard going all over town looking for jobs, and applying here and there with a little one."

Again, he shifts his gaze toward Susan. By this time her son is beginning to get tired, but he clings to her by resting his head on her shoulder. I can tell she is getting tired too.

Jim continues, "We are more fortunate than others. We still have our truck and some belongings we carry in the truck. Some only have a backpack. We traveled 2,000 miles with the promise of a good job and a good wage. It didn't happen. I guess that was an irresponsible thing for me to do with a family. I should not have a problem with my experience and licensing, but you just never know."

"What about food? Are you able to get enough to eat?"

Susan answers this time. "Jim is diabetic so that limits what he can eat, and I am a vegetarian which makes it a little difficult. My son is a picky eater and doesn't understand that he needs to eat what we have or he will go hungry. You learn to eat what is available."

"Do you have any dreams?"

Jim raises his head and his eye sparkles as he answers. "Our dream is to own our own RV Park. We love camping and the outdoors. We are just like everybody else, we just want to be happy, be free, have a job, secure work, a home, a safe place for our children. We don't need or even want extravagance."

Susan piped up chuckling, "A shower is good enough for me."

Jim said, "Just the American dream like anybody else, security and safety."

My heart was breaking for this sweet couple and child. Jim and Susan were so articulate and intelligent and even though I felt I could see despair, they were very friendly, and I still saw hope. He has a good education and experience, a veteran, and yet, he was sitting on the bench homeless. It seemed unwarranted. I wanted to pray with them as I do the others, but they backed away, and I left it alone as I knew their beliefs were different from mine. I hugged them both and told them I believed they were going to make it.

When I returned home, emotions, I thought dormant reactivated. My house, which is a modest home, suddenly felt overwhelmingly large. As I opened my refrigerator and saw the snacks and drinks sitting on the shelves, a sense of uneasy gratitude filled my heart. My eyes burned with tears as I stepped into the living room to rest in a comfortable chair. Those dormant emotions that filled my heart could not be defined. I wasn't sure what to think. Should I cry? Should I simply be grateful and go on?   Should I be sorrowful? I sought answers in my mind as I closed my eyes.

As a Christian, I am torn with mixed feelings born from not wanting to interfere with Jim and Susan's understanding of who they were, and my understanding of the difference they could find with Christ in their lives. As much as I respect the beliefs of the Indian cultures, I was saddened knowing they could not allow themselves to believe in the God who created this beautiful earth that they so revered. It was clear to me that the beliefs they clung to were simply a way to describe their journey through this life as they searched for meaning. At this time in their lives, they were walking through a fire with no one to turn to for hope and strength.

Tears began to meander down my cheeks as I contemplated the consequences this family may have to face someday. I knew that I was unable to pray with them, but I could pray for them, and so I did.

The next day, I felt convicted to fill their truck with gas and to bring them some snacks. I found Susan, Jim and baby sitting in the truck parked under the shade on the outside corner of a department store parking lot. When I handed the snacks through the window, her two year old was into them in a moment. Susan gratefully said she wanted to pay me back, but could not until one of them got a job.

I said, "Don't be concerned, pay it forward instead, and do something good for someone else when you can."

They said they would. I believed them.

A couple of years later I received this text . . .

"Hi Kris, this is Jim, Susan, and baby. Just dropping a text to let you know we are home in Tennessee and doing great. Thanks for all your help in 2011."

It seems this bad novel took some turns, and landed on a happy ending. I'm so happy for them!

CHAPTER 18 – Chains of a Different Kind

For several months, Greg became my go to person when it came to making contact with other homeless people. Almost every person I interviewed during that time resulted because of his intervention. Over those months, Greg's life and ours intertwined more closely as his life became more visible the more time we shared with him. There were days when Greg would call me, being down, sometimes crying, he would ask me to read the devotional book we shared, *Jesus Calling*. Even in happy times, he would call just so we could read together. He always wanted us to pray together before hanging up. I loved those times.

Although Greg was now a Christian, his new life constantly confronted his past. His past was bound by demons to an addiction that threatened to undermine his desire to change.

Twelve weeks after I met Greg and six weeks after he made his public profession of faith, Greg was arrested for public intoxication. I initially knew nothing about why this happened, but I did understand that he struggled with alcohol. There were times he confessed to me that he hated what the alcohol did to him. He no longer wanted to succumb to its grasp, but he would always conclude by saying something like this, "You just don't understand how hard it is."

He was right, I did not understand, at least not in the way he tried to explain it. I knew about the effects it had, I understood intellectually what he was saying, but I had never felt the grip of its power over a life. There were times he would hang his head with tears sliding down his broad cheeks, and he would pray in anguish that he could stop drinking. My heart wrenched in anguish as well seeing him struggle so. Many times we prayed together that he could quit. I suggested Alcoholics Anonymous or possibly other addiction treatment centers. He would always shake his head,

"I've tried those, know what I'm say'n. They don't work for me. The desire is too strong.

It was a late September day when he told me about how he was arrested.

"I was bored, know what I'm say'n. It was Saturday night so I started to drink inside my shed. It was stuffy so I decided to take a walk and go downtown. That girl who works at the Subway store, know what I'm say'n, the one who would give me a free sandwich sometimes. She started passing around rumors about me that weren't true, so I confronted her about it, know what I'm say'n."

"And were you drunk when you did that?" I asked.

148

"No I wasn't drunk, I had been drinking, not drunk though. She got mad at me, said I was threatening her."

"What did you say to her?"

Greg rolled his head to one side and cast a shallow grin.

"I admit, I probably said some things I should not have said. She called the manager, and he made me leave. He banned me for two years from that place, know what I'm say'n, two years. She shouldn't have been saying those things."

Greg's addictions went further than alcohol. He confessed he also smoked marijuana and that so-called legal drug known as 7H. Heavy use of these drugs can cause a person to become paranoid, and at times Greg showed those tendencies. I suspected the rumor accusation was born more from his state of mind than from reality. He continued with his story.

"I left and walked over to the park and they called the police on me. When the police came, they said I was drunk and arrested me, know what I'm say'n. Spent five hours in jail, and now I have to pay a two hundred dollar fine, know what I'm say'n. I hate being an alcoholic."

This was the first time Greg admitted to me that he was an alcoholic. He grew up in a world foreign to the world I grew up in. He experienced drastic chaos in his forty-six years. As was his habit of doing, he leaned his large frame forward resting his elbows on his knees. He hung his head low as though he was ashamed of his behavior, as though he was embarrassed for me to know about this incident.

Because Greg gave his life to Christ does not remove him from the temptations of this world. The heavy baggage of guilt he carried around weighed heavy on his shoulders. Too often when someone like Greg chooses to follow Christ, they are left on their own to fend for themselves. He needed Keith and me as friends. We needed to hold him accountable, but doing so proved difficult to execute. We never judged Greg, which he always appreciated. Had we judged him, he would have walked away from our relationship. Several times, he would say to me with a big smile and deep riveted voice, "You're different than the others."

I wanted to be different. Even so, knowing that he struggled with the chains of addiction that choked his life, my heart was broken for him, for there was little I could do short of prayer and support as a friend. Ultimately, he would have to make the choice to get help.

Greg was attending two separate church services; one on Wednesday morning for a Bible study at the small church across the road from his storage shed, and again with us on Sunday's at our church. He was also volunteering at Hope House, a local charity location in town. This volunteer work gave him a greater purpose, and helped him feel as though he was giving something back to the community.

A few days after our conversation he told me, "I love God with all my heart, know what I'm say'n. I'm try'n, I'm really try'n, I just have to take it one day at a time, know what I'm say'n. Don't give up on me."

I patted his brawny hand, "I'll never give up on you Greg just don't you give up on yourself. God can and will help you through this."

Chains of a different kind tormented Greg. They were chains of fatigue, chains of fear, chains from a past that haunted his now. I prayed that those chains would break and he could one day shout to the world, "My chains are gone, I've been set free!" What he did not realize was, with Christ already in his life those chains had already been shed. He was so new to that insight, he was unable see it. What neither of us could see at the time was where his addictions would eventually lead both of us.

CHAPTER 19 – I Am Weary - God Speaks

A couple of weeks later, having been let down by several people; I became weary. This same week I was really missing my prodigal son. I became even wearier. This same week, after hearing so many homeless people telling me their stories filled with such sadness, seeing the despair on their faces, bodies drooping, tears streaming down their cheeks, I became extremely weary.

I came home thinking maybe I would just quit, just do my own thing, crawl back into my comfort zone, sit in the box – and then God spoke.

Through my devotional calendar, He said:

"God does a complete work, and He will see it through to the end. So don't give up because it's taking longer than you hoped. Be confident that 'He who has begun a good work in you will complete it until the day of Jesus Christ.'

Then I opened up a friend's blog the same day. An excerpt from Lynn Mosher:
http://lynnmosher.blogspot.com/2011/09/alone-time-with-god.html

"My child, you are doing well. Keep aiming at the goal I have set for you. This has been a wearisome time, but keep your aim and your eye on the goal, that is, to do my will. Obedience is of the utmost importance. All my trust is placed in one of my children who places all their trust in Me. I trust them to do my work, that work which is so important for the lost world. There are those who desperately need your obedience, for without it, their pathway is hindered. There are many who depend on my obedient children even though they do not know it. I will help you rule your time. Give all your time into my Hands. I will see to it that there is time enough

for everything you need, and I need you to do. I will bring about my will in your life. But you must be willing as a little child to follow Me and do so obediently."

No one can tell me God does not speak to us. So then I went to His Word and my eyes fell to this verse:

*"My soul melts away for sorrow;
strengthen me according to your word!"*

Psalm 119:28 (ESV)

Isn't God good?! So I kept turning pages and looking up scriptures to feed me. With each word I became less weary, more at peace, and feeling the confidence returning. Are you weary? Let me share His Word to give you a jump-start.

*"He gives power to the faint,
and to him who has no might he increases strength."*

Isaiah 40:29 (ESV)

*"May the LORD give strength to his people!
May the LORD bless his people with peace!"*

Psalm 29:11 (ESV)

*"For I will satisfy the weary soul, and every languishing
soul I will replenish."*

Jeremiah 31:25 (ESV)

*"...looking to Jesus, the founder and perfecter of our
faith, who for the joy that was set before him endured the
cross, despising the shame, and is seated at the right hand of
the throne of God. Consider him who endured from sinners
such hostility against himself, so that you may not grow weary
or fainthearted.*

Hebrews 12:2-3 (ESV)

"Come to me, all who labor and are heavy laden, and I will give you rest. Take my yoke upon you, and learn from me, for I am gentle and lowly in heart, and you will find rest for your souls. For my yoke is easy, and my burden is light."

Matthew 11:28-30 (ESV)

"Peace I leave with you; my peace I give to you. Not as the world gives do I give to you. Let not your hearts be troubled, neither let them be afraid.

John 14:27 (ESV)

"I can do all things through him who strengthens me."

Philippians 4:13

Are you feeling better? I sure was. I'm so thankful God does not abandon us and leave us in our weariness! I was ready to go back to the bench and visit with more people.

Praise God from whom all blessings flow!

CHAPTER 20 – Nicole

"My dad was abusive to the whole family. I remember my mom telling the story about the time he lined all the older kids against the kitchen counter and pulled out a gun intent on shooting all of them. Mom grabbed his arm as he fired the first shot."

Nicole was not old enough to remember the incident being the youngest of nine kids. Even so, she was obviously disturbed by what had happened.

Twenty-seven-years-old, she was from Ohio and although homeless, did have a part-time job working in the food service program at Western Kentucky University. She was staying at the Salvation Army under their Honors program, which allows people to stay up to a year as long as they could afford the five-dollars-a-day fee. There was emptiness in her eyes. She searched for words to express the emotional drain she experienced for most of her life. Of the many forms of homelessness, hollowness of spirit is a prevailing trait, one that clung tightly to this young woman's life.

"Who I called mom and dad were actually my grandparents. My real mom gave me up at birth, she was an addict and my birth father was in prison at the time. My grandparents took me in. My dad was abusive physically and emotionally. My mom was so scared of him that she could do nothing. He slammed a two-by-four board to my back, punched and kicked me for no reason. My older siblings got the worst. Once they were grown, they didn't come around much as they resented him so much."

It was as though the childhood abuse was so commonplace to her that the profound wounds it created bled the emotion from every facet of her life. Resentment replaced hope at an early age, and the continuous battles that raged became a part of her and her sibling's life experience. I wanted to probe more deeply into her relationships with the brothers and sisters.

"There were nine of us, I was the youngest. Our relationships are casual at best. After my dad died, I was going through my first separation from my ex-husband. I was at home, and one of my brothers came into the kitchen where I was about to fix some rice for lunch. He started screaming and yelling at me about fixing that box of rice. He hit me and kicked me, and beat the crap out of me, all because I was fixing rice."

Her voice broke for the first time, and tears began to fill the hollowness that dominated her eyes. She turned her head to one side, and using just her fingers, she wiped away the moisture smearing her eye shadow in the process.

"I had a breakdown after that. Not long after, I caught a bus and ended up in New Mexico, then Arizona, and eventually back to Ohio. After I returned to Ohio, I connected with a friend whose husband was being sent to Iraq. She was moving to Bowling Green to be closer to other family members, and she asked me to come along. It took about two seconds for me say yes. I didn't have anything for me in Ohio."

She paused as if waiting for a response from me. I asked her if she remembered having ever attended church growing up.

"My dad never went, but my mom would take us sometimes. When I was seven I was baptized, but only because I was forced to. There was nothing real about it. I believe there is something greater than ourselves out there, but not necessarily just one God. I pray, but it's not to one, to whoever is out there. There was a time I got back with my high school sweetheart and ended up getting pregnant. His dad was a minister and forced us to get married. Neither of us wanted it. Just like when I was baptized, religion forced us to get married. I back away from religion because I feel I've always been told I had to do it. It makes me very uncomfortable when people try to push their religion on me. I need to come to it on my own or it's never going to work. It can't be forced on me because anything forced, I run away from. I have to come to terms with it on my own. I do try to work on it."

I paused a moment to allow her words to resonate through my thoughts. There are times my desire to share the love of Christ begins to dominate the interview process, and there are times I realize it is best to simply allow the moment to work its own merits. Then, there are times when the Lord speaks to me and I feel compelled to respond.

"You know Nicole, when we place our focus on people more often than not, people disappoint us. But, when we

157

place our focus on Christ, we discover that he will never fail us no matter what our circumstances."

She fought back the urge to cry. Her voice grew timid as tears overwhelmed her attempts to hold them back. She blinked several times taking in two or three deep breaths between each gentle sob, and with shaky hands she smoothed over the moisture that spread beneath her eyes. I gently patted her forearm.

"When I was younger, I prayed and prayed and everything kept going wrong. I'm struggling to keep my faith. Everyone comes at me saying don't believe this; you should believe that. It pushes me back."

I continued to pat her arm offering her time to release the emotions she had held in for so long. A few moments later, she had calmed down enough so I could ask about her children.

"I've been married and divorced three times. I have three children, but custody of none of them. One of the ex-in-laws has custody of one, and the other two fathers have the other two. I do love them and miss them so much, but being homeless and all would not be a good environment for them, so they are better off where they are now. I won't fight to get them back."

With only a slight pause, she told me about her school years. "I dropped out my senior year. One of my classes got fouled up in one of my earlier years, and the principal said I had to redo my senior year. I didn't want to do that, so my mom signed the forms to allow me to drop out. I did get my GED later. I really enjoyed marching band though. I played the clarinet. My dad, the way he was, didn't allow me to have many friends, so marching band became my saving grace during that time. I love music." Her tear-reddened eyes brightened as she relived the one good memory from her past. After a minute or so, she continued on.

"I just want to get on my feet. I'm tired of everything going wrong in my life. I'm trying to do the best that I can and it feels like every step of the way I get knocked back. I seem to attract the wrong people."

She points to Mike, a homeless man sitting on the bench across the park from us, who is also staying at the Salvation Army. She tells me they are getting married.

"Mike is different. I have chronic back pain, sciatica pain, chronic migraines, manic-depressive [disorder], anxiety and I'm not receiving help for any of it. Having him with me makes it easier, and he makes me feel better." She pauses a moment before adding, "I want to stay in Bowling Green. It's more comfortable here than any other place I've been. People here for the most part are friendly, but even here some people misconstrue us. Some look down on us. When people find out I live at the Salvation Army, I get disgusted looks. It hurts when people don't understand. People fall on hard times, and it's hard to get on your feet, working paycheck to paycheck, part time, with only minimum wage; it's hard. People presume if you're homeless, there is something wrong with you, wrong in the head or something."

I asked her if alcohol or drugs contributed to her being homeless.

"I used to drink socially, but I was turned off after seeing what it did to an old boyfriend. He drank Listerine to get drunk. I will go to bars but all I drink is a Coke or a Sprite. I go to listen to the local bands and to play pool. I'm called the mother hen because I take care of the ones who do drink. I'm a mother hen at the Salvation Army too. I love to help people. If they're happy, I'm happy. I learned to please everyone because of my childhood, and that's how I got into this position. I helped everybody else, and forgot about myself."

Nicole expressed desire to improve herself so I asked her what kind of job she would like to have.

"I love working with animals. I wanted to be a vet tech at one time. I also would love cosmetology. I actually got into a school for that, but my bad back got in the way and the position of the arms you have to use was hard. I'm severely left handed, and they could not teach me to cut left handed. I would like to go back to college someday. I need to keep a job, save money, eventually get married to Mike. It's hard to hope because when I do, it falls through every single time. It's hard to plan. You do, you get your hopes up and then they get crushed. I feel I'm on the verge of another breakdown. Right now, I live day-to-day, minute-to-minute. I do have more hope now that I've met Mike."

She throws a casual glance toward Mike across the park and smiles for the first time during our conversation. Then paused for a moment as she gathered her thoughts.

"I want people to keep an open mind about homeless people. I would say, 'Don't judge a book by its cover.' If you see someone on the street, don't just walk by, talk to them. Sometimes all people need is a hug and a smile in that moment. The littlest things help more than people can imagine. People need to understand how hard it can be."

As our time came to a close, my concern for Nicole dominated my thoughts. She was once again placing her faith in another person, the kind of faith that had failed her numerous times. I did not know anything about Mike at the time, but understood that Nicole was in many ways a fragile vase filled with faded flowers of empty promises.

When I consider our time together, what touched me most deeply about her strength was the look in her eyes as she described her abusive father's death. "When my dad was dying, I spent time with him trying to help him as best as I could."

She looked away and clinched her jaw, not speaking, just breathing deeply during silent moments. Then, with a weak trembling voice, she quietly whispered, "He died in my arms."

Her voice broke with a rough moan as she barely finished the words. Her cheeks once again glowed with moisture while she fought to hold back the tears.

"Just before he died . . . I told him I had forgiven him."

CHAPTER 21 – Mike

There are times my preconceived notions about someone interferes with my ability to remain objective. I found it is better to leave those notions behind. Doing so provides room for surprises. Nicole's story evolved into a series of dramatic events. When she indicated that she and Mike were a couple, and planned on getting married, my mind said this will lead to problems. My heart hoped they could make it.

Mike was a large thirty-two year old man. As large as he was, he appeared quite shy, but confident and well-rehearsed with his story.

"I never knew my dad. My mom couldn't take care of me even working two jobs so when I was four or five, I lived with my grandparents, and stayed with them until I was twenty-six. My grandfather died four years ago, and about a year later my grandmother died. That is when things went downhill. They were the only parental guidance I ever had. After they died, I had no one to turn too. I was pretty much a hellion all my life. My grandmother did her best, but I was just too much for them. Once I got my driver's license I was gone all the time. They even bought my first car, and gave me a second one later. They owned a small furniture store, and I helped out. They would buy old video game systems and I would fix them up, and resell them for a hundred dollars to earn some spending money."

When Mike spoke, he held his shoulders straight and his head high. His broad neck blended with his shoulders in one homogenous mass. His faded black t-shirt, although several sizes larger than what the average man would wear, clung to his bulk. I asked if he was happy living with his grandparents.

"I was and I wasn't, but I started hanging out with the wrong crowd, and that caused some problems. They were thugs, but I never got into drugs or anything. I didn't drink too much, maybe every now and then. We mostly just hung out at someone's home and drank. I was sixteen, and thought I was pretty cool."

He told me about living in Tennessee and Kentucky, and then finding himself stranded in Bowling Green working at McDonalds to pay his five-dollar-a-day fee to stay at the Salvation Army. His demeanor changed when he spoke about his son.

"I have a son who is eight-years old now. I don't get to see him; his mother has custody. It's been six months since I last saw or spoke to him. His mother and I had some words, and now they won't let me see him. He's going to be a hellion like me."

Why do you say that?"

"Because I was, and the offspring of a hellion is ten times worse."

I hoped for the son that wouldn't be true.

"I only drink twice a year now; once on New Years and once on my birthday, to celebrate a friend of mine who died."

He paused for a reflective moment. Although he did not share the story about his friend's death, I could tell the incident was a powerful force in his life.

"I went to the University of Tennessee once on a football scholarship. In my second year I opened a mini-bar in my dorm room, and sold drinks to the under-aged students. I never got caught or in trouble for it. I stayed in school playing football until I blew out my knee. Ended up losing my scholarship, and dropped out. Just as well, I could never get along with the coaches. One coach would say I wasn't being aggressive enough, and another would say I was being too aggressive. I just wish they would make up their minds what they wanted me to do".

I asked him about playing football in high school.

"I actually got kicked out of high school two weeks before graduation."

"What happened?"

"I punched the principal in the face for calling my Grandmother a bitch."

He stopped on purpose, and cast a smirk toward me as though he was proud of having done such a thing. "Ended up getting my GED and scored a perfect score on it. I was in the top ten percent on the ACT. Because of that, I still got my scholarship. After I left school I went back to help out my grandmother at her shop. That's when I injured my back. I'm a mess now, bad knee, bad back, bad hips, and rheumatoid arthritis, upper and lower back pain due to disc disease, bipolar, and depression."

Depression is understandably a common issue with the homeless. The reasons for it stem from any number of causes far more complex than what I am capable of understanding. I asked Mike to tell me about his depression.

"Years of depression. It was doing me in. I couldn't keep a job whatsoever, couldn't keep one in the factories. I just wouldn't go or when I did, I just didn't care and they would send me home. Depression and Bipolar both just get in the way. My bipolar meds make me feel like I'm a zombie a lot of the time. I try not to take the meds, but I know I need them. I take Seroquel. One of the side effects is that it can cause diabetes, so I'll probably end up a diabetic."

Mike's posture began to slump more. He lowered his head, and shifted it slightly from side to side like one disgusted with a situation. I redirected the questions and asked Mike about being homeless.

"I've been going from friend to friend off and on now for about four years. I've never been 'on the streets'. Whatever money I have, I give to friends to help with the bills. I had food stamps so would help that way. I had an apartment for almost three years. I got with a girl and she ruined everything.

"In December of '07, I lost my job. I had been coming in late, leaving early, sick a lot. Then I fell over a cart at Wal-Mart where I had been working and hurt my knees and back again. They were afraid I would file for workman's comp, so they fired me. Not finishing my education and disabilities is making it real hard to keep a job. If you don't finish school, it's going to be rough. If you don't have a high school degree or nowadays, if you don't even have an Associate's degree, you won't get nowhere."

I nodded in agreement and asked Mike if he had any advice he would like to share.

"Stay in school, go to college definitely! Anymore, you can't get anywhere without a college degree. Or at least go to a Trade School."

"Do you want to go back to college"?

"I'm going to whenever I can. I don't know when that will be. I need to get back on my feet, get a place to live, and keep up on my child support payments. If I don't keep that caught up, I go straight to jail. No ifs, ands, or buts on that.

"What hurts most right now is not being able to talk to my son or my mom. She has a phone but can't afford to put minutes on it. She lives in Tennessee. Growing up I got to see her on summer breaks and for two weeks in the winter. Tennessee is home to me, and hope to go back there someday. I'm thirty-two years old. I need to step up and help myself. I make just enough at McDonald's to pay fees at Salvation Army, my child support and that's it. I work full time, but at McDonald's that's just 35 hours a week. Only managers get 40 plus hours."

Mike's reflection on bettering himself I recognized as another common comment from speaking with the homeless. Too often, the desire is there, but the means is not. Living on the streets or even at a shelter creates its own kind of situational environment, a 'catch-22' circumstance that leads those trapped there in a constant circle of failure. I asked Mike about his future.

"Go back to school for a small business degree. I would like to open up my own business, a restaurant. I've taught myself, and my grandma taught me how to cook. I taught myself more with international foods. I would like to get a small business degree and a culinary arts degree.

I asked how Nicole fit into his plans.

"We want to get a place together, then get married and possibly have a kid. I can't stand to not be around her. If I don't see her in the morning, I have a bad day. I guess it was first sight, fell in love with her right away. I haven't felt like that since '98 with my fiancé. She was killed in a car wreck. She was 18 and I was 19. When I get on my feet, I will fight for custody of my son."

I asked him if people in general realize he is homeless.

"No, I dress like a regular person. Some you can tell and some you can't. And I'm not just going to come right out and tell people. I've seen regular people who come through the park, and see someone they know is homeless, and they frown upon them. My first day in Bowling Green, I met a guy, Albert, a guy in his 70's. He was sitting in the park with me across from him and we started talking. He said, 'I'm homeless, and I said 'So am I, I'm living at the Salvation Army." Albert said, 'I sleep right under that tree, that is, when the cops don't make me leave.'

"While I was talking to him, people were walking through, coming from the businesses around the square, getting their lunch, and he would say 'Hi' to them and they would look disgustingly at him and not say a word. But if I said 'Hi', they would say, 'Hey, how ya doing?' People just don't care if you're homeless. If you don't look like them, they are not going to talk to you.

"Case in point, I told a buddy at the Salvation Army to apply on line at McDonald's, and I'd put in a good word for him. The guy did, and then came into McDonalds's with the only pair of clothes he had on. The establishment turned him away because of what he looked like. People, citizens of the

United States, take everything for granted. They will never realize what it is like until they are like that."

"Not everyone is like that", I said.

"I know everybody is not but a lot are. Every state, every county has raised the cost of living so high, for tax reasons, but it hurts us so much more than what it was supposed to do to help us. By raising cost of living, taxes so high, it makes it where people can't have anything. If they would put the cost of living back down where it should be, then possibly people could get back on their feet, and live their lives."

Mike took a deep breath and continued, "A hundred dollars comes out every two weeks for child support, and a hundred and forty dollars goes to the shelter. I can't save at all. I have a year at the Salvation Army, but I want to be out of there by Christmas. Nicole and I have an appointment in November with the housing authority to see about an apartment. I'm hoping we get that, and we can have Christmas there and not at the Salvation Army. I have no winter clothes. I need to find some. I wear a 5x shirt and 50-52 pants. Those are hard to find. I also need some tennis shoes."

He showed me the shoes he was wearing, and the soles were parting from the uppers. I told him about Hope House.

"I've been there, and they didn't have any my size. People need to appreciate what they have. A lot don't know what they have until it's gone. I used to have a vehicle, a home, a steady job and it was all gone in an instant. The girl took all my stuff. My license got suspended due to non-payment of child support, and due to this, I lost my truck. How am I supposed to live and work and make something of myself when all these bad things happen?"

An abundance of hurts contributed to Nicole and Mike's emotional states. Childhood abuse, poverty, bad relationships, no real godly training growing up, some poor choices, and then teen-age rebellion on top of that with poor health added in, has led these two to homelessness.

Loneliness is another powerful circumstance for the homeless. Mike and Nicole found each other during difficult times. Mutual understanding of each other's situation helped to form their bond. However, what it takes to retain a lasting relationship is the more difficult of their situation to grasp.

As my time with Nicole and Mike ended, I prayed for the four children involved between their two lives, and that the cycle of abuse and broken dreams will no longer hold these families captive. I fear they may just end up in this same situation someday... or worse.

A year later I discovered Mike and Nicole went their separate ways, and I lost contact with both of them.

CHAPTER 22 – Day at the Laundromat

All through the summer, my friendship with Greg became stronger. His trust of Keith and me became stronger allowing for more relaxed and personal relationship. Greg would always stay nearby while I talked to someone he had arranged for me to meet often telling me, "I got your back, know what I'm say'n. I won't let anybody hurt you."

Before long I began to trust Greg as though he were my brother, and he would tell me I was his sister. Trust is a struggle for many that are homeless. Their situation being what it is places them at a disadvantage when dealing with the other side of life. Trust was an issue that Keith and I never took lightly. We diligently pursued any opportunity to build the connections so vital to establishing and then maintaining trust.

Greg desperately wanted to move into his own apartment, and get out of that cramped storage shed so smothering hot in the summer, and so drafty cold in the winter. "I just want a place of my own, ya know what I'm say'n." He just wanted a degree of normalcy again.

Something as simple as getting around town proved difficult for him. Although he had a bicycle he could ride for a while, his old self would sometimes resurface and one day he fell off that old bike. Before he knew what he was doing he threw it into the river.

"I guess I got a little mad," he told me, "now I'm on foot again, know what I'm say'n."

One day he called me from Hope House, and asked if I would write him a letter of recommendation. One of the low income apartment complexes in town had an opening and he needed that letter before he could apply for approval to move in.

I quickly wrote the letter and made the ten mile drive into town to deliver it to him. Although he tried to hide his excitement about possibly getting into his own place, the grin on his face betrayed those efforts. While we talked, he asked if I would drive him to the Laundromat. The mutual trust that Greg and I had developed allowed me to break the driving rule from time to time and this was one of those days.

When we arrived at the Laundromat he suggested that I go on and do what I needed to do and he could walk back to his shed from there. I didn't have anything pressing I needed to do, so I decided to stay with him until the laundry was finished and then I would give him a ride back to the shed.

A big smile spread across his broad face as he said, "Why don't you bring in your Bible and read to me while we wait?"

We made quite a pair sitting in between the washers, a five foot seven inch white woman reading verses from the Bible aloud to a giant six foot four, dark man. The stares we received could have pierced a steel curtain. Across the room were four young men all probably in their teens. Toward the back of the room, the caretaker was doing some cleanup chores. Along the opposite wall were several older men and two women, all staring at Greg and me.

The four teens kept staring at us, and talking amongst themselves. I could only wonder what they were thinking. I thought, "Lord, let them have ears to hear," as I opened my Bible.

I didn't know where to start reading at first and then remembered the reading from my Sunday School class the

Sunday before, so I opened to Psalms 118 and began reading out loud. I had to raise my voice because of the rumblings of the washing machines, but Greg listened with intensity at every word. After a chapter or two, we began to discuss the life of David from the Psalms, and the others in the room continued to stare not quite sure what to make of this odd couple.

As we were discussing what we had read, we began to smell burning rubber with every passing minute. We wondered where it was coming from. Eventually the caretaker came over, and lifted the lid on Greg's washer.

"Man, you're machine is too full. You're burning it up!" she shouted above the spinning noises that filled the room.

Greg had stuffed a large blanket along with four pairs of his large sized Jeans. No wonder the machine was burning up!

"You need to use two washers. Take some of this stuff out before you burn it up," said the caretaker.

Greg's demeanor changed and I could see his old self starting to surface. He didn't like the idea of having to spend another seventy-five cents on another washer. Seventy-five cents, for most of us it is nothing, but for Greg it could mean having a meal that day or not. More than likely, it meant not being able to buy that pack of cigarettes that he desired on a daily basis.

"You want me to spend another seventy-five cents?" Greg spouted rather gruffly. The caretaker refused to back down. "Either that or pay for a new washer."

Greg rolled his eyes and clinched his jaw. He towered over the caretaker as he stood up, but was helpless to do anything but give in to the demand.

I had to fight back the laughter as I watched him unload the wet Jeans and throw them into another washer. They were full of water, dripping the soapy mess all over the floor. He continually cast disgusted looks toward the caretaker as he slid each quarter into their respective slot. He fought hard to hold back his anger, and I suspect he might not have tried so hard had I not been there. He did not want me to see his bad side.

The caretaker came over with a disgusted look on her face and mop in hand. As she began to mop up the soapy mess, she made a remark to Greg about not filling up the machines so full anymore.

When he returned to his seat he leaned toward me with pursed lips and said, "The old Greg would pop off right about now, but the new Greg is going to sit here quietly and keep listening to you read me the Bible." Smiling big, and again trying to contain my laughter, I told him I was proud of him for keeping his mouth shut.

The washing cycle completed, and he stuffed everything he could into a single dryer. I hoped we would not smell more burning rubber. When the dryer finished its cycle, he slowly and deliberately checked each piece as he pulled them out. While he was extricating his clothes, I went to the front and sat by the big window next to a lady, and we began to visit.

"My, you have a wonderful husband, willing to do laundry while you sit here. Most men would have their wives doing the laundry."

Her statement caught me off guard. "Oh no," I said, "We're just friends."

I had no idea anyone would think that Greg and I were a couple. For a brief second, I thought this was comical, but as I began to think about it, I realized this was not good. I didn't want to give the wrong impression, and I did not want to dishonor Keith in any way by having others think Greg was my husband.

The lady seemed somewhat embarrassed by the conversation and apologized. She was a truck driver and we had a lovely conversation, mostly about her travels and I listened and we conversed well together as we would every once in a while glance over at Greg folding his laundry.

As I drove Greg back to his shed I realized that I had breached the boundaries Keith and I had set for ourselves by giving Greg the ride. All in all, it was a harmless gesture that helped him out, but for the first time since I met Greg I felt somewhat uncomfortable with the situation. By breaking this rule I had opened the door for future requests, and for similar situations to develop. Later I spoke to Keith about it and he said he would say something to Greg.

A day or two later he met Greg at the park where Greg, not unexpectedly, asked him for a ride. Keith casually and politely explained to him that he and I had a rule that we were never to give rides except under rare circumstances, and that I was never to give rides to anyone especially by myself. We didn't mind picking him up to go to church with us, but that is where we must leave it. There was never any waiver in our trust of Greg. Neither of us ever thought that he was a threat. On the contrary, we were thankful that he looked after me when I was alone downtown interviewing other homeless people.

Greg understood what Keith was saying to him. Even so, for the next few visits, he appeared a little distant and cool, and I was worried that he was upset over the conversation with Keith. Too, I worried that it had become between him and me. I prayed about it, and God in His goodness once again came through and took care of it in my fifth interview later with Greg.

For Keith and me, incidents like this one were growing moments wherein we learned how to deal with situations with tact and politeness. We strove to maintain that bonding we desired, yet at the same time, we also wanted to maintain a separation, to never cross the boundaries. Through it all God's hand was there. Our friend Greg became an even stronger and more respectful friend as a result.

CHAPTER 23 – Greg Visit 5

"Are you ready? Are you ready to go?"

"I was looking at the book. I looked at my beer, which I hadn't started. I couldn't see Him but I could hear Him, He was asking me again, "Are you ready to go?" I couldn't make up my mind, so I asked myself, "Did I want to give all of this up?"

"Are you ready?" is a question that every Christian faces. These were startling words from Greg, and he was adamant that God had come to him. I need to back up a bit to illustrate the whole story.

When it is nice in Kentucky, it is exceptionally nice and this mid-October day proved once again the flavor and character of that singular observation. The stifling heat of summer was behind us, and the day comfortable in the mid-seventies. To describe the sky as being blue is an injustice to the brilliance and depth of its color. A light breeze caressed the leaves, which were just now beginning to turn toward their fall rendezvous of boldness. Squirrels scampered across the ground looking for something to eat. One would find something, and another would try to take it away as they chased each other up and through the canopy of trees that shaded the downtown park.

I found Greg again sitting on one of the park benches. I was hoping to begin another conversation with another homeless individual, but there were none present except for him.

But before we started the interview, he asked me to keep the recorder off for a minute. He leaned forward and then looked at me with tears in his eyes.

"Why did you pick me to be part of your project?"

Tears welled up in my eyes as I could see Greg was questioning my motives. "Well, remember Greg how I told you on our first visit that I believed you were the answer to my six month prayer? I prayed asking if the book was God's will or my own. I did not want to do it for the wrong reasons, and God finally answered me by putting you on that bench the night Keith met you. I believe God brought us together for many reasons, this book being one of them. You were my first interview for the book. I don't see this as "my" project but "our" project. I don't believe I picked you but that God picked you."

Greg lifted his giant shoulders, and raised his head. A slight grin spread across his broad face and the often distant look in his eyes focused into one with a confirmation of purpose. He was more relaxed and the countenance of his expression portrayed a sense of relief. He nodded in agreement.

By now the tears were falling down my cheeks. "Please don't cry," Greg said. Let me finish what I want to say. I needed to know that I was important in this. I remember reading the newspaper article where you said we, the homeless people, had a sweet soul and you wanted people to know that. I thought to myself, it takes someone with a sweeter heart and soul to say such a thing. You have the most golden, sweetest heart I've ever seen, and I know that you are in this for the right reason, so I'm on board all the way. Please don't cry!"

"Oh Greg, you are important in so many ways!"

As he and I wiped the tears off our faces, I grabbed his hand, smiled, and thanked him for his kind words. Even the two of us can get sappy! He smiled saying, "We is good to go. You can turn on your recorder, and talk to me." So that is exactly what I did. For the next two hours, Greg shared more of his life with me. His words proved not only encouraging, but prophetic.

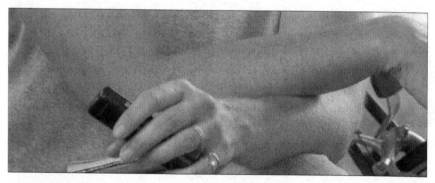

"So tell me how your life has been different now that you have changed?"

"I'm doing a Bible study with Bryan now, and I volunteer at Hope House on Tuesdays and Thursdays, know what I'm say'n. I go to another Bible study at the Episcopal Church on Wednesday mornings, the church services Wednesday night, and back again on Sunday."

"Why are you doing all this?"

"You know what they say, 'Practice makes perfect'. I'm hoping I can become a better person. If I can become a better person, others can and let's just keep this ball rolling, know what I'm say'n."

"So, you want to treat people better now?"

"I do. I didn't then. Back then it was all about Greg, know what I'm say'n. I want to do better. That's the difference".

"Do you make better choices now?"

"I try to, and I pray to. Sometimes I still make stupid mistakes, know what I'm say'n."

"We all do," I said.

"But I'm trying not to keep making the same mistakes. Enough is enough! I just want to be right with God, have Him take control over my life, know what I'm say'n. When I try to take hold of the wheel, I crash. With Him taking control, it can be nothing but fruit filled and blessings."

He again raised his great bulk upright, slightly turned his head to one side, and spread a giant grin across his face. Even if his words were simple, the complexity of his life and his struggles to change reflected in his eyes.

He continued, "Bryan said something that blew my mind. He said God is a jealous God, and Jesus saved all of us from God's wrath. By right, we is all supposed to perish but by Jesus dying on the cross for us, He wiped out all the sin so we could be right with God again."

"Hallelujah," I exclaimed!

He went on. "I thank Him every day for that, thank you Jesus, thank you Jesus! This is the most I've ever done, going to church and I want to stick with it, know what I'm say'n."

His face morphed into a sullen expression, and he paused, lowered his shoulders and his head. In a quiet voice that still carried a deep rumble, he continued, "I'll do good and then I'll do something stupid, and it's back to the same ol' Greg."

He paused again. "I'm sick of that Greg, I really am."

"You know Greg, the day you were baptized Keith warned you that Satan would really come after you and attack you where you were most vulnerable, and you said, 'Let him try, I got my armor on now.'"

"That's right, and I do have my armor on." He raised his chest and jutted his jaw physically showing his determination.

His shoulders fell again before continuing, "If I could just get this one thing off my back, the alcohol, I think I could be a really good person, ya know what I'm say'n. If I could get away from that, I'd be all right. When I was in the drug rehab years ago, I stayed sober by hanging around other sober people, when I got out, it was right back to that same old Greg."

He pursed his lips, and clinched his teeth, his jaw muscles working. His eyes stared blankly toward the ground as if searching for an elusive answer. The answers he needed I could not provide. The demons that tormented him were deeply rooted in his life, and physically he was dependent upon alcohol. My heart ached for my friend for I could see in his demeanor and hear in his anguished words the struggle from which he longed a release.

"Are you hanging around people now that tempt you?" I asked.

"It's not so much the people, you know? Everywhere I walk, you know, I see liquor stores, shops that sell beer and if I got money, that's what I do, know what I'm say'n."

"Is it physical or mental, or both?"

"Both", he says, "I'm trying to stop. I'm going on three days now that I haven't had nothing. The liquor stores give me credit. Because I go every day, they know who I am, they don't know what they're doing. They're a business, but they have no idea what they're saying to me."

"What are they saying to you?"

"They're saying, 'Come on, come on, come on, I'm gonna be right here waiting on ya, all you gotta do is walk this way'. That's what they're saying to me."

In my naivety I asked, "When you go by those places, can you not just put up your hand and say 'No, I'm not going to do it', and just keep on walking?"

"I have done that. It can be two in the afternoon and I will walk on, but by the end of the day, I have walked in. The thing of it is, this is as real as it gets, know what I'm say'n."

He remained quiet, looking down at the sidewalk. After a minute, he went on, "I just need God, that's all. I've prayed and prayed and prayed. The thing of it is, when I just got saved, and went through the baptism, I was doing the right thing, walking the way with Jesus. Good things happened. When I stop, that's when bad things happen in my life. That's why I stay in church, and doing the right things because if I stop, bad things happen in my life."

I encouraged him to seek out people who will hold him accountable and to stay in the Word because it is there we find strength.

"I know that can keep me on the righteous path. I like talking to people about the Bible. When you and I read scriptures together, I always feel better. That's a good way to start my day off. That's why I do the church things in the mornings because my life could be in shambles by 12:00 otherwise." I told him I was proud of him then allowed a few moments to pass before moving on with our conversation.

"You told me once that you used to use cocaine and crack, but that you no longer do so. Can you tell me how you were able to beat those things?"

"God always works in mysterious ways. I was selling dope at the time I was using it. I had an apartment at the time and this girl came in and bought some, but she had a wire on. As soon as she left, the police came up there, asked questions, and searched the place. They left but I knew it was just a matter of time before they came back, and kicked in my door, so I packed up all my stuff and moved it into the storage unit then checked myself into a halfway house/substance abuse program. Stayed the 90 days. I haven't seen the police since about that. I haven't used those drugs since. When you quit one thing, you substitute it for something else. I went from cocaine to weed and alcohol. Now I need to substitute something for the alcohol. I've never been much of a coffee drinker. I'm thinking about soda or something."

I chuckled telling him, "I think I'm addicted to Dr. Pepper."

"See, everyone has something, but at least yours doesn't get you into trouble," he said with a comical expression.

We laughed together breaking the lock on the serious moment.

"I am so grateful to you and Keith. You've given me a chance. Some people just walk past you out here, they could care less. I don't want to be like that. That's not how God wants me to be. I want the promises. When I was in recovery, they was always sayin', 'Don't leave before the promise happens.' That's what I'm thinking about the Bible too, don't leave before the promises, know what I'm say'n. When you do good things, good things follow, and when you do bad things, bad things follow. I try to do good things. But sometimes I do bad things, and when I do, I pay for them. I'm trying to get out of that rut, I'm trying to continuously do something positive. When I do something bad now, I feel convicted, I feel real bad. The old Greg wouldn't have, know what I'm say'n."

I reminded him that feeling convicted like he does is proof that the Holy Spirit is working on him.

"I know that, I have a place at His table now, you taught me that. You see, I have been paying attention," he said smiling broadly. A bit of sparkle returned to his eyes and he cast his gaze across the park, closed his eyes and soaked in the warmth of the fresh air.

He turned the questions back on me, and said, "We talk about me all the time, let's talk about you. What's a typical day for you from the time you get up?"

"Well, I get up and read my devotions and a piece from the Bible. Then I shower, clean up the house, do laundry if needed. On certain days, I volunteer with a lunch ministry at the local hospitals where we share bag lunches to family members waiting on loved ones being treated. If they allow us and want to, we pray with them."

Greg smiled, "See. I wish I could do things like that."

"Well, you are helping at Hope House. And that's another good reason to get plugged into a good church where there are ministries you can become a part of.

He said, "I just want to be a part of something. God knows what I do and that's what's important, I don't need recognition, I just want to be a part of something. I want to get involved."

Our conversation grew quiet again as he contemplated about possibilities of getting involved in something outside of his daily existence. He asked me to continue talking about my day.

"In the summer, I do all the yard work. I mow, weed-eat, rake, pull weeds from the beds. I enjoy feeling the sun and it's a good time being alone, and a good time just for thinking about my life, pondering."

"I like being alone to think", he says, "but I don't like to be isolated. It's just about me being in my comfort zone. I'm comfortable when I'm by myself. When you let somebody in, they can tear the whole house down. I enjoy spending time by myself reading a book."

"I wrote a story about comfort zones, I'll read it to you sometime if you would like. It is about how God brought me out of a lot of comfort zones and how blessed I was because of it".

"I'd like that," he said.

"There is a pond not far from where we live, and I have spent a lot of time there talking to God. I began to write about those encounters a while back. It was a time of transformation and renewing."

Greg was quiet for a few moments before he caught me completely off guard, "I was reading a book from Life

Fellowship in my shed. I was freaked out; I thought I was hallucinating. Let me tell you, know what I'm say'n. The pastor from the church told me to read it, and I thought, ok, I'll read it. I laid it down and glanced at it. It seemed the words just lifted off the book. I tried to close it back, I turned to face outside, and it seemed God came to me, I swear on Shanese's name (his daughter's name).

He was like, "Are you ready? Are you ready to go?"

"I was looking at the book. I looked at my beer, which I hadn't started. I couldn't see Him but I could hear Him, He was asking me again," "Are you ready to go?" I couldn't make up my mind, so I asked myself, "Did I want to give all of this up?"

About two minutes later I turned around and He asked again, 'Are you ready to go?' And I said, "Yeah, I'm ready to go."

"Well, get ready then," He said.

"I thought I was supposed to take off my shirt and shoes but then I thought where we were going, clothes don't matter. All of a sudden, I snapped out of it. I don't know what that was. But it was so real, so vivid, ya know what I'm say'n."

I said, "Maybe He was asking you, 'Are you ready to leave all the old life and follow me."

"Yeah, get rid of that ol' lifestyle, get ready for something new. That's the only thing I can think of. It scared me. I think about it every day".

"What scared you, the realness of it or the message?"

"No, it wasn't the message, it was how real it was and you know, am I ready, I couldn't make up my mind, whether I wanted to keep living this way or get ready to follow Him.

I thought about it, and it's like this, right here, this is just temporary, but that's eternal. That's what made me make up my mind. I'm like, 'Yeah, I'm going this way.' I swear, I wasn't smoking or nothing. I hadn't even had my beer yet."

I didn't know what to make of his story, but it was obvious that it had an impact on him. "Maybe the Holy Spirit is working on you," I said trying to encourage him. "Remember when you came out of the baptistery a great light shined on you and many who were there saw the peace on your face that was unmistakable. I believe that God has great things in store for you."

Before I could finish my thought Greg broke in and said, "I'm trying my best, know what I'm say'n, I'm really, really, trying. I just hope I can stick with this, to make something good out of my life. I want to live right. I want to enjoy his promises. I don't want to be miserable anymore. I'm tired of that."

We sat quietly for a few minutes before Greg broke the silence. "Tell me more about what you do."

"Next month there is a Women's Holiday Fellowship event and I've been asked to be one of the speakers."

"What will you talk about?"

"The evening will be centered around a book I read called '1000 Gifts', by Ann Voskamp. It's about how God gives us gifts every day, but we don't always notice them because we do not always pay attention. They can be very miniscule, like the beautiful color in the leaves laying in a puddle of water or the crunch of dried leaves underfoot. The message is when you recognize the gifts, name them with a thankful heart, and acknowledge them to the Father, you are entering into His presence. You become more aware of everything around you, from all your senses, and when you start seeing and focusing and thanking Him, the joy swells up inside of you because you're bringing Him into the moment. These moments, in essence, become holy moments and how can you not be joyful in those times."

Greg again raised his broad shoulders and lifted his head. His expression was one of revelation. "You know, that can go for anybody! When I'm at my church, your church, up there with Bryan at Hope House, it seems like everybody is saying the same thing, know what I'm say'n. We're all on the same chapter. That's powerful! It is!"

"Yes, even in the hard and difficult times, there are gifts to discover. Sharing about my prodigal son was very difficult for me as my heart was broken during that time. But, God led me to that pond, and it became a great and wonderful gift. The times I spent there, He spoke to me and as a result the stories I have written came from that inspiration."

Greg grew quiet again as he absorb the words. He closed his eyes, and nodded in agreement.

I shared more, "There was a log hidden behind some tall grass. Thinking about how it was hidden led to think about how we all hide something in our lives. There is a Bible verse that says we should not hide our light under a bushel. Understanding what is meant from those words helped me to step outside of another comfort zone to share about our family trials with our son and it became a blessing far greater than I could have imagined. Others came to me and shared about similar experiences, and we became prayer warriors for each other."

Greg smiled as he said, "You know by sharing it makes me feel better. God is so good. He is good all the time. We just need to let go and allow Him to hold onto those trials we face, know what I'm say'n. When we try to be our own

God, things tend to go badly. My daily devotion this morning spoke of that very thing, know what I'm say'n. When we try to act like the God in our own world, we forget about the peace that only He can give when you give it to him. I was glad to get out of that old storage shed after I read that and get going."

There was slight pause as we both allowed the power of the moment to work. Then Greg said, "I hope everything works out for you and your son. I know it will! God don't make no mistakes. My mom and I don't get along, but I still love her and respect her. I don't always agree with some of the things she does, but I love her anyway. I hope she knows that.

"Parents need to let the kids bump their heads to learn. I know you're a good person, don't let people try to change you, you're good. I always think about you saying we (the homeless) have a sweet soul. For you to say that you have to have a sweeter soul. You may get mad at me at times and disapprove of me at times, but I'm a grown man and still bump my head up against the wall at times. That's how I learn things."

I told him I'm still learning too. "That's the neat thing about grace and mercy Greg, we don't deserve it but God gives it to us and we need to do that for each other."

Greg smiled, hands up in the air and head back said, "Thank you Jesus! I can't imagine what this world would be like if Jesus hadn't died on the cross for us."

I replied, "People would be bumping their heads on the wall *all* the time and *never* learning."

Greg kept talking.

"With me before, as long as the money was coming in and I didn't have to ask anyone for anything, I thought I was doing all right, know what I'm say'n. But you know what? That was suffering. I just didn't know what it was. I was feeling no joy. I wasn't happy. I was okay, but I wasn't even content, but I didn't know no better. But thanks to you, it brought back from a long time ago, what I had forgotten. I was suffering before, but thank you Jesus, I don't got to suffer no more if I don't want. My mom always told me, 'You make your bed, you gotta lay in it.' That's the way it is, know what I'm say'n."

"Greg, you've come a long way from the old life in such a short time."

"Trust me, he says, I've got a million miles to go, but I'm going with Jesus. As long as I'm moving forward, I'll be doing all right. They told me this when I was in AA at one time. 'Just because you stop drinking and doing drugs, doesn't mean your problems are going to go away. It depends now on you dealing with them with a clear mind.' Just because I'm a Christian, that don't mean things are gonna stop happening in my life. The more at peace I try to be with God sometimes it seems like things get more screwed up for me."

I told him, "The closer you get to God the more the devil is going to attack. So if you're getting attacked, Greg finished my sentence—

"I know I'm on the right track." We both laughed.

Greg had to leave for a doctor's appointment. Before we parted, he shook my hand and said, "We are all right." I gave him a hug and did the "I love you" in sign language. I asked him if he knew what that meant. He didn't so I told him. He smiled and returned the sign.

CHAPTER 24 – John

"I've lived a hell of a life. I've made bad choices. I wish I had done things differently, but because of what I've experienced, I am more compassionate and understanding, but I don't want to be pushed."

On this day, it was extremely windy, the kind of wind that made my hair blow all over my face, and I had to keep brushing it away. As my visit went further and further, it seemed the wind was blowing other things my way.

The wind brought a respite from the warm temperatures that were still lingering the day I met John. Of all the forms of homelessness I've encountered, John was unique. At forty-six, he was divorced with four children and six grandchildren. Originally from California, he lived in Bowling Green for the past twenty-five years. Most of his family had lived here as well, but he didn't see them very often. At this time, he was staying at the Salvation Army.

He was polite always calling me ma'am. His constant chuckling reminded me of Ernest T. Bass from the old *Andy Griffith Show*. Yet he carried within him a disease of the mind called Schizophrenia, and he was also bipolar. Schizophrenia is no laughing matter, and not the fault of the person who suffers with it. He is able to function reasonably well as long as he takes his medication.

Our conversation was characterized by his random, rambling, thoughts often making it difficult to follow the point he was trying to make. Interspersed amongst his ramblings were profound insights into his life for his was a life afflicted with addictions and dependency compounded by the effects of his schizophrenia disease. Somewhere deep inside of this man, another person struggled to find an outlet. His life being what it was came into conflict with the calmer, gentler side of him. This conflict caused him to do something I could not imagine.

I asked him, "Do you ever get into any fights?"

"I try not to". He pointed to his scarred up arms. I raised my eyebrows. He continued, "Self-mutilation; I don't want to hurt anyone, so I did this to myself."

"Everything has a name. These scars are called pain. I had to cut myself to know I was alive. Cutting to let the pain out." He clenched his jaw and rambled on again.

I was fascinated in a sad way as he described the meaning of all those scars, scars that ran down both arms from arm pit all the way down to the wrists, with not more than a fourth of an inch in between each one. He had scars on his stomach from cutting also.

He points to several and continued, "This one is because of a woman, and this one because of a woman, and these to just keep from hurting somebody." As he spoke, his jaws constantly clinched tight, and I could see in his eyes a combination of pain, guilt, and anger. I wince with a minor paper cut. I could not imagine the state of mind he must have been in as I looked at the deep scars caused by his self-inflicted lacerations.

"I've also stabbed myself in the stomach. I've eaten poison too."

"And you are still alive! I think God must have a reason for you to still be here."

"Yes, ma'am."

"Do you ever ask Him what it is?"

"I just hang on maintaining balance between the dragon, leviathans, and the beast within."

When I asked him about how he ended up staying at the Salvation Army, he did not hesitate to explain about his addiction issues.

"I had been doin' drugs and alcohol and basically given up. Givin' up on tryin' to do good. They say once an alcoholic, always one, but I'm totally absent of alcohol and drugs now. I'm just hangin' in there tryin' to be normal."

"When was the last time you did anything?"

"A few weeks back, I smoked that 7H in the red package. It put me through a bad loop, I thought I was dying, slipping in and out. I went right to the face of God, trippin'. But I have a faith, a close relationship with Him (Jesus) so I would have been all right."

"When did that happen, finding faith in God?"

"I was saved by a black woman preacher."

"How did you become a Christian?"

"By believing in God, in Jesus, I confessed and repented."

"How old were you when you did that?"

In most instances his responses were quick and direct, but he paused for a few moments as he searched through his memories before answering.

"Not sure."

"Were you a little boy or grown when you asked Jesus into your heart?"

Again he paused. It was obvious that he had never thought about how to answer that kind of question.

"Hmmm, that's a good one, as far as I'm concerned, He's always been in my heart."

I try to explain that it is important to be able to look back and see our moment of decision, our conversion. We may not know the date, but I wanted him to know that we haven't always had Jesus in our heart. We had to have made that decision.

"Oh I confessed, and I read the Bible too."

I redirected the questioning, "Tell me about growing up."

"I grew up in a military family always moving from place to place. When I was three years old I was run over by a truck in Germany."

His matter of fact dialog changed energy as he reflected about his early years with his parents.

"I remember my dad crying begging my mom not to leave, but she just walked out the door. Not long after that my dad brought me back to the States."

He stopped and lowered his head; his eyes seemed focused on some distant memory. As young as he was at the time, to have his mother walk out must have had a profound impact on his state of mind and view of himself.

"I dropped out of school in the tenth grade. I skipped final exams because I just did not want to go anymore, ended up getting my GED. As a teen, I went through a rebellious period, and got into some trouble. My daddy didn't go to church but he made sure us kids went. He was brought up in a black Pentecostal church, was saved and baptized there. A black Pentecostal woman preacher baptized me. Going to church was something we did sporadically."

My experience from past evangelism classes led me to ask, "When you die, do you know where you're going?"

His answer was quick and direct, "To see God, hopefully Heaven. God puts us through all kinds of tests in life, the kind we have to pass."

John, during our conversation, would often start in one direction then in mid-statement take off in another direction. It was difficult to follow his train of thought. As soon as he made the last statement, he started in talking about another subject.

"I used to sneak behind my parents to drink and party. My mom would put whiskey in my baby bottle to get me to go to sleep. I've been drinking ever since. I was showing signs of alcoholism by the time I was ten. After I got my GED I went to work on my uncle's farm, then I worked in construction for a while. The last job I had was over a year and half ago."

He paused again and glanced across the park grounds as if deciding if he wanted to say something. "I went to the crazy house in Nashville for twenty-one days. I was on the sixth floor, you know, the one for the mental patients. That is where I was diagnosed as being bipolar and with schizophrenia. Because of that I now draw disability for being mentally disabled. I've lived a hell of a life, and I've made bad choices. I wish I had done things differently, but because of what I've experienced, I am more compassionate and understanding now, but I don't want to be pushed."

"How long have you been at the Salvation Army?"

"About a month. Before that I was living with my ex-sister-in-law. I've burned a lot of bridges from my past. I used to be a crack head."

"Have you changed?"

"I know I have, definitely for the better. A good trick, when you open yourself up to God, you become a target for evil. When you go to church, you hear, 'You fool, you fool, you fool!'"

I wasn't sure what he meant by that, so I decide to take the conversation in a different direction. "Do you have any brothers or sisters?"

"Whole ones or half ones? I have all kinds. My dad died two years ago."

"Did you have a good relationship with him?"

"There were cycles, a cycle and a cycle until somebody breaks it."

"What were your hopes and dreams?"

"To be a police officer and a military man. I trained my whole life to fight, but now I think I'll just take the path of peace. Soldiers out on the frontline fighting; that's what I would like to do. I have arthritis now, so I can't, but if I had been on the frontlines I would have been good. If it moves, it's dead."

He chuckled with his unique form of laughing then continued, "I might give them two days to leave the city and then they'd be gone. Maybe that's why I'm not on the frontlines."

At this point he began a series of unrelated ramblings and just like the wind that whipped through the trees in the park, his thoughts whipped about in haphazard veins. I tried to reel him in.

"What are your dreams now?"

"I try to have dreams, but when you watch television, there is not much worth watching anymore. I use to draw real good, but I'm not interested in that anymore."

He stopped talking and shifted his posture searching for something meaningful to say. He pointed to his scarred arms again and mumbles something I could not understand. Then I asked,

"Have you stopped cutting yourself?"

"Oh yeah, I don't do that anymore. I took twelve hundred pills, had convulsions and almost chewed my tongue off, had to be given three pints of blood. I decided after that, never again. About a year ago I became homeless. In my mind there is too much demonic crap going on so I don't be around any one person for too long. When I think someone is crazy, I up and leave, and just run around in misery all the time. Books are full of crap!"

His statement about books caught me off guard but was typical of his ramblings going in one direction and then in another. I asked him, "Do you believe in the Bible?"

"I believe in God, and I believe the book has changed so many times. One says Jesus is the lamb, then one says Jesus has to be burned and sacrificed forever and ever. One Bible says Barabbas was the son. I have fourteen Bibles.

"There is a fine line between insanity and genius. I wouldn't say I'm a genius but I am very intuitive. I always ask why. When we quit asking why, we quit accepting God. With truth and knowledge, we have help."

I asked him, "What is truth?"

"It's self-explanatory."

I asked, "Do you think God is truth?"

"Oh yes. When they took out the canon Bibles, forty-nine Algiers decided what they wanted to take out and keep in. They took out all the bad things about His wrath and said, 'We'll just make everyone believe God is good and everything will be fine.'"

It was becoming clear that John's theological views were all over the place, packed with emotion, and filled with uncertainty and contradictions. At this point it was time to redirect the conversation once again. "What would you want people to know about the homeless?"

"If we're not careful, we all are going to be homeless. But, when you are homeless there are places to go to, not to

197

live permanently. It is designed to give you structure for yourself, and to learn that we all need to come together. I'm getting a place soon, near the Salvation Army. There are a lot of good places in Bowling Green like Community Action. I like to brag about Bowling Green."

"Sum up your life in one word."

He thought for minute then said, "A walk of faith; a test."

"So, how are you doing on your test?"

"I'm trying to maintain balance like we all are."

"Would you like to join a church here in town?"

"I wouldn't want to join just one church, none of them have it right. They just want to use whatever serves their purpose. A lot of them don't give a crap about the other churches. I hate to say it, but they are prejudiced, the blacks against the whites, the whites against the blacks and Indians. They all mock the Father and one another."

"Not everyone is like that."

"Exactly!"

"Do you believe there are good people?"

"Yes, ma'am, but there is evil in every one of us, but if you invite Jesus in, it's like you didn't have a problem one, but they don't like it."

He started to ramble on again and I could not understand him.

"How can I pray for you" I asked.

"Like anybody, for good. But I *will* not pray for my enemy who is against me. He needs to be prayed for that he changes, but if not he *rots*!"

I wanted to go back to the subject of homelessness.

He responded, "There are places to go, but don't burn your bridges there! You have to do what they say, follow their rules or you're out!

"You said before those places are good."

"Oh, they are, because of their money. But all the gold is up there in the sky. Why is everybody getting rich off the United States but the United States? We don't own this country anymore, we just live in it."

He rambled on and on again about the world, the Taliban, Canada, earthquakes, running to the hills and on and on and on. His mind was racing.

I tried to reel him back again by asking what advice he would give to teen age kids.

"Be in the Word, get baptized in the waters, confess, listen, and be kind to your parents; quit trying to tell your parents what to do."

"Would you tell them to stay in school?"

"Well, what are we going to do when we get rid of shorthand, how are we going to communicate? They need to stay off drugs. But it's not a sin to drink or smoke. But too much of anything is not good for you."

John looked at his scars and said, "Everything has a name. These (looking at all his scars) are called pain. I had to cut myself to know I was alive, cutting to let the pain out." He clenches his jaw and rambles on again.

He pulled a Seroquil tablet out of his pocket.

"When I start slipping in and out I'm supposed to take this. I should be taking this pill right now."

"Please, do." With all his ramblings, I was impressed he understood that he knew he needed the pill.

"But I want 7H."

"I thought you weren't going to do that anymore," I said.

"Well, but I can handle it. It's legal you know. But they got to get it off the street."

The conversation was so erratic I decided to stop and hoped he would take his Seroquil. I thanked him for his time and for sharing with me. I told him I would be praying for him. He told me he would pray for me too.

Schizophrenia is a disease of the mind. I saw some of the symptoms right before me: disorganized speech, distortions in thought, content, feeling out of touch with people, family and friends. I saw pain in the scars of his arms. I pray for John to have peace in his sometimes rattled mind. I pray he doesn't just find balance in life, I hope he falls all the way to the side of living for the Lord, staying in reality, and can learn to be around people forming real relationships. I pray when he looks at his scars, instead of being reminded of the pain that caused them, he is reminded of the Savior's scars that will save him. The Father knows. Jesus loves John. I pray for all his delusions and distortions to disappear. May the wind blowing in John's mind settle down, and may he be able to completely rest.

CHAPTER 25 – Tony

"I feel like human refuse."

Powerful words from a man I met who, for the first time in his life, found himself living on the streets wounded of heart, discouraged in life, and distressed by his situation. Tony, a middle-aged former truck driver from Berkesville, Kentucky, sat subdued and tentative as we began our conversation. He spoke those words only after looking around to make sure no one else could hear our conversation. Leaning forward with his elbows resting on his knees, he held his head low, and his shoulders sagged from stress induced fatigue. Were it not for his deep voice, it would have been difficult to hear what he was saying.

"I've been a cook and a delivery driver too, but I'm really a truck driver by profession. Back in 2002, I had to take care of my mom. I had to let my truckers license expire, and didn't have enough to pay for the renewal. I'm kicking myself for not doing that."

Again, Tony hung his head low staring at the ground contemplating his mistake, one of many from what I could gather. His dad, a military career man from the U.S. Army died in 2000, his mom died in 2002.

"They stayed together. Mom used to be a librarian way back when, but she was a stay at home mom and Dad was military, a retired Master Sergeant/retired teacher. They were financially fine. We had our spats every now and then. My dad was always there for me. When he passed away, it's like my world just collapsed. Mom made me feel more like I was her property than her son.

"I was working at a Pizza Hut when I started taking care of them. I don't have a stable work history. I was adopted. I have four natural sisters and brothers floating around, I have never met them. I was born in Lexington but the family lived in eastern Kentucky in the coalmine area. My real mom and dad sang in the nightclubs in Lexington. I was born with a gifted voice and used to sing but I've ruined it with smoking."

Tony's history-narrative seemed almost rehearsed as he spoke of isolated key events during the time spent with his parents. Somewhere during those years, his life was influenced by those moments more than he probably realized. He struggled to maintain eye contact constantly shifting his gaze toward the ground. As he spoke, I tried to hear what he was saying between the lines. More often than not, the real story of a person's life is played out in those gaps that are left unspoken.

Sharing personal history is a common trait with the homeless people I've met. Their history carries value. Who they are today is less important, it is how they got there, where they've been that defines their lives, not what they are.

"Welfare came in and took me away, and I went to my grandparents. Then I was adopted. I didn't go without. If I needed something, I always got it. I was a happy child. But I became rebellious at age thirteen, fourteen... started drinking. I would stagger drunk into the home at night, and they never knew. I quit drinking around twenty because I knew it wasn't for me. Thought if I didn't quit, I would be dead by thirty. I've made mistakes."

In this our beginning connection, our conversation was broken by deliberate contemplative moments. Through a few opening statements, I could see a complex series of events had unfolded in his life. In many ways these jumbled and disconnected events had somehow given his words a sense of connection and continuity.

"What have you done since then," I asked.

"Well, in 2003 I was arrested, spent time in prison." Again, his gaze was glued to the ground as if he was uncomfortable having to admit that aspect of life.

"Arrested? Do you mind telling what for?"

He shifted his gaze left then right then twisted to look behind him trying to make sure no one had drifted into range who could hear our conversation. Tony said, "I'm a registered sex offender. That's why I can't stay at the Salvation Army. That's why pretty much, nobody will help me. Basically, I'm human refuse. That's how I feel."

I understood why society would turn its back on someone with that kind of a rap hanging over them, yet at the same time I could not help but feel sorry for him because of the way he felt.

"Do you understand about people's fears?" I asked.

"Yeah, I understand that, but I've done my time. I went through everything the government has asked me to do. All I want is a chance."

He chokes up fighting frustration not tears, anger not directed toward others, but regret directed toward himself and what he had done. "Just one time, and it's going to follow me the rest of my life."

"How long did you serve?"

"Two and half years, with all the jail time, more like three years."

"What about after you got out?"

"When I first got out, I got a job in a lumber yard and worked there almost 2 years hating every minute of it. They were hiring people off the street, giving them jobs that I had been trained for, paying them more than I was making. A friend of mine opened up a restaurant in Glasgow, and I got a weekend job there for two years working my way up to assistant manager. Then it closed. I haven't been able to find work since. Every time I interview for a job, everything goes great up until the felony is mentioned. Then it's, 'Thank you for your honesty, have a good day,' and I never hear from them again."

The cadence of his words slowed again, and he stared at the ground with his back slumped and jaws clinched. I wasn't sure if he was trying to hold in his anger or simply reacting to his frustration.

"If I could just get my truckers license back, then I just might stand a chance. The employment office here in town is trying to help me get it renewed, but it's taking a long time."

Tony spoke expectantly about how a contact in town could get him a job with a local trucking job. He can't go out on the road again. His record would make that impossible, as he would have to cross state lines and maybe drive into Canada.

"I'm not stupid."

He shows me papers, certification in computer repair, truck driver training papers, computer programming from Bowling Green Junior College. This is not a complete degree since the school closed. He did not graduate. He also showed me a certification in motorcycle repair.

"These don't do a whole lot of good in my situation. I just took a test for the employment office." He showed me the results form; all individual grades very high, total overall was a ninety-one.

"I'm far from stupid, but I've done stupid things."

I asked him if he would talk about the charges, and how all that happened. At this point in our relationship, he was reluctant to reveal the details. The previous June his wife left him. For two months, he sat in his house unable to pay the bills. Bank accounts closed, but he was able to sell some of his mom's jewelry to pay off most of those debts. He had a car, but it was repossessed. He had a broken down motorcycle that he could repair, but he didn't have the money or tools to do the work.

"I get frustrated. I didn't think I could be legally homeless.[2] On September 21, I got really depressed and wrote a letter to my wife, basically saying, 'I give up,' a suicide note. This was after she left. I had no electricity the

---

[2] Before this, I had never heard of this term.

neighbor was feeding me because I was too stubborn to get food stamps. I've gotten more brains since then. After I wrote the note, I got another place to stay on the twenty-third."

Tony's rambling, one-line statements of fact about how his life was playing out rumbled in his deep voice. It was like a slow motion life played in fast motion a few frames at a time. First this and then that, then another scene filled his stage. There seemed to be little connection between some of the statements, yet I knew down deep inside of this man resided a story of strength and regret.

"I left the note on a dresser, and my wife found it. By then, I had decided not to follow through with it. I was just so depressed I didn't know what to do. She called the cops and they took me to Western State Psychiatric facility for a three day evaluation." He raised his shoulders, lifted his head, and looked at the sky through the canopy of tree limbs that hovered over us.

He took a deep breath, looked off into the distance, and continued. "I had lost thirty-nine pounds in three months. I weighed 175 pounds and by the time I was taken to the ward I was skin and bones. I was watched by the ward all weekend. They kept telling me they wouldn't put me back on the street. They called all over trying to find a place to take me but no one would. That's why I feel like human refuse."

I could not imagine how difficult it was for Tony to say such a thing. His voice fell weak and tired. As he had been inclined to do, he lowered his shoulders, and shifted his gaze to the ground.

"There's not an organization out there set up for people in my situation. That's why I am under the bridge with Dave, a long time inhabitant of underneath the bridge. Dave welcomed me."

I knew Dave, a friendly ex-military man about sixty years old; at least that's about how old he looked physically. My husband and I met him a couple of years prior to meeting Tony. Dave wasn't one to talk about much. He spent much of his time in an alcohol-induced state of mind. We found Dave under the Old Louisville Road Bridge curled up on an old mattress asleep in the middle of the afternoon.

"Does he know about your felony?"

"No."

"What about your drinking? Do you still drink?

"I became a drunk in my teen years. Alcohol and I got along too well, so I decided to just quit it."

"What about school? Were you a good student?"

"I was a lazy student. I got bored one summer between my junior year and senior year, so I got my GED. In what would have been my senior year, I asked the principle if he was going to let me graduate, and he said I had two more years to go. I argued with him and said but I already had my GED."

"Why did you have two more years?"

"I was lazy. I wasn't stupid, just lazy. Since then I have learned to appreciate education. If I find something I enjoy, I study it."

"I went to college but got thrown out right away because of the drinking. That's when I decided to quit, just quit cold turkey."

"Have you done drugs?"

"Just pot. The last time I smoked any was in my twenties. After I was kicked out of college, I moved in with my parents but couldn't stand it. I didn't like the control. So I signed up for the Army. I stayed in 11 months."

"Why only eleven months?"

"My sergeant told me one morning to shave. I had to shave with an electric razor. My beard is tough, so it didn't shave well. I was going to shave again after lunch but at lunch, I was told by someone else to go clean my weapon. I didn't have time to shave before having to get in formation. Sergeant said I didn't shave. Article Fifteen (disciplinary) and $150 out of pocket fine, and fifteen days restricted post. First Sergeant asked me into his office and said, 'Do you want out?' I said, 'Yes.' I kicked myself for that. I should have stayed in. At the time, they were downsizing the military back in the eighties. They decided there were too many soldiers, so they let you out just for the asking. So I came home."

By this time in our conversation, Tony's answers to questions came more quickly, and I began to feel more comfortable with him. So, I asked about things that are more personal.

"Any church background?"

"Not really. If I wanted to go to Vacation Bible School or church, I could. We were not an organized religious family. They didn't go. I've done a lot of research on my own. I'm an Agnostic. I'm waiting for proof. I'm a knowledge seeker. I've read the Bible and there were times I got heavily into religion, back in my early teen years. In my teen years I was converted. I've been saved and baptized. A bunch of my friends and I would witness to and lead people to salvation to the Lord. Then, I quit the church"

He became more reflective. "I showed up one Sunday and half the congregation was gone. The church had split over some money issue. Everyone argued and half the church went one way and the other half went the other way. I went out the middle. I've not been into religion since."

"You know there is a difference between religion and Christianity. Why did you walk away from God?"

"I didn't really. Like I said, I've done a lot of studying. I've read lots of different books. If I had to pick a religion, you aren't going to like this, it would be Wiccan."

"Wiccan! How come?"

"Because it's about nature. A lot of people think of Wiccan having to do with witches. There is that aspect of it, but mine gravitates more to the pure side of Wiccan, the worship of nature. If you're into nature, you're into God. If God did supposedly create all this that means you are in God."

This revelation surprised me somewhat, so I felt compelled to dig deeper into what he believed in his heart, not just, his intellectual beliefs.

"Do you believe in Heaven or Hell?"

"Sometimes my wife would say to me, 'When we die, I'll go to one place and you'll go to the other.'"

"Where do you think you will go?"

"If I had killed myself, I would have gone to Hell," Tony's tone held just a note of questioning.

"Would you like to know for sure?"

"Agnostics are waiting for the proof, the evidence."

"What made you think when you were young that Jesus was the truth?"

"At that young age, I was easily influenced. Since then, I've learned. I've read a lot of books, including the Bible. The Bible leaves a lot of gaps."

He asked if I've ever read anything by Zechariah Sitchin.

"No, I've never heard of him."

"He wrote *The 12th Planet* and *War of Gods and Men*. They are about the human race being influenced by other creatures."

(Later, I searched for the books on Google. Amazon gives this definition for *The 12th Planet*:

Over the years, startling evidence has been unearthed, challenging established notions of the origins of Earth and life on it, and suggests the existence of a superior race of beings that once inhabited our world. The product of thirty years of intensive research, The 12th Planet is the first book in Zecharia Sitchin's prophetic Earth Chronicles series -- a revolutionary body of work that offers indisputable documentary proof of humanity's extraterrestrial forefathers. Travelers from the stars, they arrived eons ago, and planted the genetic seed that would ultimately blossom into a remarkable species...called Man.)

Tony continued. "If you can stand on this planet and look at the stars, all those lights up in the Heavens and honestly say this is the only planet that has intelligent life on it, you've got to be very egotistical. That's just the way I feel. If you read the Bible like the story of Genesis, that's a story of genetic manipulation. That's exactly what it is. The story of Moses, people led by a pillar of smoke during day and fire at night, to me that's the story of Moses being led through the desert by a space ship. Nobody can prove me wrong, just as I can't prove the Bible wrong. But the Bible leaves gaps."

I asked, "What about testimonies from people today who speak how God has worked in their lives?"

"Okay, if you believe something so deep inside yourself, that say you've got a friend who has cancer and you believe you can pray them well, 99.9 percent likely you will pray them well. Belief in oneself is as powerful if not more so than belief in God. I usually try to avoid religion and politics because those can upset people. In my teen years, as I said, I was influenced. I wanted to believe so much, I did. And now, I'm forty-six, and I walk around the streets of Bowling Green and I think to myself, if there is a God, where is He? I look at people staying at the Salvation Army and think, they're not homeless. Homeless is living under a bridge. I'm just thankful I have a tent."

At this point, I felt he was wandering where there was a lot of confusion and misunderstanding. Not wanting to generate any kind of a conflict with him, I tried to redirect our conversation to something less potentially difficult to approach. I noticed that his shoes were literally falling off his feet, and they were wet. He talked about spending time at Hope House where he had received a better pair of shoes that he could wear to job interviews. He seemed most appreciative of the help that they provided. He said there were plenty of blankets under the bridge; many of them we had left during previous visits.

"I will come back and give money to these organizations because they were there for me. I don't like asking for help. I made a promise. When I'm back on my feet, anytime I pull money out of my pocket, whatever falls on the ground stays on the ground whether it's bills or coins. I've had to struggle so much these last several weeks. I walk all over the place looking for pennies to just get enough to buy my cigarettes."

"How do you eat?"

"I get food stamps now, so I eat just fine. My coffee and cigarettes make me happy. I told the Western State Psychiatric place that I just wanted a chance. I just want a place, work and to pay my own bills. I'm not asking to be a millionaire; I just want to survive. It was time for me to leave, and no one would take me, so they just put me out."

"Do the homeless help you?"

"Yes, the homeless share with one another. I've always tried to help other people. When I had a home, I brought people in who needed help," Tony said.

"You sound like a giving person, so, what led you to do the thing that got you into trouble?"

"My step-daughter and her mother were always yelling and fussing. She thought she was the boss of the family. All I did was touch her; I didn't have any kind of sex with her. She was asleep, and said she didn't even know about it. She told the police it didn't happen."

"Then how did you get caught?"

"I made a pass at one of her friends, and her mom called the cops. When they came, I cooperated and told them everything I had done."

"Why did you do that?"

"I wanted to get caught. I was afraid I would go further than I needed to go, and I didn't want to do that. I'm not a violent person. I think subconsciously, I was getting even with my wife. I started scaring myself, and got myself caught."

"How do you know you wouldn't do that again?"

"'Cause I just know I wouldn't. I've been through all the treatment programs. One part of the treatment is that you have to put yourself in your victim's shoes. That is the most powerful thing you can do is put yourself in somebody else's shoes, especially, when you are the perpetrator. I would never do that again."

"Have you seen your step daughter and wife since?"

"Yeah. Up 'till June, we were living together. The daughter swore nothing happened. But I knew it did, and I wanted to be punished for it. I didn't want to hurt anyone. But that is not a fear anymore. I would never put myself in that situation ever again."

Almost all the stories the homeless revealed carried one common theme; their search for value and how that search was often misdirected by circumstance. Tony's story was no different.

"What were your dreams when you were younger?" I wanted to explore deeper into his life to discover the Tony who possessed a passion and hope.

"I've always been into science, science fiction. At one time, I wanted to be an astronaut. I've been a volunteer fire fighter. When younger, I had first aid training and some EMT training. I wanted at one time to be a cop, but that'll never happen."

"What about now?"

"When in prison, I was a teacher's aide in a GED class. I would love to help people get their GED. I have to look at life now as reality, not as hopes and desires. I will do whatever the world will let me do. What I want is to get my truckers license back, get a job, get my own home."

"Can you sum up your life in one word or sentence?"

"My life goes in cycles; short cycle of everything good, then long cycle of everything going crazy. I always seem to be the cause of the crazy part. I do something stupid and the long cycles get longer. I used to have faith in humankind and now I wonder."

"What makes you wonder? You said people here were good."

"Some good, some..." he shook his head. "I've always been the type of person that would give you the shirt off my back if you needed it. Everybody is out for number one. I've gotten worse at being selfish since this started, more than I ever wanted to be. But once I get on my feet, I won't be that way again."

"Does it make you more understanding of others who are trying to take care of themselves?" I probed.

"Of course, but there are people who come into the Salvation Army, and take off the free table, you know, flour and cornmeal. Then they come back the next day and take a bunch more of the same thing. Nobody needs 20 bags of cornmeal. They are taking more than their share. When I talk about me becoming selfish now, I'm talking if I am down to my last couple of cigarettes, I think, can I really let that last one go? I've met more nice people in the way of generosity from the homeless community. They will share. I share my coffee with Dave under the bridge." I could tell that Dave and Tony were beginning to bond under mutual circumstance even as eccentric as Dave was.

The more I encountered the homeless, I realized just how important something like that was to them. So many things in their lives have unraveled they become almost desperate to cling to that one thing that makes them feel needed. Being a part of something larger than their own circumstances, like being a friend, becomes a lifeline of sorts. It is part of that history story so many want to share.

"We talk about old television shows. My favorite was the *Andy Griffith Show* and *Star Trek*, and any other science fiction show. I really miss television. I miss watching *American Idol*. I loved that show. I'm also a Harry Potter fan. I missed the last movie. I also like *Lord of the Rings*."

I'm not surprised that he found the *Andy Griffith Show* as one of his favorites. It perhaps was one of the best family oriented programs in the history of television. Its focus on family values and community involvement helped an entire generation identify with those things. With Tony locked into the situation that he was in, I'm sure it was comforting for him to remember those Mayberry moments from his own past.

"What else do you like?"

"I like music, to read, watch television. I played the trombone in band for two years during grammar school. I would like to teach myself how to play the piano. I used to have an electric piano but I lost it with everything else."

His mood grew somber again. I've often wondered just how often people in his circumstances looked back on their lives to think about the *what-if* of their past. He cast a gentle smile for the first time. His gaze left the distance and turned toward me. He said, "One of these years, everything will work out."

By now, I began to understand more clearly the depths of his despair. Even with our short time together, I felt like Tony revealed so much more through what he did not say than through what he did say. It was through the cast of his gaze, the brooding posture of his body, the break in his voice, the deep sighs, and the tears that hovered just inside his eyes, that I began to know this gentle man who had made a single mistake that had cost him so much. I wanted to give him some encouragement without sounding like I was talking down to him.

"You know Tony, being a Christian, I place a great deal of faith in prayer. Can I pray for you?

He lifted his eyes toward me and made visual contact.

"Absolutely, I still pray every now and then, but it doesn't seem like it does any good. The Lord works in mysterious ways. He put me here in the beautiful city of Bowling Green, He introduced me to Dave, which I'm very thankful for. When you leave a psychiatric place knowing you're going to the street, that's a scary thing. When I got to the bridge, I was scared to death. I had never been in that position before. Dave welcomed me under that bridge and I got to sleep on a mattress. I was really nervous that first night. But Dave was friendly. We talked and laughed."

"I just heard you thank God for Dave and Bowling Green and yet you're not sure He's really there?"

"It's just a figure of speech. I've said that throughout my life, but I'm still not convinced."

"Will you keep searching?"

"Yeah. I've seen a lot of suffering in my life though and I don't believe a loving God would allow that."

"He didn't promise us a life without suffering. He promised to be with us through it."

"I've also heard He would never give you more than you can handle."

"You are still here," I pointed out.

"Yeah, I'm a survivor."

"I'd like to encourage you to keep looking until you find Him. You may think I'm crazy, but I've been walking with the Lord for over thirty-seven years. I wouldn't want to live any other way."

"One of these days maybe it will hit me over the head, and I will know He is real. I've paid my dues, have done everything asked of me, and I still can't seem to catch a break. What do they expect people like me to do if no one will help?"

"Can you understand that people might be afraid of you because of what you did?"

"Yeah, but a lot of that is media hype. They make us all out to be monsters, and I'm not a monster. Everyone is lumped together. You're a sex offender, level one, two, or three, three being the worst. But in the public's eye, you're just a sex offender. I was a level one, but that doesn't matter to anyone. They should take it case by case. Media hypes it up so much that there is paranoia about it. Most people who do it never do it again. When you go through the therapy that I went through, you will never do it again."

"If you had a young daughter that you loved with all your heart, and someone like that came around, would you be scared for her?" I asked.

"Yeah, I can understand the paranoia when it comes to stuff like that, but it is pushed too much. I've worked hard. I never thought I would be here. You just can't judge people by others' actions. You can't judge a book by its cover. You get to know a book by reading it. It should be the same with people. Look at people by their own merits, not by a group. I've been labeled a monster. I'm not a monster!"

"How old is the step-daughter now?"

"She's twenty-one."

"And the family relationships?"

"They're over."

It had been a long and tiring interview, and it was time for a break. We both stood, and I asked if I could pray with him.

"Sure," he said.

I placed my hand on his shoulder and prayed. When he and I stepped away from each other, I noticed tears glistening in his eyes.

With a quiet, broken voice, he said to me, "Thank you for not treating me like trash." I walked away with my own eyes glistening.

When Tony told me about his felony, I did not act shocked, I remained calm and just listened. That may be hard for some readers to understand, but I thought if I am going to ask the reader to look at these interviewees with the eyes of Jesus, then I also needed too as well. I heard repentance in this man's voice and story. He was convicted about his wrongdoing. He confessed when he didn't have to because the victim had denied anything ever happened. He didn't have to go to jail but he wanted to pay for what he did. I think that speaks volumes. I spent time researching his story and verified the details of his felony conviction. Honesty and trust are virtues that define a man's heart, and Tony revealed a great deal of both.

Remember David in the Bible? He was given the title, "A man after God's own heart." David was a betrayer, liar, adulterer, and a murderer. How could he be given such a title? Because He was repentant, he was sorry for his sins and turned from them. He loved God and felt sorry for what he had done.

Tony said at one time he had asked Jesus into his heart and was on fire for about two years, witnessing to others during that time. Something made him walk away. During our initial contact he acknowledged that he was not sure and was waiting for proof. But I think some of that early experience stuck with him, or I don't think he would have confessed to something that he knew would put him in prison when he didn't have to confess.

He wanted to pay the consequences for what he had done. How many times have we sinned that no one else knew about, and confessed, so that we could pay the consequences? I believe Tony needed to pay the consequences of his felony. Even though he paid his penalty, the world is still punishing him. I think the world's hardness towards him contributes to his hardness of heart right now. I wonder if people stepped up with forgiveness and acceptance and offered help, how this would affect his thinking towards his faith.

Tony was seeking knowledge and truth. What he needed was love and acceptance. What he did not understand was that it all is in the One who is there beside him. If he opened his heart and accepted the love of Jesus Christ, he would recognize Truth, and then knowledge would come. But he had to take that initial step of faith.

I continued to meet with Tony as he continued to seek the truth about God. There were discoveries waiting just around the corner to be revealed about how the power of God's word can have in a person's life, even a sex offender.

CHAPTER 26 – Through Tinted Glasses

For most of Greg's life, before his conversion experience, he was challenged by black and white situations, not so much racial, but he looked at life from a perspective of filling immediate needs. His tendency was to identify what he needed now and not what was best for his future.

"It's the day to day living that is hard," he would say.

For him, something either was or it was not with little room or desire for compromise. If a situation arose that would give him an advantage, he would take it regardless if that perceived advantage was short term, and might lead to a long term disadvantage.

After his conversion, he began to recognize a difference between what the old Greg thought, and what the new Greg was trying to understand. The old Greg still controlled much of his emotional responses to circumstances, as might be expected. He still approached life from a daily needs perspective, and if that meant using some aggressive pushing to obtain what he needed, he would push. This tendency at times led him into conflict with others who although might have his best interests at heart, did not always understand his point of view. As these conflicts played out they became valuable teaching moments for us to help him grasp how his life was changing.

Greg, more than anything, wanted the dignity of having his own apartment. An opportunity for him to get into a place became available. Unfortunately he still had an unpaid electric bill from a previous time. When word of this reached several friends, they graciously offered to help with paying off the old bill, and within a few weeks enough was raised to fulfill all of the requirements with some left over. The left over amount was held in reserve so Greg could use it to cover other deposit costs that might come up.

His outstanding bill was paid with those funds as a surprise gift to Greg, although it was never intended to be a secret. Most of those who donated knew Greg only superficially having never met him. I also believe there must have been an element of naïve expectations about Greg and his new life. Even though everyone recognized that he had a long way to grow spiritually, those expectations centered around believing that after his conversion, his old ways of behaving would immediately change. We understood that he was not going to change dramatically overnight. His old ways still influenced his behavior simply because that was the only way he knew how to act. A few people wanted to mentor Greg to help him grow spiritually, which in itself was a commendable gesture, but we did not see a problem was brewing.

Greg needed a slower almost child-like pace to help him grasp more clearly, how to let go of his old self-centered life and embrace all of the life changing benefits his new life in Christ could offer. He needed to learn that with Christ at the center of his life, all the other aspects of living would eventually fall into place. We hoped he would begin to understand how to rely on God's strength and not his own. As he continued to butt heads with his life issues, his lack of social skills clashed with the good intentions of others. One couple wanted to jump into the fire before they fully understood the difference between their own expectations and how Greg might actually react.

He found out about the left over funds, and that one of the couples was holding those funds for him. He did not understand that she was not to release the money except for additional deposits that might come up. Greg using his old-self style of dealing with his immediate needs did not see it that way. He confronted her demanding he be given the money. Rightly so, she refused to turn the funds over to him thinking of his best interest. Greg became angry and gruff and by doing so not only upset and disappointed her, he actually scared her. He was not acting Christ-like, and only saw how he could use that money today. Saving it for future use never entered his mind.

It was a misunderstanding of not only circumstance, but about behavior and reactions. The unfortunate outcome of this was she and her husband backed away from ever helping Greg directly again. They still held an interest in his life, yet there would never again be any meaningful connection between them. It was unfortunate, as both could have benefited from such a friendship. Although they had good and honorable intensions, it is my belief they too quickly jumped in thinking Greg was now a completely changed person. When the first sign of unfulfilled expectations arose, they just as quickly jumped out.

We tried to explain to Greg the reasons why the money was set aside, and that he should honor their intended purpose. His logic was not the same as ours, yet his perspective often served to remind us of just how different his life and ours were.

"You can never understand, know what I'm say'n, never understand what it's like for someone like me. I needed that money today, not next month."

Eventually, he did calm down and apologized to us for anyone he might have offended by his behavior. The old Greg would never have done that. What was so revealing about his words was that in a way he was right, we could never fully understand.

Most of us tend to look at the homeless situation through the tinted glasses of comfort. Too often when we are confronted with the reality of someone like Greg, we back away, and throw in the towel because it is so foreign to us.

Working with the homeless is difficult, and yes, it can be ugly, but that is where we must grasp what it means to not only accept and receive grace, but more importantly, to give it. That was a tough lesson for Greg to learn: How to receive and to give grace. It became an important lesson for not only us to understand how to deal with the homeless, but to instruct those whose good attitudes and intensions might be shattered by unrealistic expectations.

To teach someone about forgiveness means we have to be willing to forgive others. We were often placed in situations where we had to humble ourselves, and let go of natural negative reactions we might otherwise have applied. How else was Greg going to learn about grace, if we failed to show it? What kind of message would we send if we walked away from the first transgression, he might have committed?

To work with the homeless first required that we remove our flaw-tinted glasses, and replace them with spectacles tinted with humility and understanding.

CHAPTER 27 – Good Bye Mr. Shed

When Greg first told me that he lived in a storage shed I could only imagine what it might look like. Eventually, I was able to turn those imaginings into a visual reality. When I first saw his living quarters my heart broke for him. It was situated near the middle of a row of storage spaces. The entrance was a roll up garage-door type of devise and the area covered approximately eight feet by eight feet. Inside of this small cube was stored all the belongings Greg owned: an old chair, a couple of small tables, an old microwave, a few assorted kitchen utensils, and a few clothes piled together in the corner. His sleeping space barely fit his six foot five inch frame. His bed was a blanket spread on the concrete floor.

There was no electricity, no window, no air conditioning, and no heat. That tiny space held his life. It was no wonder he valued the time spent in the open at the downtown square. The shaded park provided a refreshing respite from the dark confines of that miniature living space.

In many ways, this existence defined his entire life. His was a life of contrasts. A dark war raged inside him. Pain and disappointment fought against the goodness that struggled to surface. It was an existence of chaos and trials. His memories filled with constant reminders of failure and abuse, were as stifling as the dark confines of that storage shed, smothered by the stale heat of a future hoped for but never realized. Those memories were filled with the cold drafts of a life almost lost. To find relief from his dark past, he sought the openness of the park where a clean breeze and a fresh day helped to air out his thoughts.

He was haunted by guilt because of the much too early death of his daughter. She was one of the few joys in his troubled life. Greg was ordered by the courts to pay those accrued amounts of back child support payments even though she no longer needed that monetary support. His meager finances were drained as a result. Fortunately, he was able to garner another court hearing, and found a sympathetic judge to have those payments reduced. That along with the elimination of a back electric bill gave him the wherewithal to afford a small apartment.

The apartment was about the size of a large bedroom in most homes, but to Greg it was a castle. Move in day dawned with drizzle and gray skies but those ominous clouds did little to dampen everyone's spirits. A few friends and I borrowed a small truck from Hope House. We emptied his shed and transferred his belongings to the new home in one trip. Greg looked happier than at any time I had known him except on the day he was baptized.

As we were all making trips with boxes in hand up and down the stairs from the moving truck to his apartment, I heard Greg mumbling, "Door... window... bathroom... bed." when I passed by him.

I yelled at Greg as we passed on the stairs, "What are you mumbling about Greg?"

"Just countin' my blessings, you know what I'm say'n."

My heart jumped with glee for him remembering about the counting.

One of the mattress stores in town donated a new queen size mattress with an iron frame. Some other friends kicked in new sheets, comforter, and pillows. We girls made sure we kept it all masculine. No flowered sheets or pink anywhere, just black, gray, and cream. Of course, I added a couple of blankets.

After sleeping on a cold concrete floor for so long, Greg said with a smile, "I'm going to sleep like a baby now."

To see his spirits lifted filled our hearts with joy for him. Hope House donated a love seat and two wicker chairs. My friend Leigha bought new towels and soaps for the kitchen and bath. A new lamp sat on his table and we all pitched in to stock the kitchen with some food. While Greg set about running some errands, Leigha and I fixed up the place, putting furniture in just the right spots, washing the dishes and stocking the cabinets, hanging up new towels in the bathroom.

His mother traveled from Ohio to share with us on this special day. She was so sweet and genuinely moved by what was happening. We were as excited as schoolgirls moving into a dormitory room. Now, we waited for the king to return to his castle.

"Welcome home Greg!" We shouted as he walked through the front door. God had answered many prayers.

Before we left, Greg, his mom, Leigha and I stood in a circle, held hands, and prayed thanking God for his provision, for salvation, and his unending love. We prayed for continued blessings and guidance as Greg traveled down that narrow road. We left with, "Sleep tight," and Greg flashed his giant smile.

As Leigha and I drove away, we felt a sense of accomplishment. I felt, possibly with a bit of naïve understatement, that his life was starting to turn around and he could begin to grow more in his relationship with the Lord. Perhaps he would not have to expend so much effort just to survive. At first, that is exactly what happened, but what was to transpire over the next few months we could never have foreseen. As brightly happy as that day was, there were dark ominous clouds hovering over us that proved prophetic.

CHAPTER 28 – Struggling

Greg possessed within him a dark hole from his past that constantly haunted his life resulting in circumstances that often overwhelmed the child like perspective of what his new life could become. He was a strong man physically. Emotionally, he fell short of understanding what it meant to be a man, and what was required of a man.

In his perspective, lived for most of his forty plus years, being a man meant drinking alcohol for just about any occasion. Although he now recognized that his old friends were not real friends in the sense that they did not concern themselves with his situation, they were just drinking buddies. If there was money, and they were together, that is what they did. He was unable to recognize the contradiction that was his life. On the one hand he wanted to change and live his life with God as his focus. On the other hand, drinking was just who he was. There was no difference to his perspective than if he ate popcorn watching a movie or drank a beer watching a ballgame.

He volunteered to work at Hope House, which was a good thing. But on his first day back after moving into his apartment, it was obvious that he had been drinking. He was lovingly confronted about it, and asked politely to come back another time when he had not been drinking. To his credit, he understood their concern, but from his perspective, he found it difficult to differentiate between what he had done for so long, and the expectations of others. Alcohol carried such a hold on him. He thought nothing of satisfying its call. The next Friday he failed to show up and everyone who had hoped for and prayed for him were disappointed and concerned.

Within a few weeks we began to recognize a troubling pattern. We could see his struggle generating confusion. With a genuine heart, he sought to change his life, that I am certain. But, with naïve expression born from inexperience he often fell back onto the old-life security options.

While Christ gave him that sense of peace he never before experienced, he allowed his old life to dictate how he reacted to circumstances that confronted him. He did not yet understand what surrender meant. He had been self-reliant for so long he could not allow himself to do otherwise. He failed to grasp the significance of how strong a tempest would be generated when his new life confronted his old life.

What he needed more than anything was encouragement and discipling. He certainly had never lived nor had he ever been taught what it meant to live a Christ-centered life. God laid it on my heart to write down scriptures that I hoped would speak to him. What he did not understand was that his old life and new life were not compatible. It was like dirty oil trying to blend with clean water. The two were made of different specific gravities, and could never mix. All that would happen was that the dirty oil would ruin the life giving properties of the sparkling clean water.

Keith and I went to Greg's new apartment one evening, and spent some time talking to him. We expressed concern about how his old life still commanded such a strong hold on him.

He politely listened with an attentive heart, then, spoke about how much he enjoyed going to church with us, "When I'm with good folks, I do good things, know what I'm say'n. When I'm with bad folks I do bad things. I need to stay with good folks. I need to keep going to church with you."

At least he recognized there was a distinction, what he failed to understand centered around how he placed too much dependence on another person and not enough on Christ. Even so, I could never fully comprehend how difficult of a struggle he faced. I was raised in a Christian home and with that history came a more in depth understanding. For Greg, it was all still so fresh he struggled to find his place in his new life. We could see it in his eyes the remorse and confusion, as he did not fully understand what he was supposed to do.

Many Christians incorrectly believe that because a man undergoes a conversion experience, his life suddenly changes. At one time I probably believed that as well. Certainly miraculous conversions do happen, and lives can suddenly be transformed, but not always. My experience with Greg opened my eyes to just how difficult that struggle to change can be for someone with his kind of background. Christians go through a metamorphosis throughout their walk. We are all placed in a cocoon where the struggle occurs and eventually we are changed from the inside out emerging a new creature. For some, the struggle takes longer, the cocoon phase more difficult, and while encapsulated within its web the old creature slowly morphs into the new. Greg's cocoon was heavy and tough; his life choices and struggles destined for a long reconstruction. The fact that he was inside a cocoon was a miracle of itself.

I handed him the scriptures and suggested that he carry them with him every day. As we sat on his balcony, he asked me to read them aloud. As I read, he sat quietly with his eyes closed and listened intently.

"...fully pleasing to him, bearing fruit in every good work and increasing in the knowledge of God. May you be

strengthened with all power, according to his glorious might, for all endurance and patience with joy, giving thanks to the Father, who has qualified you to share in the inheritance of the saints in light."

Colossians 1:10 – 12 (ESV)

"Set your minds on things that are above, not on things that are on earth."

Colossians 3:2 (ESV)

"Let your speech always be gracious, seasoned with salt, so that you may know how you ought to answer each person."

Colossians 4:6 (ESV)

"For God has not called us for impurity, but in holiness. Therefore whoever disregards this, disregards not man but God, who gives his Holy Spirit to you."

1 Thessalonians 4:7-8 (ESV)

" [You} were taught in him, as the truth is in Jesus, to put off your old self, which belongs to your former manner of life and is corrupt through deceitful desires, and to be renewed in the spirit of your minds, and to put on the new self, created after the likeness of God in true righteousness and holiness."

Ephesians 4:21 – 24 (ESV)

"And let us not grow weary of doing good, for in due season we will reap, if we do not give up."

Galatians 6:9 (ESV)

"I can do all things through him who strengthens me."

Philippians 4:13 (ESV)

"Rejoice always, pray without ceasing, give thanks in all circumstances; for this is the will of God in Christ Jesus for you."

1 Thessalonians 5:16 – 18 (ESV)

"He who calls you is faithful…"

1 Thessalonians 5:24

"… do not grow weary in doing good."

2 Thessalonians 3:13 (ESV)

"So flee youthful passions and pursue righteousness, faith, love, and peace, along with those who call on the Lord from a pure heart. Have nothing to do with foolish, ignorant controversies; you know that they breed quarrels."

2 Timothy 2:22-23 (ESV)

For the grace of God has appeared, bringing salvation for all people, training us to renounce ungodliness and worldly passions, and to live self-controlled, upright, and godly lives in the present age, waiting for our blessed hope, the appearing of the glory of our great God and Savior Jesus Christ, who gave himself for us to redeem us from all lawlessness and to purify for himself a people for his own possession who are zealous for good works."

Titus 2:11 – 14 (ESV)

"Do not be conformed to this world, but be transformed by the renewal of your mind, that by testing you may discern what is the will of God, what is good and acceptable and perfect."

Romans 12:2 (ESV)

"Blessed is the man who remains steadfast under trial, for when he has stood the test he will receive the crown of life, which God has promised to those who love him."

James 1:12 (ESV)

Greg ~ I always thank my God as I remember you. . .

Philemon 1:4

We love you Greg!

(Keith and Kris)

When I finished he raised his head and opened his eyes. The words from the scriptures soothed his tired soul and he said with a forlorn look, "I'm tryin', I want to change, know what I'm say'n, please don't give up on me, I don't know how to change. I hate the old Greg, know what I'm say'n, but he won't go away."

His words reminded me of what Paul said in Romans 7:15 and 18-20:

"For that which I do, I allow not: for what I would, that do I not; but what I hate, that do I.... For I know that nothing good dwells in me, that is, in my flesh. For I have the desire to do what is right, but not the ability to carry it out. For I do not do the good I want, but the evil I do not want is what I keep on doing. Now if I do what I do not want, it is no longer I who do it, but sin that dwells within me."

In these passages, Paul explains to us that becoming a Christian does not automatically stamp out all sin in our lives. He emphasized that becoming a Christian requires an act of faith, but learning to become Christ-like is a process that can take many years of struggle. Paul's struggle with sin was very real and he had to return continually to his basic beliefs in the strength of Christ to combat those desires because fighting with his own strength was insufficient (Romans 7).

We are still influenced by the desires of the flesh and Greg in his Christian infancy found it difficult to reconcile this. He could not understand how to use the power of Christ to

233

fight his battles for him. He felt he was unworthy because of his failings with alcohol, when in fact he was no different from the rest of us, or Paul. His situation was simply compounded by his addiction to alcohol.

How I wished I could help the old Greg to let go. All I could do was to encourage and pray, and allow God in his own timing to work on Greg's life. He agreed to keep the scriptures nearby and to read them often. We arranged to meet again the next day, Sunday, and take him to church with us. This was a prayer I lifted up for him before we left.

Dear Heavenly Father,

Please shine your light into the dark corners of Greg's world and expose the evil schemes of the enemy that makes Greg struggle so. I pray for the chains that still bind him to be broken for good and for him to be free, totally free. I thank you for the freedom he has in Christ now. Please teach him how to walk away for good from his old world. Take him by your righteous right hand and hold on to him. When he stumbles from temptations, pick him up with Your courage. Where he is weak, You are strong. May your strength overtake his weakness. Help him to endure, to grow, to become stronger in every way.

May Greg always hear your whispers of "I love you and I have a plan for you." Help Greg to find that plan and continue to move towards it, seeking it with all his might, never looking back. I praise you Father for your loving kindness and mercy.

In Jesus name, Amen.

As we left his place he yelled out from his balcony, "I love you guys!"

And I yelled back, "We love you too!"

CHAPTER 29 – Eucharist and Gifts

The Lord's Supper some call it, others call it Communion, and still others call it Eucharist. No matter the name, it is the symbolic remembrance of the last supper, the Passover, Christ had with his disciples before he was crucified. For those of us who grew up in the church, this reenacting of a sacred moment is a familiar act. For someone who has never before been through the ceremony it carries with it a fresh expression of obedience.

During the next visit to our church, Greg was able to experience this act for the first time. He was curious, uncertain, and excited at the same time. He watched intently as the plate of wafers and tray of juice cups passed from aisle to aisle. He was uncertain of what to do, and cast a questioning look my way. As is the tradition in our church, the ceremony waits until all have received the wafers and juice. At that time, our pastor presents a mini-sermon on the symbolic nature of the event. Greg listened intently and absorbed every word spoken. The tiny wafer was barely noticeable in his great hand, and the small plastic cup that held the grape juice bent as he tried to hold the fragile vessel delicately in his powerful hands.

When the pastor spoke of how the bread symbolized Christ's body, the congregation in unison ate their small wafers. I cast a glance toward Greg as he lifted his hand. When he lowered it, his gaze focused on the cup. He spun it slowly between his index finger and thumb, waiting for the cue.

The pastor spoke of how the juice symbolized Christ's blood and again the congregation drank. Greg slowly lowered his hand, and held onto the empty cup. It seemed so small and insignificant in his grasp. Everyone else placed the used cups in the small cup holder on the back of the pew in front of them. Greg held on to his, and as the pastor completed his mini sermon, Greg closed his eyes, smiled, and nodded gently. For the longest time after it was over, he continued to hold the cup before finally placing it in the holder.

Greg gently rocked forwards and backwards as the songs were played, his eyes closed, his head nodding in time with the music. Contentment filled his broad face, and I could see a measurable level of peace fall upon him. Thirty minutes later, toward the end of the Sunday sermon, he lifted the cup again holding it close to his heart as he cast his gaze toward it. When the service was over, he returned it to the holder.

(During our next communion service, Greg was not able to be with us. As I held my cup, I remembered how important it was to him, so I *borrowed* the cup and the next time I saw Greg, I gave it to him.)

On our way out, he carried a smile as wide as his chest. He leaned toward me and said, "You may think I'm crazy, but I think that Pastor was speaking right at me, ya know what I'm say'n, like it was written just for me."

I smiled and said, "I think that was the Holy Spirit talking to you Greg."

"Well, something was," he replied.

Keith said later when we were alone, "You know Greg has forty-six years of crust built up, and God is slowly chipping it away bit by bit."

Greg said one time, "I know I'm a bit rough around the edges, know what I'm say'n, but Jesus is smoothing me out. I'm like the clay that the Bible talks about, and Jesus is molding me."

I couldn't help but think of a song I heard many times in church and began humming it, singing the words in my spirit.

Have thine own way, Lord! Have thine own way!

Thou art the potter, I am the clay.

Mold me and make me after thy will,

while I am waiting, yielded and still.

Have thine own way, Lord! Have thine own way!

Search me and try me, Savior today!

Wash me just now, Lord, wash me just now,

as in thy presence humbly I bow.

Have thine own way, Lord! Have thine own way!

Wounded and weary, help me I pray!

Power, all power, surely is thine!

Touch me and heal me, Savior divine!

Have thine own way, Lord! Have thine own way!

Hold o'er my being absolute sway.

Fill with thy Spirit till all shall see

Christ only, always, living in me!

(Words: Adelaide Pollard, 1862-1934)

That evening I wrote five additions to my list of one thousand gifts;

865. Experiencing Greg's first communion

866. The wafer

867. The juice

868. Hearing Greg sing the praise songs deep from his heart

"And he took bread, and when he had given thanks, he broke it and gave it to them, saying, 'This is my body, which is given for you. Do this in remembrance of me.'" Luke 22:19 (ESV)

"And likewise the cup after they had eaten, saying, 'This cup that is poured out for you is the new covenant in my blood.'" Luke 22: 20 (ESV)

CHAPTER 30 – Melanie

It is remarkable how resilient and strong the human spirit can be when confronted with impossible situations. One such spirit crossed my path on a Saturday afternoon and became a steadfast friend with a welcoming heart.

Keith and I found Melanie sitting on the corner of the bridge one bright, sunny afternoon. There were several others milling around, who soon became awkward and difficult people to deal with. We have never been threatened in all of our encounters, but this particular group of people bulled their way into our space and created an uncomfortable situation. They were not homeless, but seeking a handout from anyone willing to supply them.

Melanie on the other hand was a delightful, yet homeless lady. She was dressed in dark heavy clothes, and carried a small bag with a few meager belongings tucked inside. Her hair desperately askew, was needing a shampoo and a brush. Her angular, sunburned face belied her real age of about forty-five; she looked twenty years older. Her fingers were bent and callused with an abundance of dirt caked under the fingernails. But, her hands were strong. Across her wide cheeks stretched a smile that embraced anyone fortunate enough to get to know her. I was drawn to her immediately, and I sat beside her.

One of the others, an older man was so drunk he stood with a pronounced leaning to his right. For each step forward he took, he staggered two sideways. Keith found himself surrounded by the others, two women and another younger man. One of the women we discovered was the daughter of the older man. All of them had been drinking, and were in various stages of inebriation. While Keith talked to the others, the older man kept interrupting my conversation with Melanie.

"You sure are a perty little thing," he kept saying over and over as he progressively encroached on my personal space. I smiled and tried to ignore his awkward advances turning my attention to Melanie each time. When he reached across with his wobbly hand and tweaked my nose, I was forced to back away. I don't believe he was trying to do anything. He was just so drunk. When he placed his hand on my shoulder and stumbled so his face came to within a few inches of mine, Keith came to my rescue, and politely ushered him away toward where the others were milling around. This allowed Melanie and I some time to talk without interruption.

She seemed to jump around in our conversation as though she could not quite place events in any meaningful order. Most of what she spoke about was disjointed, single statements of facts. She was raised in Henderson, North Carolina until she was thirteen when she became pregnant. She moved to Florida. She attended Western Kentucky

University. She had medical problems and surgery on her neck. She also has multiple brain injuries because of accidents.

"I know I seem normal, but I'm really not," she interjected.

She had a sister who was on drugs. Her mom and sisters were alcoholics. She had a daughter, and at one time she had a miscarriage. Her attempts at conversation lacked the sophistication most people use. Yet, within those first awkward moments, I began to see Melanie as someone with a strong spirit in spite of her circumstances. I will present her conversation as she spoke the words to me, although it was a bit disjointed.

"My sister is on drugs so I broke ties with her. My daughter is also messing with drugs. Even though she is on five years of probation, she keeps crossing state lines. I don't speak to her anymore. I raised her on my own though. I was only thirteen, but I was declared an adult by the courts. I worked."

"Are your parents still alive?"

"I know my dad is, last I heard mom was. They never divorced but split up when I was a baby. I grew up in a tabernacle home until I was eight. Then the state of North Carolina took custody of me. From thirteen on, I was on my own."

I asked her how she stayed off the drugs and alcohol.

"I had a baby to support so I worked in a rehab center hospital with adolescents. I learned a lot about drugs and alcohol there. Drugs will fry your brain. My dad used to be a smart guy, but after the drugs, he wasn't no more. I'm a workaholic by nature. I even took psychology at WKU."

241

She paused for a few moments. The other people on the bridge began to get loud, which interrupted our conversation.

After they calmed down, Melanie continued. "I was just trying to support my daughter, and half the time my dad and my mom. When I would get aggravated at my dad, I could take him down to my uncle's place, but my mom had no place to go. They stole from her."

She barely paused to collect her thoughts before she continued in a new direction.

"Potassium depletion put me in the hospital and in a coma. I almost died. I was working on a construction crew and the whole crew went in with heat exhaustion. My dad stole my medications. When my daughter and mom both got sick in 1996, I had to leave WKU and go back home. I never was able to go back to school, but I did make it back to Bowling Green. Everyone here in Kentucky are the nicest. It's the only place that ever felt like home. Some of the people who move into the area have an attitude. They're not true Kentuckians 'cause your true Kentuckians are nice people."

I ask her how long she has been homeless.

"Off and on for a few years just to stay away from my family. For now I am staying at the Salvation Army, until my time runs out."

"Is there anything you'd want people to know about being homeless?" I asked.

"You gotta be tough to survive! In Florida, they would come through on horseback and run them out. Here it doesn't seem to be bad. I think with the economy the way it is, it leaves people with no choice. Some people are not capable of surviving this."

"What makes you tough?" I probed.

"All those years being on my own. When my daughter was a baby, we lived in the swamps of Florida for two and half years along with the gators and snakes."

"Where did you stay?"

"We camped out, and I worked to feed us. I hope to get into vocab/rehab. Maybe they can help me. They did back in 1996, so I am hoping they can do it again."

As independent as Melanie appeared, I was curious about what kind of relationship she had with God, so I asked her about her faith.

"I've had four traumatic brain injuries that should have killed me. I told them they couldn't kill me 'cause it wasn't God's will. Dad hit me in the head with metal spikes, grabbed me by the throat. Drug addicts flocked to my dad, so I moved back to the boonies. He was overdosing me with seizure medicine, so I got in my truck and said, "God, you lead the way, and wherever my truck breaks down, that's where I'll stay. It broke down in Bowling Green. For years I thought I was non-denominational, but I keep seeming to go to Pentecostal churches. I believe in a higher power. I believe that God has a plan for me. My plan is not up yet."

"Do you believe in Jesus, and about repenting and inviting Jesus into your heart?"

"Yes, I feel the spirit in me. I can feel the devil too. When you feel evil on you strong, you'll never lose your faith on that one. My mom took me to a church one time, and as I was walking through the doors, she felt evil, so we left. My mom said she saw angels pulling her away. A week later, that preacher was arrested for raping the kids in that church."

A train horn blared. The giant machine roared down the tracks not far from where we were. I got a chill shivering up my spine.

After the roar of the train died away, Melanie continued, "I'm a firm believer. When you feel it, you know it."

"If you could sum up your life in one word or a single sentence, what would that be?"

"Get better. I want to get better. God's preparing me for something. My premonitions normally give me more detail. He's just given me enough to let me know I will survive. I will be better. I think it's going to be global; all the fights and riots going on. Enjoy what you have, what God has given to you."

"What has He given to you?"

"Survival! I survive on the knowledge that He's going to take care of me through thick and thin. I took Psychology and social work at WKU. I passed all the tests."

"Would you still like to do that?"

"My brain is so messed up now, I don't think I can. I think once I get my body back in shape, I think my brain will be better."

"What would you like people to go away with after reading your story? What do you want them to know about you?"

"It doesn't have anything to do with me, it's all about God. You gotta believe in God. Belief is the number one trait of faith. I wouldn't have survived what I've been through if I hadn't had that."

"What would you say is the worst and the best thing in your life?"

"I don't really relate to things as best and worst. I think it's just a path you take, and sometimes you take a path God doesn't want you to take. He has to give you a wake- up call, which I think He did with me when I got all my brain injuries. If you follow God, you're following in the right path."

By this time, the drunken man and the others were beginning to gather around the back of our Jeep that was loaded with blankets and other items. They were helping themselves to as many blankets, scarves, and gloves as they could carry. Keith tried to explain to them that they could take what they needed, but only what they needed. That is when one of the women became belligerent. Her father, the man who was stumbling around was clearly not able to walk even the short distance to home. She wanted Keith to give him a ride. After he explained that one of our rules was to avoid giving rides, she started to scream at him at how awful we were, her tirade interlaced with explicatives. The whole time she was reaching into the back of the Jeep and helping herself to more blankets.

Keith reached over and offered her a Bible. She grabbed it and promptly threw it on the ground.

"This never worked for me. I don't need it."

By this time her dad was also growing more belligerent, but was so unstable he fell down the steep slope next to the bridge. We were concerned he might actually fall off the bridge onto the rocks below or even into the river some sixty feet down. Keith decided for the old man's safety to call 911. He stepped far enough away so they could not hear him and placed the call. A moment later, he took me by the arm and said it was time to go as things were starting to unravel with the others. I said good-bye to Melanie and vowed to reconnect with her.

As we drove away, I felt sad for all of them. I could not help but see the stark difference between someone who is truly homeless and those who are simply needy. The homeless woman was gracious and kind, the others were unappreciative and looking for what they could get, greedily carrying away more than they needed potentially depriving someone truly in need.

Melanie proved how tough she was, but I was touched by her vulnerability. I wished there was more that I could have done, but for now that was where the Lord led me. I was there to offer warmth through blankets and the love of Christ. I knew that Christ would take what little we had to give and make something remarkable with it. As Melanie said, it has nothing to do with me; it's all about Him. After additional conversations with Melanie, she became a beacon of hospitality and warmth as I continued to gain her trust.

CHAPTER 31 – Those Hands, Those Feet

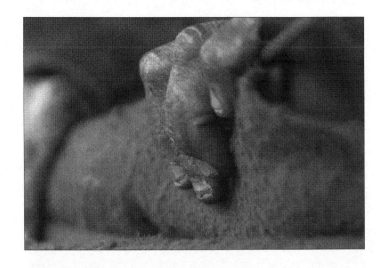

I couldn't get Melanie out of my mind so I sat down to just write. Sometimes just writing what comes to mind is all we need to do in that moment.

Those precious hands. What do you see? I saw hardship and survival.

Those feet have taken her many miles.

Those hands have held a baby of hers at thirteen years of age.

Those hands worked hard to take care of her daughter.

Those hands have worked horses, even thoroughbreds.

Those hands were raised to protect herself when her father hit her on the head with metal spikes.

Those hands took care of her mother and father when they could not take care of themselves.

After 40 something years, those hands were thrown up in the air and those feet walked away after having all she could take.

She got into her small truck and said Lord, take me where you will. The truck broke down in our town of Bowling Green.

Her stay at the Salvation Army was up.

She went to stay under the bridge.

Do you want to judge her?

Not until you've walked in her shoes.

Those feet walked into the hospital. and she heard the diagnosis of Crones Disease. She could not buy the medicine. The feet walked back to the bridge empty handed.

Those hands were blackened by the ashes from the fire built to stay warm and make coffee.

Blackened ashes covered her face, a face that held beauty.

She was told so, but all she could do was point to her once broken nose and once broken fingers.

She saw dirt and brokenness. I saw a beautiful face beneath it all.

And God sees our beauty beneath the dirt and brokenness and offers His red blood to make us white as snow.

I saw survival in those hands. I saw endurance in those feet.

Does God see himself in her heart?

She says yes.

Only she and the Lord know this.

I prayed for those hands to fold in prayer. I prayed for those hands to lift up to Him in glory and honor.

I prayed healing for those hands in whatever way she needed.

I prayed for complete healing in the heart.

I prayed for the gift from the manger to be truly inside of this homeless woman so that one day she will be truly at home with the Lord, the Savior, the gift from the manger, homeless no more.

CHAPTER 32 – This is 90.7

This is for all you out there that hear God calling you to step out of your comfort zone, but you are reluctant to do so. Please listen.

I grew up painfully shy and quiet, never one to speak much. I always wanted to be at the back, to blend into crowds. And this was not a pleasant way to live. So why do we do this? For me, I believe I let the devil whisper those insecurities into me so much that I believed them more than I believed God's promises. As I became an adult, I should say an older adult, I began to realize where those feelings were coming from, and I began to stand up to the enemy, fighting him with the strength and power of the Almighty God. I also realized that in those insecurities, I was thinking solely of myself and finally realized just how selfish that really was.

Over the last twelve to fifteen years, God has been empowering me little by little, pulling me out of comfort zones of one kind or another. And with each one I stepped out of, blessings abounded. I became a little bit stronger.

Never did I ever think I would go onto the radio waves for *all* to hear. But I had a passion that God laid on my heart for a group of people, and those people became more important than me. God had been taking blinders off my eyes for quite a while now and it was so liberating to see, feel, and share with the love of Christ. As I grow, He is giving me more and more opportunities to do just what I never wanted to do, be out there in the public's eye. But now, instead of feeling the old insecurities, I stand strong on the promises of God.

God opened a door for me. December 15, 2011, I stood on those promises once again and found myself about to enter this place.

I walked through the doors and saw this.

I thought I better go to the little girl's room and have a quiet time. I went in, shut the bathroom door, and this is what I saw taped to the back of it.

"Okay, God," I told Him. I was ready to step out of the box and into the radio booth.

This is 90.7 Christian Family Radio and in 3-2-1

I told my blog readers before they heard the taped interview, "WARNING! My Oklahoma drawl and the Kentucky southern influence may have blended just a tad bit."

I didn't stumble one time. God was holding my hand.

"For I, the LORD your God, hold your right hand; it is I who say to you, "Fear not, I am the one who helps you."

Isaiah 41:13 (ESV)

CHAPTER 33 – "I'm tired, really tired Kris"

"I'm so tired Kris, I'm just so tired. Please help me. I need help," Greg was pleading.

As I was driving to the radio interview at Christian Family Radio, I felt the need to call Greg and ask him to pray with me about the interview that all would go well. While on the phone he prayed the most precious, heartfelt prayer, and I fought back tears as I listened to his staccato voice as he prayed for the moment. When he finished there was a moment of silence, and I could hear him take a deep breath. Then he started to cry. Inside he had a tenderness that desperately wanted to find an avenue of expression, but it was an emotion so new to him, and he was often confused by what he felt. On more than one occasion the tears over took him, but he would never explain those emotions to me. I thought he was just moved by the power of his prayer.

After the radio interview, I found several messages on my phone, all from Greg. Each message was the same, "I need help", "I'm tired", "I don't want to live like this anymore."

I was concerned for Greg, but I was not sure what kind of help he was asking for. I suspected it had something to do with his drinking. I could hear the desperation in his voice. I did not know who to call or what to do, so I bowed my head right there in my car and prayed. I then drove to Hope House. My friend Linda, who also had a heart for Greg, was there as was Brian who ran the house. I spoke to both about the situation and Brian prayed, but was unable to leave because of the busy nature of the day. Linda came with me and we drove to Greg's apartment.

We found the front door open with Greg sitting on the sofa in a robe. Surrounding him were several beer cans and a

254

large almost empty bottle of Vodka. With his head in his hands he kept saying over and over, "I'm so tired, so tired. I want to get away from all of this, from the alcohol, from the people I hang out with. I don't want to be this Greg, I want to be the new Greg."

He raised his head away from his hands, his eyes glowing red mostly from the tears but also from the alcohol binge he was just now coming down from. Through the redness a pleading soul reached out to us, "Please help me. Put me into an institution or something. I don't want to be this person anymore."

Linda and I prayed with him, and as we did he kept rocking forwards and backwards mumbling words to himself. I felt like Greg had reached a turning point and was ready to get the help he needed to beat the devastating dependency on alcohol that for so many years had robbed him of the man he could be. With a stern and direct voice I spoke to him.

"Greg, if you mean it, then the first thing you need to do is get rid of all the alcohol in your place. Will you let me pour it down the drain?"

"Is that what you want me to do," he replied with a shaky and uncertain voice.

"You need to want to do it Greg."

"But, is that what you want me to?" He said again.

"Yes," I nodded with tears in my eyes. My voice cracked because of the lump that had invaded it. I picked up the Vodka bottle and started to pour it out, but Greg snatched it from my hand and took a large swig."

"Greg!" I shouted. "You either mean it now or you don't. You want help, you have to make a choice now."

He handed the bottle to me and said, "Throw it down the drain."

He watched with despairing eyes as the clear liquid gurgled and disappeared.

"Do you have any more alcohol?"

His large hand shook as he pointed toward the refrigerator. Inside were five cans of beer from a twelve pack. One by one I popped them open and started to pour them down the drain. Before the first one emptied, Greg again grabbed it from my hand and took another long drink.

"Greg!" I shouted again. "Decide now, once and for all!"

He handed the half-empty can back to me, "Do it," he grumbled, and I finished pouring it down the drain along with the other four. As they drained, he shook his head and grumbled, "I've got a white woman in my apartment pouring my beer down the drain." He sat down with a heavy plop onto his couch continuing to shake his head.

I sat next to him, and Linda stood to one side. He gave me a reassuring hug, but the alcohol was still affecting him, and he became extremely sleepy, and finally passed out rolling off the sofa onto the hard floor. As she was looking down on him, Linda said, "Well, he's going to be there awhile."

He was too big for us to lift, so we just covered him with a blanket, and placed a pillow under his head. I left a note that Keith and I would be back at the end of the day, and we would take him to the hospital.

Linda had called several rehab locations, and asked about getting Greg some help. All of them said he would have to be detoxed first before they would take him in. He could obtain that by being admitted to the hospital under their detox program. So that was our plan. When he had sobered up enough to travel, Keith and I would take him and get him admitted. Before we left, Linda lovingly patted him on the head, and we closed the door behind us.

When Keith got off work, I met him at a McDonald's and together we drove to Greg's apartment. He was still lying on the floor having not moved for at least six hours. We shook him awake, and helped him to the sofa. His eyes seemed to be out of focus, his gaze drifting around from point to point, staring at the wall then looking at us. He shook his head, placed his face into his hands, and started to cry again.

"I'm so tired," he repeated over and over.

"Greg, we're going to take you to the hospital so you can get the help you need." Keith said.

Greg raised his eyes that were still red, closed them, and nodded in agreement. It took him several minutes to get ready, and before we left, he picked up the Bible we had given to him, and the picture of his daughter.

Uncertainty permeated the situation. We did not know for sure how Greg would react once we got him to the hospital. I was afraid he would change his mind, but I was proud of him for facing the issue head on, and at least taking the first step to get the help he needed.

I was relieved to find only one person sitting in the waiting room at the emergency entrance. We told the receptionist what we were there for, and a nurse took his blood pressure and entered him into their records. Only one person could go back with him so he asked me to go. Keith waited in the waiting room. Once in the back room the first signs that Greg was having second thoughts began to show.

A nurse came in and asked him several questions. "What have you been drinking, any drugs, any history of mental illness, do you know what year it is?"

That last question triggered an old Greg response. "What? Of course I know what year it is, 2011." He cast a disgusted, good-grief kind of look toward me. I couldn't help it; I wanted to giggle. Instead I patted his massive arm, and asked him to not get upset.

We expected to see a doctor in short order. One hour, then two, then three passed. Still no doctor came. As long and irritating the wait was, God blessed us during that time as Greg wanted to thank us for what we were doing.

"Let's pray," he said. First he would pray and then I would. After we finished, he asked me to read from his Bible, and as I read he would stare at the picture of his daughter.

"I think she would be real happy to know that her daddy is finally getting the help he needed," I said.

"You're like a second mother to me."

"Mother? I'm not that old. I'll be your sister."

We both laughed, and mixed between the happy chortles he said, "That will work."

To keep him from becoming too antsy I tried to keep his mind occupied, and asked him to tell me about his childhood, favorite foods, and favorite books. Food seemed to be his favorite topic so we talked at length about his cooking skills. It made me hungry.

We actually stepped outside so he could smoke a cigarette. He was always the gentleman around me, opening doors, making sure I was comfortable. During our wait, a nurse entered into the room, and during that conversation the old Greg let out the 'S' word. Immediately he looked at me and apologized. Later the nurse acknowledged that Greg seemed to have a great deal of respect for me. I explained our friendship, and that he always treated me like a big brother would.

After waiting for hours, and still not seeing a doctor, both of us were getting antsy. We were all tired, and Greg said, "This is the kind of thing that makes me want to drink."

I laughed and said, "Another hour or two and I just might join you."

Greg laughed hard for the first time that night. He wanted Keith to join us so he stepped into the waiting room and brought him back. Even though they had said earlier he could only have one of us in the back, they did not stop him from getting Keith.

I kept trying to ask a nurse how much longer the wait. I knew Greg's resolve was dissolving with every tick of the clock. The nurse simply said there was no way of knowing. The doctors just had to work through the emergency room issues from who needed the most care the quickest. I must admit, it appeared as if they were ignoring us. I would stand at the edge of the doorway, and hear the doctor and nurses chit-chatting about non-medical issues. When we first arrived there was only one person in the waiting room. Three hours later there were a dozen. Had they pursued the issue when we first arrived, Greg would have been admitted by now.

"You know, we do not have a detox program here," the nurse said. I was floored.

"What? That's what we're here for. All the rehab places said to bring him here to get detoxed."

"Well, we don't do that here," was her answer and she left.

Maybe it was because I was tired, but I was starting to feel rather agitated and weepy. Greg had finally reached a turning point in his life, and was willing to get the help he needed. We followed the instructions given to us, but now it seemed to all be falling apart. As I tried to ask more questions, I began to cry. The head nurse approached me and I explained the situation about Greg. She again said they did not have a detox program. All the doctor would do was order some blood tests to test for infections. No detox admission.

"We didn't bring this man in here to get blood tests. We brought him here to get him the help he needs to get off the alcohol."

The nurse simply repeated her words. It sounded to me like they did not want to deal with Greg. I returned to the room, and explained it to him and Keith. Greg was ready to go. I began to cry feeling as if we had failed him. He was so sweet.

"No, you didn't fail me in nothing, know what I'm say'n. I don't like to see you cry, please don't cry." He said as he raised an arm to my shoulder and looked to Keith for help. A few minutes later we walked out of the hospital. I cried the entire way down the hall. I was angry at the hospital for letting him walk out when he had been begging for help.

"You didn't fail. I promise. I won't let you down. Just don't cry no more." Greg tried to console me as we walked across the now dark parking lot. We dropped him off at his apartment, and as we drove away, Keith and I prayed for him.

A side note here. I just have to praise my husband for just a little bit. Keith worked all day at the office, left there at the end of the day without anything to eat to meet me in town, went with me to Greg's apartment, then to the hospital where he sat in the waiting room for over three hours. He never once complained, whined, whimpered, got angry, or lost his patience. I think he should be nominated for sainthood! I am blessed!

CHAPTER 34 – Christmas Party at the Bridge

December 25, 2011 we met at the walking bridge. The day was crisp, clear, and clean with a magnificent cobalt blue sky. Long shadows angled across the bridge and a chill filled the air. On this Christmas day we held a special party for our homeless friends.

They came from under the bridge, from a dilapidated abandoned barn, the woods, one walked for miles from who knows where and others came out of nowhere; lonely people who tentatively joined our party given in their honor to celebrate the One we give glory and honor to.

My friends, family, and strangers with oversized hearts filled with compassion became like Santa's elves setting up tables, preparing food, hot cocoa, hot cider, and hot coffee to serve our cold guests. A pianist and a violinist serenaded us with Christmas music and a Christmas puppy added a cuddly comfort to all with a wag of his tail and lick on the cheek. We sang Christmas carols and even the homeless joined in with genuine enjoyment that comes only from the feeling of Christmas, the feeling of love, something they don't feel very often. One stood to the side for the longest time, unsure, checking us out, but slowly made his way over. I caught him casting a wide smile not for the camera, not for me, but simply because the Christmas spirit and a warm drink filled his otherwise, lonesome life.

My heart leapt with joy when several said how wonderful it was to see people out there for them, that they would take the time and effort to throw a party just for them. They live in a part of the world where they only see selfishness, people who want to hurt them or shun them or steal from them. It was a gift for them to be around a group of people that just wanted to share a special day so they could relax, and know they were safe, to have a real Christmas filled with love, joy, turkey and dressing. As they walked away, they were given a lime green tote bag filled to the brim with goodies. Many kinds of gifts were exchanged that day but we received the best gift of all; to see the smiles on their faces as we shared the love of Christ.

267

When the party was over, and everyone was leaving, Greg helped carry boxes to my car. As we were walking through the parking lot, I said, "We'll have to do this again next year."

Greg replied, "Yeah, if I'm here next year."

"What do you mean, if you're here next year?" I asked.

"I may not be here next year," he said.

"You're not thinking of moving away are you?"

"No, he said, I'm not moving anywhere."

A chill went up my spine as we loaded supplies into my car.

CHAPTER 35 – God Is In the Details

The Bible tells us God knows the number of the hairs on our head.

"But even the hairs of your head are all numbered." Matthew 10:30 (ESV)

He knows and names the stars in the Heavens.

"He determines the number of the stars; he gives to all of them their names." Psalm 147:4 (ESV)

He knows everyone of us ever born, and sent His son to die for all.

"For God so loved the world, that he gave his only Son, that whoever believes in him should not perish but have eternal life." John 3:16 (ESV)

God knows everything under the Heavens. Everything down to the smallest of details, even the need of green tote bag supplies.

When the forty tote bags were being prepared for the Bridge Christmas Party we were gathering forty of everything to go inside them; forty pairs of socks, forty jars of peanut butter, and so forth.

Keith was at work one day when one of the ladies came up to him and said the Lord had laid it on her heart to donate hand warmers to our blanket ministry. She had no idea we were planning a Christmas party or about the tote bags. When Keith brought them home to me and I counted them, I couldn't help but smile. There were forty.

While the girls were packing the tote bags with the goodies we got down to the stocking caps and somehow we came up eight short. I told them not to worry about it. Not knowing at the time, but God was already taking care of this.

I have a wonderful friend who lives in Texas. She had taken an interest in the Blanket Ministry, and because of her big heart she wanted to donate. She too had no idea about the Bridge Christmas party. She just wanted to help the Blanket Ministry. The day after discovering we were eight caps short, I received a large box in the mail from my Texas friend. When I opened it, I found hoodies, gloves, and at the bottom of the box . . . eight stocking caps.

It does not surprise me at all that He would lead someone to give us forty hand warmers and eight caps, the exact number needed for each bag. He is God after all, but it is still exciting to see Him work, and I did the happy dance and praised Him for taking care of the details. What an awesome God we serve!

"For he looks to the ends of the earth and sees everything under the Heavens."

Job 28:24 (ESV)

CHAPTER 36 – Teresa

Teresa didn't ask for her mother to die when she was little. She didn't ask for beatings as a little girl from her father, the man who should have protected her. Hers is a story of triumph over failure, strength over weakness, love over hate and courage over fear.

"We lived in Florida. My mother died when I was nine years old. I was the oldest of three girls," she began, "and we lived with an abusive alcoholic father. I was homeless when I was fourteen years old."

I first met Teresa at a Homeless Coalition Meeting. The people there were handing out applications to help low-income homeowners with repairs. At the time she needed help with minor repairs that she could not make herself.

Teresa was not a shy introverted young lady; she was anything but that. I was impressed with her confidence and beautiful smile and the twinkle in her eye. During most of our conversation her story telling was direct and confident, but there were moments when she had to pause to reflect on the enormity of her situation. It was during those moments she revealed the most about her life.

"The abuse was bad. When I would come home I could read the look on my dad's face and tell what kind of night it was going to be. I would hide one of my sisters in one part of the house and the other one in another part, and then confront my dad. I would think, let's just get this over with."

"I became rebellious because I just had too much free time. I would come in late, and my dad would get mad. He told me if I came in late one more time he was locking me out of the house for good. As luck would have it I was out with my boyfriend, and he had a flat tire that made me late.

273

When I got home I found some bags packed and a ten-dollar bill sitting on the porch. The locks had all been changed."

"I slept on the beach, under the piers, and with friends until they got tired of me. Then I slept with other men just to have a place to stay. I got pregnant at fourteen. I wanted to have the baby, and give it up for adoption. But when I told my dad, he said no and insisted I have an abortion. By then it was late term, but I had one anyway."

Her eyes went hollow as she remembered, and her voice fell shallow as if the shame of having done such a thing had not yet disappeared. It took a few seconds, but her resolute nature began to take hold again. She straightened her shoulders and raised her chin high. She tightened her jaw, took a breath, and continued.

"The doctors said I would never be able to have children again after that. They were wrong; I had five. When I was sixteen, I moved back in with my dad and stepmom. He had remarried by then. Not long after, we went through an emancipation proceeding. Basically my dad divorced me. After that I had to lie about my age to get a job so I could get an apartment. During that time I was promiscuous, I guess I was looking for love."

At sixteen, Teresa found herself pregnant again and alone. Before continuing, she looked down and took another shallow breath. "I worked with an older girl at McDonald's. I was pretty gullible, and one day she asked if I wanted to go to Kentucky with her and her husband and maybe get a new start. They ended up dropping me off at her mother-in-law's home where I stayed for quite some time.

"During that time, I started dating her son, and he eventually asked me to marry him. I wasn't in love with him, but I felt obligated because they had been nice to me. We were married for thirteen years, and we had three children.

"We moved back to Florida. When his mother died we returned to Kentucky. But while we were in Florida, both of us became involved with a church and became Christians, but we really didn't understand what that was all about. It was the first real church either of us had had, except when I was little when my grandmother took me. The church we were going to in Florida was a very legalistic church."

I've heard this kind of description from other homeless people. Often, they are searching for answers, but simply do not know where to look or what to look for. When a church home offers a sense of place and purpose, having no other strong biblical foundation to compare it to, they tend to latch on to that feel-good teaching because it fits what they envision their life should be like. Too often, they are taught misleading doctrine that serves more to confuse them, and give a false sense of security based on works.

"After we returned to Bowling Green, Kentucky, my husband started running around with his old friends, and we ended up splitting company. I started cleaning houses to earn some income. One of the men I worked for said I could stay there, and being gullible like I was, I eventually got involved with him. This quickly turned into another abusive relationship, and I ended up homeless and pregnant again. But this time I had three kids, plus one on the way. I was scared, and didn't know what to do, so I ended up going to the police station. They took me to BRASS (Barren River Area Safe Space) where we stayed for a month.

"BRASS was a great place, and treated us very well. I was able to work, and save some money up until I gave birth. With that savings and the time BRASS gave me I was able to find some housing, but had to go on welfare to get by.

"Welfare is a good stepping-stone to help you get through a down time, but it is not good when you have kids. What happens is that you get accustomed to what is provided then if you do go to work you lose it all. It creates a cycle of dependency that becomes harder and harder to break. I didn't want that for me and my kids. I wanted to control my own life, be my own provider. Transitional housing should only be a place to help you get back on your feet, but for a lot of people it becomes a lifestyle.

"I continued to clean houses in the mornings, and managed to enroll at Western Kentucky University, and went to classes in the afternoon. I had to pay a babysitter in paper food stamps, but in time I was able to save enough to buy a mobile home. Because I was gone much of the day, my kids, who were now teenagers, had too much free time and eventually started getting involved in drugs.

"At this point in my life, all I had was God. He helped me over some issues, but not all of them. I kept making bad choices, and ended up with another man, Bobby. We had a son together. It just seemed like everything I did was the wrong thing, and bad stuff happened to me all the time. I cried out to God asking him why because I didn't understand. Then He must have answered me because I realized that I had never really allowed God to be in my life. I always kept him at arm's length."

She slowed down for a moment hesitating before she continued. "When I met Bobby, I was daddy shopping. I needed a protector and provider. He appeared to be a good man who would be good to my kids." She pauses again. "Bobby molested my kids. That's why we split up. But, he turned himself in and went to prison, and while there he became a Christian."

"Because of what he did, I was broken. One day while sitting at my dining room table I know I heard God speak to me. He said, '*If you will let me, I will be everything you ever wanted. I will be the father you never had. I will be the husband you long for. I will be your friend who will counsel you and help you.*' For the first time I began to realize, that the reason my kids were hurt was because of the lifetime of bad choices I had made. It was at that point I surrendered my all to Him."

"I thought I was going to have to go back on welfare. I didn't want to, I needed and wanted to work, but God had other things in store. I felt like he was telling me to stay home and take care of my kids. I was uncertain of why I felt this way, so I opened my Bible to look for an answer. My eyes fell upon 2 Kings 14:10. These are the words that moved my heart:

"*Thou hast indeed smitten Edom and thine heart hath lifted thee up; glory of this, and tarry at home; for why shouldest thou meddle to thy hurt, that thou shouldest fall, even thou, and Judah with thee?*" (KJV)

"I'm sure there is a more historical meaning to this verse but at the time it spoke directly to my heart; to me it represented my five children as the Lord was speaking to me. There were five letters in that word, Judah, the son of Jacob and Leah, fathered five children, and I knew that if I fell or 'perished', my children would too. I just knew in my heart that this was it, this was my moment of visitation, that I had to make a decision for the Lord or we would all be lost. Funny the different ways God uses His Word to speak to us."

"I read those words over and over and felt like I had my answer. For the next six months, I was obedient to his calling and all of my bills were paid, everything was taken care of. Someone from a local church called me and said '*God placed*

277

it on my heart to give you seventeen hundred dollars.' My sister was moved to send me eight hundred dollars. I didn't ask for any of it. Eventually I felt a release from God to go back to work, but for those six months, all of my needs were met."

While Teresa attended WKU, she received a degree to become a paralegal assistant. Unfortunately, she could never find a job in spite of that training.

"I filled out application after application many of them not related to being a paralegal assistant, but nothing ever worked out. Eventually I did receive a call from a lady about working with Meals on Wheels. I was willing to do anything by this time so I prayed asking God about needing to make ten dollars an hour and that the job be on the side of town where I was located. Well, the job paid seven dollars and hour and was on the other side of town."

She half giggled with that last statement and continued, "I told the Lord, 'You missed the mark a little on this one,' but I feel he said to me, 'It's going to open the doors to the job you need', so, I accepted it. That's when I became affiliated with Community Action. Before long another job did open that was on my side of town. The pay was the same, but it was a better job. In time, I was placed as an interim supervisor but they never increased my salary. After three months doing that kind of work, I asked my boss about the pay situation. He was very understanding and talked to the CEO and before I knew it, my pay went to ten dollars an hour, and they also paid me the difference for those three months."

Teresa enjoyed cooking as a hobby. Doors opened up for her to break into the catering business, but she still prayed, "Lord why not a paralegal job?" After praying, the Lord brought to her attention a proverb that says, '*your gifts will pave the way*."

During our conversation Teresa would at times jump back and forth to address different points in time trying to connect current events with past mistakes or situations. When it came to Bobby, her last husband and the father of her fifth child, the one who had molested a couple of Teresa's children, she prayed, "Lord I can't have this root of bitterness and unforgiveness inside of me, I just can't. Please help me to see him differently as You see him. Not long after, I had a dream and in that dream I saw Bobby as my son. It was in a desolate place, nobody was around and he was about four years old. He had on a pair of blue jeans and a striped shirt, there were tears streaming down his face, and he was holding out his arms for someone to come and get him, and to love him. When I woke up from that dream, that's how I began to see him."

I was curious as to how she knew God was speaking to her so I asked her to explain.

"A lot of times, it's just an impression. When I really need to hear from Him, it comes and you just know. And when I really need confirmation, I open my Bible, and He always has something there for me. Now God is leading me in a different direction, and I'm scared to death. 'Popcorn Lord, really?' But He led me to people who are connected to Orville Redenbacher. I'm scared because I don't like to fail. I've made so many mistakes, but He always pulls me out."

Someone I knew once said that God spoke to him saying, "If you will be faithful in the small things, I'll be faithful in the big." I shared with Teresa how it seemed she had learned to be faithful in those small things, and it appeared that God had been faithful to her in much bigger things.

She agreed. "God has given me a creativity to create good meals on a budget, and He has challenged me to do just that—to cook healthy meals on twenty-five dollars a week. I've been able to do that."

"I see a cookbook in your future."

Her face lit up with a big smile, "I do too. God has told me to start writing my recipes down. Whew, it's been a crazy, crazy ride!"

I was not exactly clear about her relationship with God. She indicated that she was saved, but her actions in the past indicated she did not have a true ongoing relationship.

"Not a relationship, I had a fear of God. It was after Bobby went to prison, and I was sitting at the dining room table when I heard God say to me, 'If you will allow me, I'll be your all,' That is when I started to realize that I had always kept God at a distance."

I shared with her about hearing Charles Stanley say one time how some people become saved but they haven't made Him Savior. I asked if this had been her situation.

"Yes, I mean no, I did not have a relationship. He had one with me. He was very merciful. I had made Him at that time more a fair weather friend. I had the seed planted in me a long time ago, and later I did invite Him into my heart, but I held Him at arm's length. I was a control freak, and that is something God had to deliver me from. I wanted everything the way I wanted it. God had to deliver me from myself.

"It was when my kids got hurt because of my bad choices, because of me, that was my moment. After that moment I started going to a different church. It was there I learned about grace for the first time, and from the book of Galatians. My life was still somewhat in disarray because I was attracted to abusive men who drank. My dad told me to go to Al-Anon Family Groups to try and figure it out and he said, "If this has anything to do with me, I'm so sorry."

She did go to Al-Anon learning a great deal about herself. They taught her about the relationship situation and consequences of being the adult child of an alcoholic. In one of the meetings, she told one of the counselors, "It's like I'm a magnet for these men, I don't understand." The counselor told her it was because they brought to her what was familiar.

"I started praying for that 'familiar spirit' to be broken. Hopefully now, that was the last issue, and I can move on with my life. You know, we're like onions. We have layers and God deals with our layers. I hope that was my last layer. I may be destined to be single now, but I'm finally at a place where I don't care anymore."

Her sisters had no idea of the seriousness of her situation because she never told them, all because of pride. She dropped out of school in the ninth grade. She did not graduate high school because she became homeless for the first time. Years later, she got her GED and went on to Western Kentucky University. This was after having her fourth child and after leaving BRASS. She told me BRASS, the Adult Learning Center, and housing all were steps to better her life. She did not want to live in nor raise her kids in the projects. "I'm not being a snob I just didn't want my kids to get trapped in that cycle."

She shared, "I looked around one night in my home. My son was happily playing on the floor, and my daughter was talking with a friend on the phone. It was cold and snowy outside, but the house was warm. I had a big pot on the stove for dinner, and I just stood there and thought, 'I am SO blessed!' I've really learned to appreciate those things. When I can go to Goodwill and find a purple pillow for my

281

daughter's bedroom for fifty cents, I feel blessed. Everything in my house is used. It comes from yard sales and Goodwill stores."

Teresa spoke about some of the lessons that she had learned. "God is the answer to everything. Go by the rules. People who have more wisdom than you and try to give you advice, *take it!* Don't be so prideful that you think you can do everything yourself."

Then she quoted Proverbs 16:18 (KJV): *"Pride goeth before destruction, and a haughty spirit before a fall."*

Because her mother had died when Teresa was very young, I purposely shied away asking about it fearing it might stir up memories that were too painful. She shared her thoughts with little hesitation.

"I prayed when my mother was sick, *God, if you will let her live, I'll serve you the rest of my life.* I thought I would become a nun", she said laughing. She thought at the time that He had not answered her since her mother had passed away. Later in life, as an adult, she looked back on that and asked again, "Lord why didn't you let her live?" His reply to her, "I did let her live." Her mother was a Christian and loved the Lord with all her heart. But coming from an alcoholic home herself, she also attracted an alcoholic man.

"She was in the process of leaving him when she became sick. She did leave him, and she did live just not on this side of Heaven."

With barely a breath after talking about her mother she began to tell more about her dad. "As I got older, I confronted my dad more about his drinking. To his credit he did go to Alcoholics Anonymous, and he eventually beat the alcohol problem. For the first time he actually started trying to be a real dad.

"On a whim, Dad drove to Kentucky to see me. We went to the Whistle Stop Café for dinner. Later that night we were sitting at my kitchen table and he said, 'Is there anything you want to talk about?' I said, 'Not really.'

"'Are you sure?'

"Do you want to bring up the past?" I said. Then Dad answered, 'I'm sorry if any of the things I did had anything to do with the horrible choices you've made.'

"I suppose I had forgiven him in my own way."

She went on to bed that night and later after he made sure all the doors were locked, before going to be by himself, he went to her doorway and said, "Good night Teresa, I love you."

I saw tears glistening in her eyes.

She told me that she had learned about his father. Her grandfather molested the children in his family, and he too was an alcoholic. Sins just pass from one generation to the next unless they allow God to break the cycle to deliver them from that cycle.

"Dad started going to church two years before he died. I felt compelled to go to Florida to be with him at the end. I had three days with him, and was there holding his hand when he passed away. He was having a hard time forgiving himself for what he had done and what I had gone through. I said to him, 'You need to forgive yourself; God has already forgiven you. Dad, you are worthy to be forgiven, forgive yourself now, and go be with God'. He squeezed my hand and died."

She returned to the present, and she began to tell me about teaching candy making at the Community Action Center during the holidays. "On a whim, I decided to take

283

my candy recipes and start mixing them with popcorn. It was really good so I started giving them as gifts. Everyone loved it. They told me I should start selling it.

"I was at work one day, and the Lord impressed on me to start a business with the popcorn candy. I said, 'Ok Lord, what are we going to call it?' And I heard clear as a bell, Popcandy."

"Since I became obedient, things have just started falling into place. I believe God gave me the gift of mercy. I'm not as sweet as I can tell you are", she said giggling, "but I can be very forgiving. I don't want to judge people. Everyone's got a story."

And then she made me smile with her next sentence, "You know what I'm say'n?"

I once was blind, but now I see.

More often than not the homeless have not felt real love or safety for most of their lives. This tends to harden their heart and spirit. Before we pass judgment we should ask ourselves some difficult questions that have no simple answers. Are we showing them there is a love greater than what man can offer? Are we telling them about this great love? Are we telling them about the Hope we have received through the love of Jesus Christ?

I wonder what would happen if we were to share the love of Christ with them. Would it soften their hardened and often broken hearts? I wonder if homeless people were shown unconditional love, taught who Christ is, if we exhibited patience and kindness, grace and mercy as the Father has shown us, what would happen? If we could point them into the direction of the cross, and then into the direction of more help for their situation, what would happen? I wonder, could homelessness end? With God all things are possible!

We live in a fallen, sinful world but God didn't leave us alone to deal with it. Teresa felt alone and tried to fill that with men. It wasn't until she totally surrendered to her Savior and made Him Lord of her life at her dining room table that she realized He was all she needed. She doesn't need a man anymore. God may bless her one day with the right man, a good man, if He so chooses. That would be a blessing. But her hope is not in a man anymore, it is in Jesus Christ, her Lord and Savior. He has blessed her with forgiveness in her heart for others, a good job, a good home, and with five beautiful children. She is a loving godly mother, and she has found a church home where she faithfully serves.

We have a responsibility as believers where we've been commanded to tell the Good News. The Bible doesn't say to only share with the friendly people in the salon, or with only your next-door neighbor, or the guy in the three-piece suit. Jesus came for all people, even the homeless who live on the street, in the alley, underneath the bridge, under the boardwalk at the beach, and on the park bench. Sometimes it means breaking away from your comfort zone to expose yourself to the often confused and uncertain world that is the realm of the homeless. By doing so, unexpected blessings will often find us.

CHAPTER 37 – Homeless Hospitality

We who have so much can complain over the simplest of things. On a frigid Saturday with the air temperatures sinking into the twenties, Keith and I, along with another friend, saw firsthand just how absurd our grumblings often become. We were re-introduced to what true hospitality means.

Our relative luxury is so distant from the lives of the homeless. Our emotions were tugged toward the end of a spectrum we rarely encounter, one where complacency confronts reality, our complacency, their reality.

We parked our vehicle in an open area above the Barren River on the edge of town, and made the short walk across the field toward the Old Louisville Road Bridge. A biting winter wind raised goose bumps across the back of my neck, and cut deeply through our clothes. I tucked the collar of my jacket tightly against the upper part of my shoulders trying to shield myself from the cold. Keith carried a large box filled with firewood, hoping to drop it off as a gift to our friends, Melanie and Tony, who lived under the bridge.

A journalism student from Western Kentucky University was with us. She cradled a camera, the strap across her shoulder, and tucked her gloved hands into the pockets of her coat. She seemed unsure and tentative, but determined to follow through with our meeting. We had forewarned her about the camera—to be discrete with its use, asking permission first before photographing anything—something we had learned in chronicling our time with the homeless people we've met over the past couple of years. For the better part of a week our WKU student had spent time talking with us about the Blanket Ministry, and now for the first time she was being introduced to the reality of homelessness.

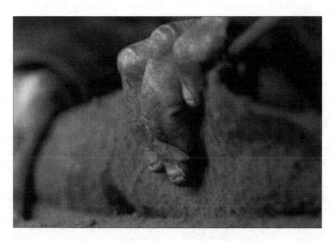

On the underside of the bridge, near one end where the concrete embankment and foundation secured the steel girders, a large plastic tarp was draped across a small four-foot wide shelf, a porous and feeble curtain of protection from the wind. Through one open corner we could see the small flame of a fire as it flickered in the dark recesses of the enclosure, the pungent odor of smoke drifted out of a small opening at the top.

There was no doorbell to ring, nor a door upon which to knock, yet we understood that this rustic, unsecured place was someone's home.

We yelled, "Hello!"

The outside flap of the tarp opened, and there stood Melanie her gray-streaked hair tussled, and soot covered face adorned with a giant smile. She greeted us with welcoming arms that engulfed us with a big hug. From what we could tell, she was wearing all the clothes she owned trying to stay warm. The smoke from the fire had saturated them so that they carried a strong, but not unpleasant, campfire smell.

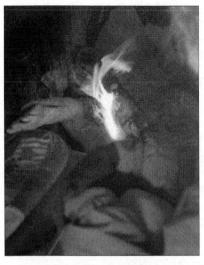

Inside the darkened tarp enclosure, the small fire actually provided smoky warmth. Melanie's face carried that strong, angular look about it, making her seem older than her forty odd years. Her hands were black with soot, and the nails broken and jagged. Her knuckles appeared gnarled and deformed broken by her father when she was younger.

"I was beginning to wonder about you two," she said. "You haven't been around for a week or two. Come on in out of the wind."

We had purposely stayed away to avoid making a nuisance of ourselves by intruding into their lives at every opportunity. In reality, though, they enjoyed our visits, and we always enjoyed their company. We introduced our WKU student friend and they, as we suspected they would, greeted her warmly. She offered each of us a stale, three-day old donut and a cup of hot coffee.

Tony also greeted us with a hug, a handshake, and a cough. His scruffy, unshaven face was haggard, and his nose dripped from a cold he was suffering. The grimy cup he held was black from soot. Still, he sipped on the warm liquid that helped to sooth his raw throat and warm his chilled insides.

We had to traverse some rough terrain and a steeply angled concrete slab that dropped off suddenly toward the edge of the rapids on the river below to get to their abode. In years past, several homeless people have been injured falling off this precarious perch. Tony understood my fear of it.

"I'm so proud of you, Kris." He said as I stepped over an old mattress and sat down on a log, "for coming all the way in this time."

I smiled and made some remark about finally being brave enough to cross that steep slope.

Keith held out his gift, "I brought you some firewood, thought you might could use some." He said as he searched for a place to secure the box.

Firewood is readily available along the timbered banks of the river, but it is often too wet and sandy to burn efficiently and must be dried first. It takes a lot of firewood to get through a single winter day, much less the entire winter.

Tony remarked, "We can always use firewood. It will dry soon enough up here out of the weather."

Along the top edge of the concrete embankment, a shelf-like ledge offered a pantry where they had stacked a few canned foods and bottles of water. It was filthy, but they used the available space as best as they could. Their refrigerator consisted of two canvas bags hung from the steel girders and cooled by the winter winds that whipped under the bridge.

"We had to run off someone the other day. He was causing trouble." Melanie said.

I have from the beginning admired the streetwise confidence and inner strength she carried that allowed her to confront serious if not dangerous situations without flinching. I have never felt threatened by any of my contacts with the homeless, but at the same time I am able to remove myself from that environment. Melanie and Tony must face it every day of their lives.

I asked her, "Do you ever worry about someone coming down here and bothering you? Are you afraid of anyone trying to hurt you?"

Her answer was typical of her stoic manner.

"I got a sixteen inch machete over there that says No! It tends to even up the odds a little."

All of us burst out laughing, not quite expecting a comeback like that. She stepped across the narrow slab, picked up the machete and waved it around in a comical manner.

Tony spoke up, "Yeah, she don't take no crap from anyone. She makes me feel real safe too."

Tony and Melanie are not a couple. They are just two people who met at the bridge, and connected for mutual support. They found friendship and companionship together. Loneliness is a predominant symptom of homelessness. It digs deeply into their emotions and adds a dimension to survivalism that makes daily living even more difficult. That disconnection with life often drives homeless people deeper into depression, a cycle that manifests itself by a constant wave of bad decisions. Keith and I were glad Tony and Melanie could ward off the worst of those symptoms together.

As I mentioned in the first part of Tony's story, when I first met him late in the previous summer, he had departed from the Christian upbringing and the Bible teaching he had enjoyed at an earlier age. Disillusioned by life, he drifted away from the beliefs he once clung to. The longer he drifted, the more deeply cynical he became, and this lifestyle led to a choice that eventually got him into trouble and time in prison. Tony was not proud of what he did, and he paid his debt, but the stigma still followed him. Because of that stigma a life as a homeless person living under a bridge became his reality. The fact that his demeanor still retained a positive element testified to his understanding that he had to move forward and make some life changes.

"You'd be proud of me Kris" Tony said. "I've started reading the Bible again."

My heart was lifted up when he said that.

"I am proud of you!" I said. "Just keep on reading, you'll find answers there you won't find any other place."

"I have a Bible, too," Melanie said. "I read it all the time. My earthly home may at the moment be under a bridge, but I know where my eternal home is. I've got Jesus in my heart. You know, we're probably the happiest homeless people you will ever meet."

For the next thirty minutes, we continued to visit and our WKU student took a few pictures and asked a few questions for the study she was doing. When we finally stood to leave, I gave Tony and Melanie another hug. I could feel the strength of their genuine embrace. It said more than words could convey. Keith gave Tony a strong handshake and pat across the shoulder. Our WKU student gave Melanie a candid hug. Touch is something most of the homeless people I've encountered crave as much as anything.

"They needed that visit," Keith said after we left. "And so did we!"

Showing unconditional love to those less fortunate, being willing to step into their home, is not always an easy thing to do, but it is necessary. A home is not so much what is inside, rather it's the people who live there. Does it matter if there is no door, no window, no electricity, and none of the amenities we take for granted? After we left I began to realize that during our visit, I never once felt cold, but was warmed by their hospitality. As simple as their lives were, they carried a measure of wisdom and attitude that many people that are more fortunate fail to carry with them. I felt welcomed and at home.

Sometimes I wonder why God led me to work with the homeless. When I hear things like what Tony and Melanie said, I realize that maybe instead of me helping them, they have in their own way, helped me.

It's not that they are happy about being homeless, but for the time being, until things change, this is the best place for them, and they will make the most of it. Their sweet attitude toward others and their situation provides an uplifting force that will carry them through these difficult days.

When I arrived back home, a home filled with furniture that collects dust, carpets that need vacuuming, hardwood floors that need sweeping, I pondered about the "home" I had just left. They possessed little in the way of things, yet I believe that if Jesus were to have walked into that home, he would have felt welcomed. They did not worry about the dust or fussing over a meal. They simply offered a stale donut and a warm cup of coffee to augment a genuine, heart-felt conversation. Melanie and Tony never complained about their circumstances.

Next time someone comes to my door, I will invite them all the way in, without looking around first. I will look at them and give them my whole attention, not sharing that attention with the cobweb. I'll enjoy their presence, their entire being. I'll leave my dust rag in the cabinet, and I'll leave my machete under the bed. Just kidding, I don't really have a machete.

CHAPTER 38 – Lasagna and Basketball

When I first met Greg, he was sleeping on a concrete floor inside a cramped storage shed. In the winter he froze, in the summer he sweltered. One could not help but understand why he was depressed. A year later Keith and I along with our friends the Fredrick's spent an evening eating lasagna, salad, bread sticks, and watched a basketball game on Greg's secondhand television inside his very own apartment. We visited, laughed, and read devotionals together. Only God could have envisioned this ever happening, and through His work Greg seemed happier than any time I had known him.

This evening of fun began two weeks before when Greg called me and said he realized that he needed to quit hanging out with the wrong people. In his defense, that is all he had ever known. He migrated to what was familiar as is common with people caught in the same kind of environment. For the first time he was seeing another side of life; he recognized the difference. He wanted to jump start the process that would move him away from the chaos that had always defined who he was.

We accepted his invitation with excitement and anticipation. We did not know for sure what to expect. Greg still struggled with alcohol and the last time I had been to his apartment was the day he called out in desperation for help. He had shut himself in, and drank until he could no longer stay awake. His room was filthy with trash everywhere, the toilet was clogged, and dirty dishes scattered across the kitchen counter. That was the low point in our relationship. Even so, because he invited us over and seemed excited about sharing a positive part of his life with us, we were filled with hopeful anticipation.

When we arrived, the first thing I noticed was how clean, orderly, and welcoming the apartment was. The bed was made, the kitchen and bathroom shined, everything in its place, no clutter, no chaos. Greg met us at the door with a glowing smile. He had a freshly shaved head and was clean and most importantly, sober. His skin shined in the soft light inside his apartment. His eyes were sharp, mind clear, and I could tell right away he was filled with joy and happiness. Just seeing this filled my heart with the same kind of joy.

Watching Greg throw his head back and boom out loud with his deep laughter brought me to tears at times. Happy tears because I remembered that long evening at the hospital after his long alcoholic binge. That is when he decided he wanted to change, rather than living the life he was living. He looked healthier. He was volunteering again at Hope House. He was being a friend and sharing his life, not asking for anything except that we accept him as such.

Half way through the evening, Greg's phone rang. It was his mother. Greg had admitted that his relationship with his mother was up and down and was not the best it could be. He handed the phone to me, and we had a wonderful talk as she seemed pleased that we were with him. When Greg told her he loved her, I as a mother knew how much that meant to her and how much it cost Greg to be able to say such things.

I had seen God's redemptive work in him. It was an awesome revelation to see how a broken man could begin to change for the better when he allowed God to work in his life. There were those who gave up on Greg, but they missed out on an extraordinary blessing. Blessings can be found in the most unusual circumstances, but those can become the most powerful and meaningful blessings one can experience.

I am reminded of a statement by Dostoevsky, "To love a person means to see him as God intended him to be."

For the first time Greg's life appeared to be moving in the right direction. We were beginning to see Greg as God intended his life to be. We all understood that he still had a very steep climb ahead, but to see him laugh and glow with a genuine excitement only experienced through true friendship, gave us optimistic hope for his life.

The mountains Greg had to climb proved very steep indeed and in the months to come our optimistic hope was tested far beyond what we ever imagined.

CHAPTER 39 – Brownies and Bibles

"It's Jesus. He's been there all along, I just wasn't seeing Him, now I do."

I wanted to keep up the friendships with the people I had made in our community. I always remember Denver Moore's statement in his book about good people coming to help on the holidays, but then go home the rest of the year while the homeless are still out there. I wanted to go out on this normal, average, non-holiday day to greet one of our friends at the bridge, and I didn't want to go empty handed. What's better than dessert? So out came the baking pan and measuring spoons and wa-la, brownies as a host/hostess gift.

As soon as they came out of the oven, my husband and I jumped into his jeep and headed down to the bridge thinking we might find Melanie and Tony. But whoever we found would be the recipients of our gift. Melanie was not there. Keith and I drove to the other side of the bridge where we knew Tony stayed. This side of the bridge is much more precarious and I became a wimp. I'm not afraid to talk to the homeless and ex-cons, but I am afraid of steep climbs with big rivers raging below. My hero of a husband took the pan of brownies and scurried down the path and up to underneath this side of the bridge.

No Tony. As we came walking back through the parking lot, we spotted a red t-shirted man sitting on the park bench under the shade. From a distance, it looked like it might be Tony. We walked towards him and he waved at us with a big smile.

He was reading.

I was elated to see what it was.

"See what I'm reading Kris," he said with a confident grin, "I read the whole Bible end to end, King James Version, and now I'm re-reading it in the NIV version. It's easier to understand."

"I'm so proud of you," I replied.

"You ever hear about a group of WKU students called Hilltoppers for Christ? Well, some of them started visiting with me last spring bringing sandwiches, and we started doing a Bible study together. I started going back to church with them too, every Sunday, Sunday night, and Wednesday night."

I was pleasantly surprised, and told him how he seemed to be different now. Tony had changed a great deal since I first spoke with him in the fall some nine months before. Back then he was scared, confused, and depressed. After surviving under the bridge through the winter and spring, he was a more confident and relaxed person.

When I shared with him about recognizing the difference, he responded, "It's Jesus. He's been there all along, I just wasn't seeing Him, now I do."

I understand there are many who might question how I could get involved with someone with Tony's background as a sex offender. In all honesty, there was a time I probably would have been scared to do so. But God also places discernment inside our hearts. When weighed on the scales of justice, in God's eyes, Tony's sin was no different from mine. Jesus died on the cross for all of us, not just some, and we are commanded to share the good news with everyone. I felt in my God given discernment that Tony was a changed man. He was a redeemed man. And he was now a friend of Keith's and mine; we were connected and the connector was Jesus Christ.

We offered the brownies to him, and his eyes lit up. Brownies were his favorite dessert. We also gave him some information about a program Hope House offered called Job's For Life. It is a Biblically based program to instruct those who struggle to get or keep a job about the importance of a good work ethic. After graduating from the class, Hope House has partnered with several businesses in town that will at least offer an interview and the possibility of a job. He said he would check into it.

We all stood up to part ways. Tony still had issues with feeling worthy. I hugged Tony, and whispered to him that he was worthy in the Lord's eyes, and he was our friend. He smiled as he walked away with tears in his eyes.

Brownies, blankets, and sandwiches won't fix homelessness. But they are great tools to get you to someone out there, feeling helpless and lonely, where you can offer friendship and in God's timing, His Good News, a prayer, a hug, and who knows, you might find them later on a bench reading that Good News. What a gift, for them and for you!

Keith and I are thankful for Tony and our visit with him this day; on this day, the connector was Jesus and chocolate. I prayed Tony felt a little better after our visit. I've always heard God can use whatever you bring. I know of nothing sweeter than chocolate and the love of Christ.

As a postscript to Tony's story, he did complete the Job's for Life Program with honors, and eventually did land a job. He was a guest speaker for a fundraiser banquet held for Hope House.

Within a few weeks, he was able to get into a room and out from under the bridge. He still struggled with feelings of being unworthy, but living under a bridge for a year and half will do that to most people.

Every homeless person we encountered had to deal with similar issues, but each story was different in how it played out. Tony had made a mistake, paid for it legally, and wanted to move on with his life. He was not a habitual offender and felt terrible about what had happened. His biggest obstacle was a society that would not allow him to forget about it. Most businesses simply will not hire someone with that kind of rap hanging over them. When a potential employer discovered what he had done, the door was shut over and over.

He was continually told he was not worthy by those kinds of actions. But because Tony accepted the actions of Jesus on the cross, because of Jesus Tony is worthy. He is in a much better place now because of redemption, but still struggled to hold a job, and secure a home with a roof.

Keith and I pray society will be able to see in Tony the man that we see. We pray Tony will be able to see the man in himself that Christ sees.

CHAPTER 40 – Scars

I met a young man named Dallas, nineteen years old, who had been temporarily homeless living at the Salvation Army. I met him through his caseworker. He had just had a birthday so my family took him out to dinner to celebrate, and to get to know him. A precious lady, a stranger to him and a blog follower of mine who had read the short version of this young man's story on my blog, gave me a Bible to give to him. She had his name engraved on the front. He smiled big when he saw his name, rubbing his hand over it taking it all in. The next week, he allowed me to interview him for this book. I didn't want just a story; I wanted to be his friend. His life had been hard and filled with pain that created physical and emotional scars.

Dallas had a heart so full of the painful memories. That kind of pain brings tears to the eyes, and makes the head droop in sorrow. His feelings of anger, sorrow, and throbbing pain were sharp. He had memories of ripping his skin until the red ran down his body onto the floor. It was almost more than I could take.

I wanted him to see I cared. So much was taken from him. I wanted to give him a listening ear as well as a listening spirit. It's so much better to let out all those feelings this way rather than taking the ripping sharpness to the skin. His physical scars were healed, but I wasn't so sure about the other scars. I prayed silently as I listened.

A few days later, as he and I faced each other in a reserved, glass incased library room, this polite young man began to share his story with me.

"Other than my stepdad and my counselor, I don't trust men much. My real dad was out of my life by the time I was five years old. I don't have one single good memory of him. But I do have memories of all the stuff he used to do to my mom and brother and me. One memory that stands out is the time when I was five, I decided to make some chocolate milk thinking I was big stuff. I put the glasses on a tray with some candies. I spilled the tray breaking it and the glasses."

My dad wanted my brother to help me clean it up. At first he wouldn't help because it was not his fault. My dad took one of the long, hard plastic light saber swords and started beating my brother on the legs. He hit so hard that it broke, and the pieces inside fell out. They had sharp edges and my dad took them and started cutting my brother all along his back and legs. Later, when my mom saw my brother, she took him to the hospital."

Dallas began the first of his many pauses to catch his breath, which fell short and fast as though he were trying to catch a lump that floated in his chest.

"Another memory I have is when my brother and I were little, we were scared of the dark. So we would have a night light on. My dad didn't like that, I guess he didn't want his boys to be sissies, so he threw my brother and me into a dark closet and locked us in there for eight hours straight.

"My real dad lives in Missouri now. To see him again would just stir up drama, drama I don't need in my life. I have an adopted dad. He is the dad who has always taken care of me, the only dad I remember ever being there. He is the one who raised me."

From this point on when he referred to his dad, he was talking about his adoptive father. His voice became somber and matter of fact as he spoke about the closeness the two of them shared. After a long pause he revealed with a shaky

306

voice interspersed with rapid shallow breaths an event that happened one terrible day.

"My mother died when I was thirteen. She committed suicide. She and I were real close. We talked a lot. She was so big-hearted, and would try to help people. She would try to teach us. As kids, we would want to watch TV, but we would have to read the Bible and sit down and discuss it. The day before she died, there was something different about her. She left for hours, and when she came back, she wouldn't say anything to me. I followed her to her bedroom, she's digging around in her closet, and I see her get the gun case and her bag of pills. I didn't say nothing. I just followed her out the door, and she just drives off. She drove all around, and then she parked about a block from our house.

"We heard the gunshot. She shot herself, then called Dad as she lay dying. She was slurring her words. Dad called the police. By now, we were all awake, Dad is freaking out, and we know something is wrong. Cops and family are at my house. We ended up going over to my grandma's house, and we kids were told to stay outside. Everybody is coming over, crying, and they're all just looking at us. No one will tell us anything so I sneak inside pretending to get a drink. Grandma is crying, and she says what happened. Grandma didn't see me. I just went back outside. I wouldn't believe it. Dad gathered the boys and he was crying. I'm just hoping it ain't true. He tells us. I froze. Everyone else started crying. I just sat there. I couldn't cry. She was my best friend, she was everything to me."

As Dallas described that terrible day, I tried to keep my emotions in check. I breathed in deep and slow then slowly let it all out. That helped me to regain my focus. I would not allow my tears to flow, but I could feel the tightness in my chest pinch my heart. His eyes shifted from left to right as though he was back in that moment. While he spoke, he would constantly raise his shoulders, his expression changed from bewilderment to disgust to a blank stare.

His words flowed nonstop from his heart, a torrent of troubled memories. "After a while I went into the bedroom and cried and cried. Then I went out, climbed up the hill, and just sat there for the longest time. The next day they planned the funeral. I went to the visitation. I was the last one to see her. You just don't believe it till you see it. I froze. I couldn't breathe. She was there in the casket. I felt so empty. The next two days, I stood by her, and greeted people as they came up and talked. I had that empty feeling for a long time after that. My smiles were faked. And then I was either really angry or really sad. There was nothing in between.

"That's when I started hurting myself by cutting. My dad went to jail 'cause after Mom died, he fell apart. The night before the funeral, someone gave him cocaine to help him, and my dad took it. He became an addict after that, and things spun out of control for him. My brother and me went to my stepsister's home. She treated us like crap, and then sent us away. There were two other half-brothers there also. Her and her boyfriend would hold them down and beat them. We all eventually ended up in foster care.

"I was fifteen when I went to a hospital for a year, and then into foster care. I was in Rivendell (Behavioral Health Services) twice, nine months the first time and a month and a half the second time. I went in for depression, self-mutilation, and I was suicidal. I tried to kill myself a couple of times by cutting my wrists. While I was in the hospital, I was on three different medicines. It was like being high. My heart would beat so fast, everything would tingle. It always felt like I was in a daze. When I would stand up to walk, I would wobble side to side. Words would slur and I couldn't think straight. My body ached, and I would have cold sweats. It sucked!

"I was then moved to Cumberland Hall in Hopkinsville where I spent a year, and really got help there. But a lot of people said I wouldn't make it. I was so hard headed at the time. But there were two people who thought differently. They wouldn't give up on me. That was my drug counselor/therapist and a nurse, Ms. Trish. At sixteen to seventeen years old, I was in bad shape. I was getting in fights every day, and hurting myself. But they saw potential in me that I couldn't see in myself, and neither did no one else. I was sneaky though. I would get knives from the cafeteria and pieces of metal here and there to cut myself. You can find things if you want it bad enough.

"My brother also has problems. He's reckless, on drugs, always high, drunk. He doesn't want to face reality. He wasn't helped like I was. I think he knows if he starts to talk about it, he'll have to deal with the pain of it all. I'm scared for my brother. He was sent for help, too, but it didn't work.

"It took me about a year and a half to want to get better, to even try. All other nurses just took care of me physically, but Ms. Trish would ask me how I was every day. I wouldn't talk to her at first but she never left me alone. I finally started talking to her, and a bond was formed. I could tell she cared. I had so much respect for her, and my counselor.

"Also, at the time, I knew God was real, but I was mad at Him. I blamed Him just like I blamed my dad. It took a lot for me to overcome that, to forgive Him and my dad. I started reading the Bible, started praying and that's when I started getting better. That's when I started to forgive people. The hardest has been trying to forgive myself. I also had to do assignments, journal, stay out of trouble, no self-harm. I graduated from the program and then I went back into foster care.

"It was hard for me to get back into a foster home because of my age and my troubled background, but a family took me in and they were good to me. It was a therapy foster home, a home for kids on medication. I liked them a lot; they really cared about me. I lived with them for nine months, and then I moved back in with my dad.

"He was out of jail by this time. I didn't want to see him at first. I blamed him for doing drugs, blamed him for me being in the hospital. Anger had built up towards him. He had become a drug infested, abusive father after Mom died. But now I was seeing the old, loving father he used to be before Mom died. Dad had changed, and I saw that he was trying, so I started to come around. He has been clean for five years now, and has built relationships up again. We're both hard headed, so we butt heads all the time, but I know he would do anything for me. It's all good.

"I drank after I got out. I thought I could handle a couple of drinks. It didn't turn out that way. One would turn into more, I don't know how many because I couldn't remember. When I would get depressed, I would drink. But I eventually deal with things.

"That's where my brother and I are different. Sometimes, if it's not around I'm fine, but if I'm in someone's home and they offer it, I take it. Once I start, I take more than I should. For the most part I'm pretty happy go lucky, but everyone has their bad moments. Sometimes I still get depressed, and that turns into anger. That's something I still have to work on.

"My anger is what gets me into trouble. I would have what's called black out anger/rage. It's like going into a dream. It doesn't happen often anymore. I've learned to control it where I don't start hitting people. I don't hurt myself anymore, but I will yell and throw stuff.

"I was sad for a long time over my mom and then that turned into anger for what she did. Dad gave me her Bible. It had her name written in it and when she was baptized. I found letters inside the Bible pocket she had written before her first suicide attempt. I'm sad that she won't get to see all her grandchildren grow up.

"Mom left a note for Dad, but I never read it. I'm told it didn't state a specific reason. She knew she was saved but felt she was a bad mom. She just couldn't handle all the depression anymore. She tried, really tried. She had a prayer journal inside her Bible, and I read some of those. I had never known anyone to write prayers down word for word before. She prayed for it to get better."

His eyes drifted toward the distance as his breathing became shallow, but steady. His spirit seemed so heavy like a thick fog hanging over the room. He found the courage to look forward, and spoke about what he wanted to do with his life. I remained quiet, and just listened.

"I've accepted it, but I don't want to forget all that happened. I want to help others someday, and if I cover it up, that won't happen. You know, I always thought two things were unforgivable, suicide and blasphemy and that eats at me."

He cast a questioning expression toward me, and I was compelled to respond. "I'm no expert but, I've never heard that suicide was unforgivable. I don't believe that is true, Dallas."

"My church said it was, but I've never been able to find it in the Bible, and they can't seem to show it to me. After everything my mom had been through with her mother, father, ex-husband, family, her childhood, she didn't really seem angry about it."

"Maybe she had forgiven all of them," I responded.

"I know she forgave her dad. She didn't go into a whole lot of detail because we were kids, I was her son but I know he was a really bad alcoholic, and he was abusive. My grandpa had a good side to him though. He's the one who got me to love music and the guitar. He's the most gifted musician I've ever known. He would hear something on the radio and be able to play it back perfectly. He told me, 'When you learn to play guitar, you can have mine.' When my grandpa would play his music, he would get such a look on his face, like almost going into a daze. People say I do the same thing. When I play music, it's like nothing can hurt me. I feel happy when I play. I'm not the best musician, but I'm just happy when I play. I love to talk about it."

During our lunch a few days before my youngest son was with us. He's a drummer for his youth band at our church, and about a year younger than Dallas. The two of them exchanged a few comments about music in general. I could tell music was an important part of his life.

"I'm learning theory," Dallas said. "I've never been good at anything in school, but music is like second nature. I'm severely dyslexic. I can't read notes like other kids. I just recognize. I can't count in my head. I'll get lost, but I can click my tongue or click my teeth. I can memorize the music so I don't have to look at it. I have a really good memory. I can read music, but I can't read it and play at the same time, so that's why I memorize."

His mood lightened somewhat. It was good to see him shift away from the sad part of his life to something positive.

312

I said, "I think that is a gift God has given you, a good memory, the ability to memorize music."

Dallas beamed a giant smile. "I want to become a nurse. One of the things in Mom's letter was her saying to us kids, 'Make me proud.' My stepmom was a nurse. I was impressed with her hard work ethic and commitment. That was so cool. Ms. Trish is one of the reasons I want to be a nurse. I told her when I was getting ready to leave, 'I don't know how I'll ever be able to pay you back,' and she said, 'Pay it back in full.' I didn't get that at the time, but I took it as to help somebody else. She cared. She never gave up no matter how bad I wanted her to, she just wouldn't. That has just stuck in my head.

"I know God has a plan for me, probably more than I can imagine. I know He'll help me along that path, but it's confusing right now to me. I don't know why the things that happened to me did, but I can't wait to see how He will use me to help others. Sometimes I get impatient and just think, 'God, would you just tell me now?' I know what I want to do, but don't know if that's His plan. I want to be able to work in a place like Rivendell."

For the first time during our conversation, there was long pause. I diverted the conversation toward something new. "I'm going to say some words and you tell me what comes to your mind, okay?"

He smiled and nodded his head.

"God, Jesus, Church."

"I wouldn't be here if it weren't for God. I was always raised in church. Some of my best memories are from church. My immediate family was always real big in church. That's what pulled us through right after Mom's death. Afterwards, it all went to crap."

"You told me that the nurse and counselor helped you to forgive, so where is the anger coming from now?"

"Myself. I think about things like how I watched my mom get the gun, and I didn't do anything to stop her."

"So you have forgiven everyone but yourself?"

"Yes. Nobody really knows everything I've been through; all the stuff that happened, stuff that should never happen to a kid by another adult. I froze up." His shoulders drooped, and he heaved a heavy sigh.

"And that's why you can't forgive yourself?"

"I didn't really fight it off. I didn't know what to do."

"That's not your fault Dallas, do you know that?"

"It disgusts me, I can't even have a girlfriend, I just can't. I don't know."

"You still need to heal from that."

"I don't really talk about that. My family doesn't even know."

"Can we talk about prayer?" I asked.

"I remember sitting in the dark in my room one night and saying, 'God, if you can forgive me for all I've done and help me to get better, I'd appreciate it so much, and I won't give up this time.

"I went to sleep, and woke up the next day. I felt like so much had been lifted off of me. I prayed and asked Him to continue to help me. I asked for courage to do what was right, to give me the strength to make it through the days. 'Just help me make it for ten minutes,' I would pray in the beginning. I dream about my mom. Sometimes I hear her telling me loving things, and when I've done something stupid, she tells me to get my act together. I know that sounds crazy but that's what I dream. And the only bad thing about those dreams is I want to reach out and hug her but I can't."

His eyes grew empty, and once again his shoulders drooped. Not being a trained counselor, there was little I could do but listen and provide encouragement.

"I asked God to let me know where my mom was. I thought I knew but I needed to be sure. I didn't hear anything for about a month, and then one night I was sitting by myself, and just heard in my spirit, 'She's in Heaven with me, she's okay.' She prayed all the time, and read her Bible all the time. Did I tell you her Bible was next to her in the car when she shot herself?"

I stepped in and said, "She probably made her peace and now it's time for you to have that peace. When you die, do you know where you're going?"

"I hope I go to Heaven."

"I'd like to tell you like I told Greg, you don't have to hope, you can know. Would you like that assurance and that peace?"

"I would so much! I'm afraid that I have blasphemed God because I had been mad at Him earlier in life, and I'm afraid that would keep me out."

"Oh Dallas, blasphemy is turning your back on the Holy Spirit, and that is not what you did. I think many have gotten mad at God for one reason or another. That's not unusual. God created our emotions, and He knows how we feel. Being mad at God is different from turning your back on the Holy Spirit."

"I've asked Him to forgive me. I think he's waiting for me to forgive myself."

"Maybe when you invite Jesus into your life, He will help you to forgive yourself."

"I believe in God."

"But He's waiting for you to accept His Son."

"I don't see what the difference is."

"Jesus died on the cross to pay the penalty for our sins. He's waiting for us to accept that gift. It's there, but we have to reach out and take it. Do you know that you are a sinner Dallas, just like all of us are?"

"Oh, yeah! I was baptized when I was little, but I didn't know what it was."

"You did that for someone else."

"Yes."

"When you're ready, you need to do it for you, and for Him."

"I thought baptism saved you."

"Dallas, baptism is a step of obedience we take after we have accepted Him. It is just a symbolic way of showing, 'I have trusted Jesus Christ as my Savior, and believe that the debt of my sin is fully paid through His sacrifice.' Jesus was baptized but he didn't need to be because He was perfect. He did it to show us the example of acknowledging Him and our acceptance of His gift before men. You know Dallas, we all come into this world a sinner, but Jesus died on the cross to pay the penalty for our sins. When we pray, ask Him for forgiveness, and repent of those sins, the Bible says our sins are wiped away. We are made clean. We have a clean slate. You don't ever have to go back and worry about past mistakes."

Dallas was smiling again looking like a light bulb just came on for the first time. "I've never understood that until you just explained it."

I quoted John 3:16. "For God so loved the world that He gave his only begotten Son, that whosoever believes in Him shall not perish but have everlasting life. That's the gift."

"When my mom shot herself in the chest, the medics who got there said she was still awake, praying, and her Bible was open as if she had been reading. I want to know for myself."

"Do you acknowledge that you are a sinner?"

"Yes."

"Do you believe that Jesus Christ died on the cross to pay the debt for your sins, and that He rose again three days later, and that we can have a home with Him in Heaven if we choose Him?"

"Yes, what do I do?"

"You just did it Dallas. You acknowledged your faith and repentance. But we can pray what is called the sinner's prayer. The prayer does not save you any more than baptism does. It's a meaningful expression of what you have done. You are acknowledging with your mouth that He is now Lord in your life. Would you like to pray?"

"I'm not sure what to say."

"We can pray together if you want. You can follow after me. We'll just pray what we've already talked about and what you have acknowledged here. Are you ready?"

"Yes," he replied as he removed his hat then bowed his head, and he repeated after me, "Dear Lord, I believe You died on the cross for my sins and that You rose from the grave. I ask You to forgive me of my sins and to save me. Thank you. In Jesus' name, amen."

Dallas raised his head, put his hat back on, and smiled big time.

"That is the most important decision you will ever make because it determines your eternal life. You don't have to hope anymore Dallas, you know now don't you?"

He nodded. "I can't stop smiling, I just feel so happy."

I fought to prevent happy tears from flowing, not sure why. I should have just let them spill. "Dallas, you said awhile back that you didn't tell a lot of people what you have told me. Why did you tell me?"

"I think I'm a pretty good judge of character, and I can tell I can trust you. If this can help somebody else somehow, then that's great. I just felt comfortable with you. When you asked me to do this, I prayed about it and felt I should."

He and I both were drained emotionally as I closed our interview. I could not help but let the mother in me take control of my thoughts. "There are many on the streets who are alcoholics and they started drinking around fourteen to sixteen years of age. Now they are in their forties, fifties and sixties with their lives ruined because of it. They will tell you that. Alcohol gets such a bite on them, and most can't get away from those teeth. I want to warn you and ask you to stop the drinking for good. Now. While you're still young and still have a chance to go school and become a nurse and not end up on the streets."

Dallas nodded as if he understood. "They say I have an addictive personality. That's why I worry about it sometimes."

"That's why I say this to you. Stay away from it now, while you are still young before it grabs so tight that you can't get away from it. I'm sorry, that's just the momma in me. You have a passion to be a nurse. I want to see that happen for you."

His demeanor had transformed dramatically from when we first started. Before he was timid and uncertain, now he could not stop smiling. It was heartwarming to see this young man who had gone through so much have a smile as big as life on his face. He gave me a hug, and we went our separate

ways. It was Valentine's Day, and Dallas had received a new heart.

He healed from the broken skin, bleeding, and the desire to tear, but the scars are there. My pastor said from the pulpit that scars are blessings when we give them to God. Not curses but blessings. They can be reminders of God's mercifulness and faithfulness to bring one through a trying time. Oh, how hard this must be for the one who carries so many scars. God did not bring about these scars but He can use them for good, for His glory. Now that this young man has the Healer in his heart, I pray he will learn to see the scars as blessings and use them for God's purpose. May his heart become healed now that the Savior is residing with this young man, and may this young soul begin to know the unconditional love that Jesus gave to all of us.

If you see scars on someone, do not pity. Be encouraged by Dallas' strength to come out on the other side to healed flesh and newness of heart. Let this strength be what you fall on to bring you through whatever may be hurting you.

Do you know this love? If not, receive from the One who bore scars for you out of love. Do you know someone who needs it? Go, give, and love with the love of Jesus. That kind of love can heal the deepest of scars. Does your skin bear the image of scars? Wear them as a badge of courage. It says you survived. It says you are strong. As a scar-wearer, you are in the best of company.

Dear Readers, I would like you to join me now in prayer for this young man . . .

Dear Heavenly Father,

We pray blessings to rain down on this young man and his future. First of all, we thank you for his new salvation. Thank you for what you did on the cross for him and for all of us. We pray that he would be healed of any emotional wounds that are still there, and that he would learn to thank you for the scars, to use them to share a testimony that is his only to give glory and honor to you Father for all of it. May his future be strong and bright, and we pray that he would always remember to look to you for that strength and guidance, and for answers that he seeks. We pray that you would continue to bring strong Christian people into his life to befriend him and help him grow in his walk with you. Thank you for being with him, and bringing him this far. We thank you for what you are going to do in this young man's life. We now give you all the glory and honor for all that you have done and will do in this precious young man.

*We pray this in the name
of Jesus, amen*

* Dallas started coming to church with us on Sunday mornings. A couple of weeks after the interview, we watched Dallas being baptized in our baptistery, this time doing it for himself, doing it for the right reasons.

Three months later he graduated high school, moved from the apartment, and we lost touch with him. But God knows where he is.

CHAPTER 41 – Loy

Our very first encounter with a homeless person occurred during the Thanksgiving Day dinner hosted by the Salvation Army in 2009. We had on hand a few hundred donated blankets, but did not have a clear outlet for distribution. The Salvation Army graciously allowed us to set up a table during their meal and hand out blankets to anyone who needed one.

My friend Karen, along with Keith and a couple other volunteers, arrived early that morning before mealtime to set up just inside the main entrance to the cafeteria. We really did not know what to do, we just asked those who walked in if they would like or needed a blanket. Almost everyone accepted the offer. We had no way of knowing who were homeless, although we could guess because of their appearance, but that was not always an accurate way to determine who was. A good number of those served were not homeless. From what I could tell, all of them probably could have used a blanket, so we made no distinction.

At first, I was tentative and unsure how to approach those who were there. I did not want to ask blatantly if someone was homeless for fear of offending. My friend Karen brought a large tray of chocolate goodies. She began to walk around, and offered to all who were there. A few minutes later, I noticed she was talking with a young man. I thought, yes, this is what we came here for. I needed to get over my uncertainty, and do the same thing, so I joined her. I have often given credit to Karen for being the one to show me the way, and for helping to get the Blanket Ministry in motion. She was the one who, by her natural ability to make friends, showed me how to approach the people and begin to visit.

She introduced me to the young man whose name was Loy. He was very quiet and always polite saying, "Yes Ma'am and thank you." His clothes needed washing, but he was otherwise clean. I thought he was about twenty-five or maybe a few years older, but he said he was closer to forty. Within a few minutes we discovered that he was currently homeless, had been a trucker at one time but lost his license because of various violations involving official paperwork. As a result, he had accumulated almost five thousand dollars in fines with no way of paying them. He had also spent a short time in prison.

He told us about his mother who was a Christian, and when he was young, she led him to the Lord. He admitted that he had never walked closely with Him, but knew he needed to. He felt sorry for the bad choices he had made, and he was now suffering the consequences of those choices.

Loy was sincere, and his gentle demeanor stole our hearts. His time was up at the Salvation Army so it was back on the streets for him. We offered him a blanket, but he spotted a sleeping bag on our table, and asked if he could have that instead. We gave him both, but he would not take the blanket, "I don't want to take more than my share."

Loy told us about his family, and how he and his father, who lived in Texas, had become estranged. We prayed with him that someday they would restore their relationship.

Karen told him about Hope House where he could get a box of food and a heavier coat if he needed one. When the lunch was over we parted ways, but we could not forget our new friend.

A few days later Bryan, the director of Hope House, met with Loy and spent time hearing his story and ministering to him. They read the Bible together, and Bryan was able to get him connected to a local downtown church. They rallied around him with love and understanding. Someone would pick him up every Sunday for church services. One couple even took him into their home for a while.

A few months later Bryan told me that Loy had indeed made his way to Texas, reconnected with his father, and was working on his brother's ranch. Not long after that, Loy called Bryan and told him that someone had paid his fines, and he was able to get his truckers license again. He was heading to Alaska to begin his new life.

Loy was our first contact, and in many ways may have been the most important. He became our confirmation that God's hand was directing the ministry. By ourselves, we could accomplish very little, but knowing that God was involved gave us confidence and encouragement. Our experience with Loy proved the merit of the ministry. All we did was provide a sleeping bag, and spend time talking to him. From that point, God took over and changed a life.

A couple of years later, I heard he was working as an ice road trucker and loving it in Alaska. He is in a small church that he loves and at the time of this writing, was in a serious relationship.

CHAPTER 42 – Pulling Away

Life experiences are not unlike driving along a foggy and winding road. The unexpected can easily rise up to inflict harm especially to an inexperienced driver. Greg lived most of his life in the hazy fog of drug and alcohol addiction. Although he sought a straighter, clearer road on which to travel for the rest of his life, he was uncertain as to how to get off the road, which had trapped him for so long. He didn't know how to slow down. Even though he had found hope in Christ, forty plus years of hard living could not end overnight. His old self continued to cling to what he knew best and the fog that had been his life would not evaporate easily.

A day came not long after our lasagna dinner and basketball game evening when he succumbed to his old temptations. In a drunken state, Greg called a lady friend of ours and he made some suggestive remarks that shocked and upset her. She had befriended and loved Greg as a brother, and had prayed for him to overcome his situation. To have him do such a thing caught her off guard, and she was disappointed and saddened by his actions.

The next day Keith received a call from Greg who said he wanted to talk to him. He said he had done something terribly bad, and needed to speak with Keith in person. He left work and drove to Greg's apartment not knowing for sure what to expect. When Greg told him what he had done, tears began to flow from our friend's eyes, his shoulders slumped, and he hung his head. Keith tried to reassure him that everything would be okay, but Greg was adamant. He was so ashamed of what he had done that he could no longer face any of us. He wanted to pull back and needed some space.

After Keith came home and told me about their talk, I called Greg. I was proud of him for confessing and understanding what he had done was wrong. He could have kept it to himself, but did not. I said, "Greg, if you are truly sorry, all will be forgiven."

"No, I just can't see you guys anymore, know what I'm say'n? I broke our trust and hurt our friend. I can't forgive myself."

I tried to explain to Greg about forgiveness and repentance. He would hear none of it, and insisted that he had to pull away so he would never again do such a thing to hurt his friends. I told him that Keith and I still loved him and would always be there for him when he was ready to reconnect. I felt empty inside and so sorry for Greg who struggled so with his past. Before I hung up, he wanted me to pray for him so I did.

My friend who received the call from Greg sent a text message to me several times during that week letting me know that she and her husband had forgiven Greg. They wanted him to know they still loved him and were praying for him. Her post-reaction about the incident was a true application of grace and mercy. So many others would have cut and run, never again allowing Greg back into their lives. But, my friend was a true woman of Christ who wanted to see the best in Greg bloom into a beautiful creature. He just needed all the weeds surrounding him removed. Those weeds absorbed the life moisture and choked off his growth. I was proud of her.

Having no other choice, we went on with our lives, but prayed for Greg every day. I thought about him as much as I did my own family, and over the next several months I began to miss him more and more. I knew he was convicted of what he had done, a sign that the Holy Spirit was working on him. The old Greg would have never thought anything about what he had done, but he was so young in the Spirit he simply did not understand how to forgive himself. By pulling away from his trusted friends, he began to fall backwards.

Too often, those of us who have grown up in the church do not understand the struggles that someone like Greg must endure. Too often, we've come to believe that when someone makes a decision to follow Christ, their lives change for the better overnight. In reality, the old struggles, the old temptations, the old addictions cling desperately holding back the new Christian's growth. In many ways Satan uses those faults and past sins to shame us into believing we are not worthy of the grace Christ gave to us.

The range of emotions that Greg wallowed in often seemed conflicting and counterproductive. Simply saying to him, "You have Christ in you now," did not change the fact that for most of his life he lived a troubled and questionable existence. All he had ever known was chaos. All he had ever done was to exist within a confined lifestyle where he covered his troubles with alcohol and drugs. They were his gods for most of his life. They were what he trusted. He knew not what the love of Christ meant for all those years.

What he failed to understand in his newly found faith was that faith in Christ was not something you had to earn. He seemed unable to shake loose from the idea that all of his past sins no longer held power over him, that he was released, no longer held captive based on performance. The fact that it was a free gift paid in full by Christ on the Cross seemed foreign to him. He didn't understand that because of that act, we were set free from the power of sin in our lives.

You see, we all struggle with this thing called The Power of Sin. It is what resides in our carnal nature. It is part of our inheritance as descendants of Adam. The carnal mind is at enmity with God, and those who are in the flesh cannot please God. Paul wrote to the Corinthians saying that since they were babes in Christ (carnal), he could not speak to them as spiritual. They had received Christ, had received some parts of Christian principles, but had not matured in their understanding or in their faith and holiness. The world still had a strong grip upon them.

Sin is what separates us from God. But when Christ died on that cross he took the punishment we deserved. When he rose again, he defeated Satan's plan to destroy us. When we accept this gift then who we were, in regards to what we deserve, no longer exists in God's eyes. He now sees us through the filter of Christ.

What Greg and many of us fail to grasp is that even though we have a new life in Christ, we are still prone to sin. I mentioned earlier what Paul wrote to the Romans in chapter seven. Sin dwells within each of us. We know what God wills us to do, but we don't do it. We endorse the noble biblical principles, but miserably fail because we are consistently trying to live out those principles within our own muscle. All have sinned and fall short of the glory of God. We are still influenced by the power of sin because we live in the flesh in a fallen world.

The difference between the old and the new is that before, we did what we wanted to do. Now, we no longer desire to do those things, and when we do sin, we are convicted by the Holy Spirit to call us back into communion with God. Every time we sin, we distance ourselves from Him. We experience a disconnection of sorts that separates us from the life giving experience our heart now desires. Repenting of those sins reestablishes that fellowship.

Without professional help, that old addiction of alcohol still held Greg hostage. He often felt like he was unworthy, that he had failed in his conviction, that he was weak and that God could never find favor with him because of his constant failure. Somehow, in his mind he felt like he had lost his place of importance with Christ. In reality, his conversion was as real and strong as the most ardent of believers, but Satan wanted nothing more than to attack him where he was most vulnerable.

I've often believed that to those who offer the greatest threat to him, Satan will attack with the most vigor. Somehow, he must have known that Greg's life could become a powerful agent against his power, and so his attacks on Greg were persistent and strong.

Too many years of abuse, too many years of misinformation, too many years of living a life based on what was best for himself, to fill his needs now, that letting go of those old ways would not come easy. He complicated things to the point of being confused. He was almost child-like in a way as someone who needed an abundance of special attention, understanding, and guidance. Even though he tried to embrace the goodness of having Christ in his life, his lack of understanding caused him to continually fall back into his old ways of thinking. He was an example of a Corinthian. That is what generated the powerful conflicts in his life.

I prayed every night for the Lord to heal Greg, to break the chains of addictions and set him free. Sometimes when we pray, we have a certain way we see it played out. God will often clear it up by saying, "I have a better way."

By doing so, He gives us the answer to our prayer but the picture doesn't always look the way we envisioned it. I wanted God to heal Greg on this earth. I wanted Greg to remain by my side as a friend and brother in Christ. Together we would work on this book project to the end. I envisioned him being truly set free and at peace, maybe even going around sharing his testimony. I am reminded, "...not my will Father, but yours... my soul whispers."

I always hear back, His whispered "Yes."

A battle was raging inside of Greg and it was about to grow more fierce.

CHAPTER 43 – The Battle

August 19, 2012, was the day Greg decided to come back to church with us after months of not going. We made plans to pick him up as usual at ten thirty so we could make the eleven o'clock church service. When we arrived at his apartment, he did not answer the door, but it was open and we could see him inside, so we walked in. We found him wearing only his bathrobe and he seemed surprised to see us. It was clear that he was intoxicated, or at least recovering from another drinking binge. In his agitated and emotional state of mind, he didn't remember that it was Sunday.

Every time we had been to his apartment, it was clean and tidy. But on this morning, I could see nothing but a mess of cigarettes all over the floor, on the end tables, and on top of the stove. Empty gin bottles and beer cans littered the floor and were scattered across the tables and spilling out of the garbage can. He was embarrassed and told us he had been binging all week and how much he missed his daughter.

He wanted to pray. So we listened quietly as he prayed a gut wrenching prayer for himself, his emotional expression of remorse mixed with sense of helplessness reverberated in his words.

I had not planned to tell him yet, but he was so despondent, that I went ahead and mentioned about the Quest House, a rehab facility close by where he could get treatment. I told him our church was going to pay for it, and that he would not lose his apartment.

Greg fought many battles in his life, some physical and many emotional, but on this day, his battle became a raging darkness that scared me. I could feel the pull of forces. It was as if the enemy's demons were tormenting him; their claws were ripping at his soul. On the other side were the angels of the Lord with their swords drawn. The war already won, they were fighting for Greg to find peace. The enemy wanted Greg to be miserable, and they knew his weaknesses.

Keith and I were standing with the angels, offering what help we could muster. Never before had we witnessed anything like this. He would cry out with a loud brawl, "Please help me!" and rock back and forth with his hands covering his face, but then quickly sink into remorseful despair and proclaim that he was unworthy.

I tried to reassure him by reminding him about that day on the park bench, and how because of his decision, he was now redeemed in Christ—no longer had to fear anything. I spoke about the power of Christ that he now had. We reassured him that with that power he could beat his alcoholism. We told him there would be people there to help every step of the way, including Keith and myself.

He rocked back and forth on his bed, holding his face in his hands trying to hide the fear in his eyes, crying. It was heart wrenching to watch such a physically powerful man succumb to his internal fears. I felt helpless with a tight knot in my gut. I prayed a silent, determined, and angry prayer demanding that his tormentors leave. I don't know if my efforts worked, but he seemed to calm down, and asked us for another prayer. We bowed together and Keith prayed this time asking for calmness in place of conflict, for courage in place of fear, and for our friend to find peace in his life, while I tried to comfort him by rubbing his shoulders.

We stayed until he became drowsy, which was a good thing. We felt he was too emotionally distraught to have any serious discussion about enrolling him at Quest House. He rolled onto his side and closed his eyes. We told him to get some rest and sleep, and we would talk with him later.

Greg mentioned the men's gathering at our church that evening and asked if he could go, and Keith told him he'd come by to get him later. When we walked out the door, he said he felt better, and thanked us for coming by. Keith walked ahead of me, and as I stepped through the door, I glanced back for one final look. He had covered himself with one of the blankets we had given him, and was curled into a loose fetal position facing away from us. He seemed calmer and I hoped he would fall asleep and rest. I told him we loved him, that everything would be okay. That was the last time I saw him.

That evening—

Greg called and asked for Keith about an hour after he had left for the men's meeting. We knew Greg would be in no shape to go to church that evening. Greg wanted him to come over again; he had done something really bad. Then he called me, and started in with a crazy story. He said that the police were going to come looking for him so he was going on the run and wanted to say goodbye. I asked what he had done.

"I shot someone, a man in front of my apartment."

I didn't believe him. I told him I knew he didn't have a gun, that I had packed everything he owned when he moved into the apartment. He kept insisting that he had one. I asked where it was and he said he threw it into the trash bin. I asked about the "victim". He said he went to the hospital in an ambulance. I knew if Greg had shot someone, the neighbors would have known, and the police would have been all over the place. I also believed in my heart that Greg could not have done such a thing. But, I was concerned and called Keith suggesting that he not go over there until Greg settled down. He was just about ready to leave to go over there, but decided it was probably best to give Greg some time to come to his senses. He also called a friend who was a paramedic to verify if any calls had come in about a gunshot victim. There were none.

None of it made any sense. He did not sound like my friend Greg. I could hear the television in the background. I figured he was either drunk again, high, or both and probably had a cop show on with a scene like he was describing thinking it was real.

Keith and I dismissed his words attributing it to confusion, and told him again just get some sleep that we would talk in the morning. He said he was going on the run and could he call us collect. I said yes knowing he was probably hallucinating, and would sleep it off eventually.

The next morning—

Lisa, a homeless woman I had met through Greg a few months earlier, called me squealing that Greg was dead. I didn't believe her. She also was an alcoholic, and I thought she was confused. But she kept insisting that it was true. I called Keith, and we both scrambled to find out what was going on. The hospital told us that Greg had been brought in but that he wasn't there anymore. They could not reveal any more information because of the HIPAA laws. We knew someone who was in the medical field so Keith called him and asked if he could check into it. A few minutes later he received a return call. It was confirmed. Greg had died early that morning.

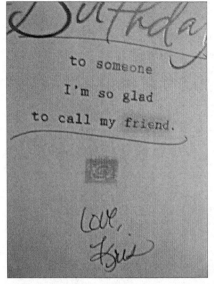

My heart sank and my breaths grew short and heavy. I wanted to, but could not, cry. My eyes just stared into blank space. My heart thumped so hard I could feel it in my chest. My throat tightened; my strength sank as I tried to awaken from this nightmare. For the next hour, I simply paced around the house. I called some friends and asked them to pray. I was antsy feeling as if I needed to do something, so I grabbed my purse, got into my car and drove over to Greg's apartment. I still thought maybe, hopefully it wasn't true, and I would see him when I got there.

The door was closed, and I prayed for Greg to be sitting on his couch on the other side. It was unlocked so I went inside. Inside the single room, the mess still there, but he was not. His giant tennis shoes were scattered on the floor. In my uncertainty and bewilderment I thought about cleaning the place, but then felt maybe I shouldn't move anything around. I wish now I had cleaned it up. I saw the birthday card I had given him sitting on top of the television.

I stepped over to the table where he kept all the books and his Bible. All of them were stacked neatly organized, a stark contrast to the cluttered apartment. The tidy stack was Greg's statement to the value he placed in those symbols. I took a few pictures of them.

Also on the table was the note I had written inside the Bible Keith and I had given him.

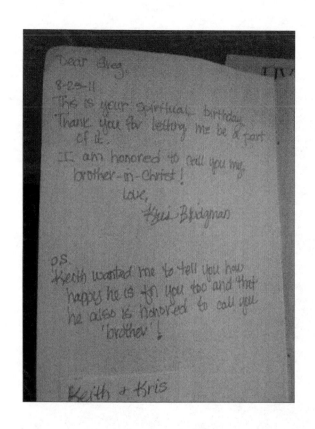

Dear Greg,
8-25-11
This is your spiritual birthday.
Thank you for letting me be a part
of it.
I am honored to call you my
brother-in-Christ!
Love,
Kris Bridgman

p.s.
Keith wanted me to tell you how
happy he is for you too and that
he also is honored to call you
"brother"!

Keith + Kris

I took pictures of his first and only
communion cup,

The picture of us,

and the one of his daughter.

I sat on the floor and saw beneath the table his Alcoholics Anonymous book.

I opened it and discovered wonderful messages written to him by others.

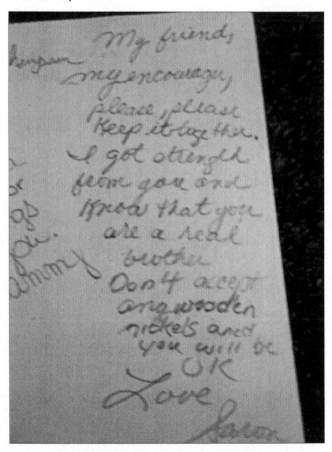

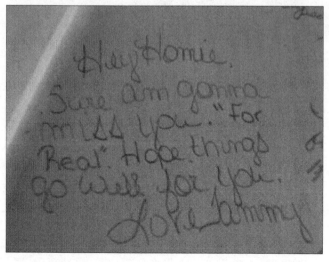

ALCOHOLICS ANONYMOU

e show, humbly saying to day "Thy will be done."

He had highlighted throughout the book and I took pictures of those special icons of his journey to recovery.

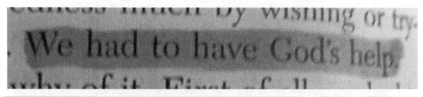

We had to have God's help,

r. We were reborn.

Then there are types entirely normal in every respect except in the effect alcohol has upon them. They are often ble, intelligent, friendly people.

I don't know why. I guess it struck me that these words stood out to him and I wanted to remember what they were. As I started to close the book, I saw where he had taped this on a back page...

Sitting there on the floor of his room with his big tennis shoe beside me, my grief got the better of me. The tears started to flow slowly at first, and then turned into gut wrenching sobs. I was angry at the alcohol, I was angry at Satan for all the grief and pain he causes. I was broken to think my friend was not going to be there anymore, no more time on the park bench together. I was angry that my friend was not able to live more of his life redeemed, set free from alcohol. He would not be there to see the completion of the book, our book.

Then God gently reminded me of how Greg always said he wanted to see Jesus and how he wanted peace, one hundred percent total peace. I realized Greg finally had what he wanted. He had a new body now. No more pain, no more fear, no more dependency. He was face to face with Jesus and he had finally found peace.

I walked out and closed the door, number 19.

I said good-bye and walked away.

The coroner's report said he died of an overdose of Hydrocodone, a prescription for painkillers prescribed to him after his colon surgery.

"I will ransom them from the power of the grave; I will redeem them from death; O death, I will be thy plagues; O grave, I will be thy destruction . . ."

Hosea 13:14 (KJV)

O death, where is thy sting? O grave, where is thy victory?

First Corinthians 15:55 (KJV)

Let no one caught in sin remain

Inside the lie of inward shame

We fix our eyes upon the cross

And run to him who showed great love

And bled for us
Freely you bled for us

Beneath the weight of all our sin
You bow to none but Heavens will
No scheme of hell, no scoffer's crown
No burden great can hold you down
In strength you reign
Forever let your church proclaim

Christ is risen from the dead
We are one with him again
Come awake, come awake!
Come and rise up from the grave

O death! Where is your sting?
Oh hell! Where is your victory?
Oh Church! Come stand in the light!
The glory of God has defeated the night!

Lyrics from Christ is Risen
By Matt Maher

Final Words

Losing our friend Greg ripped away the final curtain that separated us from the homeless stage. Such struggles had never before played out across our lives, and we discovered just how ugly and heartbreaking that kind of story could become. Our understanding of homelessness changed forever because of Greg and the others. No longer can we look upon a homeless person without first sifting their lives through the filter of Greg's life. His struggles became the standard by which we determined our understanding of struggles. We are no longer distant observers, but players scripted by God's word.

As difficult as it was to witness how his life played out, we now grasp more clearly, why some of the most important blessings do not always come easy. There are times God places us in the middle of a difficult situation often filled with muck and mire, yet he wades through it with us to the other side. When we finally get there, we discover almost unexpectedly, how the beauty of faith in the midst of chaos was all around us. I am reminded what Isaiah 43:2 (ESV) teaches us about faith.

"When you pass through the waters, I will be with you; and through the rivers, they shall not overwhelm you; when you walk through fire you shall not be burned, and the flame shall not consume you."

It takes a lot of faith to walk through the fire or cross a raging river. Keith and I understood the importance of holding on to God in times of trial as we took this life-changing journey with Greg, but he was new in his faith, and struggled to learn how to apply it to his life. Although his life was characterized by trials of fire, he was not given much time to learn how to walk through that fire with God as his guide. In thinking about it, it has taken me years to be able to trust enough to step out in faith like that. To his credit, he desperately wanted to change his life, but he struggled to let go of his old world. It was the only world he had ever known and it kept colliding with his new desire to change. Even so, we do not see Greg's death as a lost battle, but as a war that was already won.

I used to recite a verse to Greg that helped me during times of despair; Isaiah 41:10 (KJV)

"Fear thou not; for I am with thee; be not dismayed; for I am thy God; I will strengthen thee; yea, I will help thee; yea, I will uphold with the right hand of my righteousness."

I suggested several times to Greg that whenever he felt down and defeated, that he do the same thing as I would, raise his right hand, reach out and take the hand of God. I'm not sure if he ever physically did such a thing. I am confident that in his heart he did, and on August 20, 2012, Jesus in His compassion extended His right hand to Greg, and brought him into His kingdom.

Through all of this Keith and I felt blessed to have walked with Greg, and he told us many times how he felt blessed to have real friends who loved him unconditionally. He is fully set apart now in the presence of the Lord. He will always reside in our memories. As he strolls through Heaven, we will remain in our faith. Whatever waters or fires we must walk through, we are well served in what we learned by having merged our lives with his.

As for Greg and all the other friends I made sitting on the downtown park bench, I have pondered what they did for me. Initially I set about this journey hoping to make a difference in their lives, and maybe in some small way extend a rope that might provide a means of rescue for anyone who reached out. I am sure, unbeknownst to them, they rescued me.

They rescued me from sinking deeper into my own sense of despair. They rescued me from the confining clutches of those most comfortable of comfort zones. They rescued me by revealing their lives if only for a moment so I could share what I could give best: a listening ear, a compassionate heart, and a prayer.

They gave to me the gift of respect, of manners, politeness, honesty, and a piece of their lives. They allowed me to give back a piece of myself, which proved to be a powerful, personal, healing process in itself.

I pray the gift I leave with them is for all of us to have a deeper understanding spirit towards those in a homeless situation, or as Tony would call it, structurally challenged.

I do not promote that we randomly give "things" to the homeless. That is between the individual and the Lord. What I am promoting is that we see with new eyes that can look past appearance and attitudes, and to pray for people for their needs whether that is physical, mental, emotional, spiritual, or monetary in scope. I promote becoming a friend to whomever the Lord puts in front of you, even if that person is a stranger on a park bench with a backpack beside them, worn out shoes on their feet, and a beat down look on their face. I'm sure there will be blessings exchanged back and forth.

This story does not end the way I wanted it to. I wanted Greg to be healed this side of Heaven. I wanted to see him healthy and whole again. I wanted him to share the moment when this book became a reality. I wanted to continue having special moments with my brother-in-Christ. But, this story was never mine to script. It was the Lord's, and as I think about it, it's not really an ending. Greg's new life finally began in earnest when God called him home. What a glorious beginning it must have been!

The Blanket Ministry will continue to meet new people and Greg's shadow will follow us. The stories of those who shared with us will give us new insight, and a simple blanket warmed by the love of Christ will continue to change lives. I know this to be true, because it is not about me. It is about my Savior and His love for you and everyone. I can hear Greg say with his booming voice, "AMEN!"

"You know what I'm say'n?"

Words from Charles Wesley

If death my friend and me divide,
Though dost not, Lord, my sorrow chide,
Or frown my tears to see;
Restrained from passionate excess,
Thou bidst me mourn in calm distress
For them that rest in thee.

I feel a strong immortal hope,
Which bears my mournful spirit up
Beneath its mountain load;
Redeemed from death, and grief, and pain.
I soon shall find my friend again
Within the arms of God.

Pass a few fleeting moments more
And death the blessings shall restore
Which death has snatched away;
For me thou wilt the summons send,
And give me back my parted friend
In that eternal day.

Author Biography

Keith and Kris are both Oklahoma natives who have been married since 1981. They currently reside in Alvaton, Kentucky. They have two grown sons.

Kris homeschooled their sons for fourteen years. Since that time, she began writing her thoughts at a nearby pond and thus began her widely read blog *Ponderings*. Her devotions have been published in *Our Daily Journey* (a devotional site of RBC Ministries), *PCCWeb Daily Devotional*, *Ruby for Women Ezine Magazine*, and she is a contributor in the book *Alabaster Jars, Life in Abundance Collection 2*. She began a Blanket Ministry for the homeless in 2009 and is currently involved in a Homeless Outreach Bridge Ministry. She also discovered a love for photography. You can find her at

www.ponderingsbykris.blogspot.com

Keith has been a mainframe computer programmer since 1987, and has worked for a number of major corporations.

He enjoys writing and outdoor activities such as canoeing, fishing, hiking and incorporates nature photography into those activities. Many of his photographs and outdoor/photography articles have been published in various major magazines including Outdoor Oklahoma, Oklahoma Today, Kentucky Living, Country Magazine, and Back Home Magazine. His photography and outdoor stories can be discovered at his blog site

www.beyondthecampfirebykeith.blogspot.com.

For more information, please join us at,

https://www.facebook.com/YaKnowWhatImSayn

Interview with Kris

What have you learned from this experience?

Homelessness is one of those aspects of life that most people simply ignore. More often than not, our attitudes toward those caught within its grasp is one of indifference or complacency believing that they are homeless because they want to be, and there is not much any one person can do to make a difference. When I began to explore the world of the homeless I discovered people with broken hearts, lost hopes, and destroyed dreams. I saw firsthand how addiction to alcohol and/or drugs could diminish a person's self-worth to the point they simply give up and no longer try to change. I've also witnessed incredible strength and perseverance.

Almost all of them are searching for value in their lives, all too often finding it inside a bottle. When I began talking with the people and listening to their stories, an entirely new perspective materialized. These are people with a history who desperately cling to one important good element from their past lives. That is what gives them a semblance of purpose to show to those around them that they do have value, so they can find within themselves a small spark of importance.

Many of them claim to know God. Most of them only know him superficially as some kind Helper to get through hard times. Rarely is there any kind of meaningful, spiritual connection. Almost all of them are searching for the very thing that only God in their lives can provide, they just fail to understand how to reconcile who they are now with what they can become with Christ in their lives. The Blanket Ministry opens doors to share with them the value that only Christ can offer to them.

353

It is amazing at how many tears are shed during some of the conversations. Emotions locked inside search for release, and when a simple prayer is offered for them, many times even the most hardened will let go of pent up emotional needs and begin to cry. I've seen long term alcoholic homeless men encapsulated with a thick crust of distrust have tears pool across their cheeks, and walk away after we have shared with them. The homeless are not devoid of good emotions, they just need some kind of trigger to allow it to surface, and listening with a caring heart combined with a gentle hug or touch will often allow those good emotions to be released. It is during those times that hearts can be changed.

How have you been changed by this experience?

No longer can I look at a homeless person without first understanding that a back-story, a history exists for that person. I've discovered that regardless of their current situation, there was always something from their past that contributed to them being there. Those histories reveal a great deal about who they are, and why they have allowed themselves to be negatively influenced by their current circumstances. It has helped me understand how to answer the question, Who is my Neighbor? When we begin to understand that our neighbor is everyone, especially those who are hurting, we can then identify how to direct our own lives.

No one person can solve the problem of homelessness and all of its causes. But, it is not so much a matter of solving the problem as it is understanding that the problem exists then being willing to doing something to help. Churches are very good at teaching their congregations all the *Ought To* scenarios, but they are less effective at teaching and encouraging them *How to*. I may not be able to travel to other countries to share the love of Christ, but I can sit on a park bench and share Him with those I meet. As worn down and forgotten as the homeless are, they are still precious souls to God. When we stop looking at those we encounter through the tinted glasses of preconceived notions, and begin to see them through the filter of Christ, how can we not be changed?

Where to now?

I've learned that when God is in control, He will lead you where He needs you. At this point, I'm not sure where He is leading me other than to stay where I am. The Blanket Ministry has grown from handing out blankets to those we encounter, into a homeless outreach ministry, in concert with HOTEL, INC. at the bridge that offers not only basic necessities such as blankets, socks, coats, personal hygiene supplies, but also hot meals once a week and food bags. It offers an opportunity to befriend those who may not otherwise have that opportunity. We spend time speaking to and praying for those we meet, and offer encouragement and direction about finding other resources for assistance.

For now, I will continue with the Blanket Ministry and Homeless Outreach Ministry until God decides otherwise. We are experiencing amazing stories from the bridge, and I am in the beginning stages of using that as a theme for a follow up book. We are developing trust and friendships with not just the homeless, but many who are simply lonely and have few resources on which to survive. We are establishing bonds, and we are sharing Christ's love with those we meet. For now, I am convinced this is what God wants me to do.[3]

------

[3] https://www.**facebook.com/**YaKnowWhatImSayn

Made in the USA
Charleston, SC
24 September 2015